Everyman, I will go with thee,
and be thy guide

Aischylos
THE ORESTEIA

AGAMEMNON,

LIBATION BEARERS,

EUMENIDES

Edited and Translated by
MICHAEL EWANS
University of Newcastle, NSW

EVERYMAN
J.M. DENT · LONDON
CHARLES E. TUTTLE
VERMONT

Translation and critical apparatus
© J.M. Dent, 1995

First published in Everyman in 1995

J.M. Dent
Orion Publishing Group
Orion House, 5 Upper St Martin's Lane,
London WC2H 9EA
and
Charles E. Tuttle Co., Inc.
28 South Main Street,
Rutland, Vermont 05701, USA

Typeset in Sabon by Deltatype Ltd, Ellesmere Port, South Wirral
Printed in Great Britain by
The Guernsey Press Co. Ltd,
Guernsey, Channel Islands

British Library Cataloguing-in-Publication Data
is available upon request.

ISBN: 0 460 87548 5

CONTENTS

To my sons Tobey and Shea

NOTE ON AUTHOR AND EDITOR

AISCHYLOS, son of Euphorion from Eleusis in Attika, was born in 525/4 BC. The ancient biographical testimony is largely speculative, and material was invented to compensate for the lack of reliable information at the much later dates when it was compiled. The historical record for the period in which Aischylos lived is also relatively slight, compared to the wealth of surviving sources for the last thirty years of the fifth century. As a result little is known for certain about his life beyond the facts and dates recorded in the Chronology. We do know that Aischylos was of noble ('Eupatrid') birth, that he fought against the Persians at Marathon, and paid two visits to Syracuse in Sicily; he died in 456/5 during his second visit, at the age of about 69. He probably became an initiate in the Eleusinian Mystery cult.

He created at least eighty tragedies, and won at least thirteen prizes during his lifetime in the tragic contests at Athens. Only six dramas composed by Aischylos survive complete, together with *Prometheus Bound* (ascribed to Aischylos, but probably created later in the century by another poet). Numerous fragments – most of them very short citations – are extant from the lost works.

After his death the Athenians conferred a unique honour on Aischylos: the Archon (the elected official in charge of the Festival of Dionysos) was required to grant the necessary funding for a choros to anyone seeking to produce his dramas. Aischylos was therefore the first Athenian dramatist to have his work revived.

MICHAEL EWANS read Classics at Oxford and wrote his Cambridge PhD thesis on Aischylos, supervised by George Steiner. He was appointed in 1973 to a Lectureship in Classics at the University of Newcastle, NSW, and began teaching Drama when the discipline was introduced at Newcastle in 1974. He became Associate Professor of Drama in 1982, and was Head of the Department of Drama from 1982 to 1985. His publications include scholarly articles and programme notes on

Greek tragedy and opera, his other main research field, and three books: *Janáček's Tragic Operas* (1977), *Wagner and Aeschylus* (1982) and *Georg Büchner's 'Woyzeck'* (1989). He has directed and supervised numerous productions at the University, both of Greek tragedy and of twentieth-century drama, especially expressionist plays. He has since 1985 been a consultant to the Australian Opera and a leading member of the committee responsible for the new Drama syllabus for secondary schools in New South Wales.

CHRONOLOGY OF AISCHYLOS' LIFE

Year   *Age*   *Life*

525/4   Aischylos born at Eleusis

499   26   Competes for first time at Festival of Dionysos

490   35   Fights at Marathon; his brother Kunegeiros is killed

484   41   Wins his first prize in the competition for tragedy

480   45   Fights at Salamis

479   46   Possibly fights at Plataia

CHRONOLOGY OF HIS TIMES

Year	Artistic & Historical Events
528/7	Hippias succeeds Peisistratos as tyrant of Athens
c. 514	First Persian attempt to invade Greece thwarted by the Skythians
514	Hippias' brother Hipparchos murdered by Harmodios and Aristogeiton
510	Hippias expelled from Athens by the Alkmeonidai
508	Constitutional reforms of Kleisthenes at Athens
508–6	Defeat of attempts by Sparta and Boiotia to intervene in Athens' internal affairs
501	Performances of tragedy first incorporated into Festival of Dionysos
499	Ionia revolts from Persia, led by Miletos; Athenian troops sent to assist
498	*Pythia 10*; first known poem by Pindar, the great composer of choral lyric poems from Boiotia
494	Persians defeat Ionians at Lade; fall of Miletos and collapse of revolt
493	Phrynichos produces *The Sack of Miletos* and is fined
490	First Persian invasion of Greece, repelled by Athenian victory at Marathon.
480	Second Persian invasion under Xerxes Unsuccessful defence of Thermopylai by Spartan King Leonidas Sack of Athens by Persians Decisive Greek victory at Salamis Withdrawal of Xerxes
479	Final defeat of Xerxes' lieutenant Mardonios by combined Greek army at Plataia

Year	Age	Life
472	53	Wins competition with a tetralogy which includes his first surviving drama, *Persians*
470	c. 55	In Syracuse. Restages *Persians* and produces *Women of Aitna* to celebrate the foundation of the new city of Aitna by Hieron
468	57	Defeated by Sophokles' first entry in tragedy competition
467	58	Wins competition with Theban tetralogy: *Laios*, *Oidipous*, the surviving *Seven against Thebes*, and the satyr-drama *Sphinx*
463	62	Wins competition with Danaid tetralogy, which includes surviving first drama, *Suppliants*
458	67	Wins competition for thirteenth and last time with the *Oresteia*
456/5	69/70	Dies at Gela in Sicily

Year	Artistic & Historical Events
478	Withdrawal of Sparta and allies from combined Greek league Athenians form Delian League
476	Phrynichos wins competition with *Phoinikian Women* Pindar visits Sicily, and composes *Olympian 1* celebrating Hieron's victory in the horse race.
470	Themistokles ostracized Pindar, *Pythian 1*. His masterpiece, written for Hieron (though Pindar, unlike Aischylos, did not revisit Sicily) to celebrate both his victory in the chariot race at Delphi and the foundation of the new city of Aitna.
469	Victory of League fleet over Persians at Eurymedon ends Persian threat to the Aigeian
466–5	Themistokles condemned; flees to Persia
465–3	Athens crushes attempted revolt by Thasos from the Delian League
462	Ephialtes and Perikles curtail powers of the Areopagos
462–61	Pindar, *Pythians 4 & 5*. Two of his greatest compositions, written for Arkesilas, king of Kyrene.
461	Ephialtes assassinated; Kimon ostracized Alliance between Athens and Argos
460–45	War between Athens and Sparta, the 'First Peloponnesian War'
c. 456	Pindar, *Isthmian 7*, critical of Athens' expansionist foreign policy.
455	Euripides competes for the first time

INTRODUCTION

The surviving Greek tragedies are the prisoners of their eloquence. They have been admired since the Roman Empire for the beauty and rhetorical power of their language, and predominantly studied for their literary qualities. Commentaries are for the most part confined to philological and cultural approaches, and the majority of modern translators are scholars or poets, writing primarily for readers rather than for actors.

Professional companies, when they attempt a production, pay little or no attention to the nature of the original presentation. All too often the imposition of a preconceived style or idea takes priority over any attempt to re-create for a modern audience the effect created by the ways in which the dramas were originally performed. Either the text is treated with almost religious reverence, declaimed in a sombre, static production style which owes more to neo-classicism than to the real ethos of Greek tragedy; or the splendour of the language is rejected entirely, and the text is often freely adapted, cut and rearranged before being submerged in frenetic activity, in a quest for some fundamental, 'mythic' truth which is wrongly supposed to lie behind and apart from the words.

As a result, students and audiences often approach Greek tragedy warily, and with the expectation that they will be mystified or bored (on occasion both). To the vast majority of theatre-lovers today, the works which founded our western tradition, and which gave us the very words 'drama' and 'theatre', seem undramatic and antitheatrical.

Almost no other theatre form could have been more damaged by this reception. *Drama*[1] means something enacted, not something written; the Greeks spoke of Aischylos as the *poiêtes*, the 'maker' or 'creator' of the *Oresteia* rather than its writer or author. This usage should make us constantly aware that 'the

---

[1] All italicized Greek words are defined in the Glossary.

Oresteia' meant far more to Aischylos and his Athenian audience than just the spoken words preserved in the script, which alone survives.

As a *poiêtes*, Aischylos was responsible for realizing, in each year that he was selected to compete at the festival, a new unified performance event which was displayed, on one occasion only, to his fellow-citizens and their guests. He combined in his own person the roles which in the modern theatre we divide between the writer, director, composer, choreographer and lead actor. In a Greek tragic performance two complementary mixed media alternated as seamlessly as possible: the more emotional lyric mode, in which sung lyrics and choreographed dance unite to form a whole; and the more dialectical spoken mode, in which speech and freer, blocked movement unite to form a different whole. These were supported throughout by richly decorated costumes, a small number of very significant props, and the façade of a wooden building behind the acting area.

For Aischylos, therefore, the script which we have treasured for its literary genius (because that is all that is immediately apparent from the surviving text) was only one part – though a vital and major part – of the tetralogy composed in dialogue and song, in movement and in dance, with which he competed successfully for the prize for tragedy at the Festival of Dionysos in 458 BC. The meaning of the *Oresteia* was enshrined in a close combination between verbal imagery and visual, between patterns of sound and patterns of movement. We possess one of these two elements of Aischylos' tragedies, and we need to reconstruct the other.

This is not a wholly subjective process. If the dramas are workshopped and performed in a replica of the Greek theatre shape, in a style faithful in the relevant aspects to what is known of Athenian dramatic conventions and theatre practice, we can recover some sense of how these dramas communicated with their original audience. Though many possible movement patterns can be imagined by the armchair theorist, practical work with a scene from the script often yields only one overall blocking which is effective. This is because Aischylos knew only one theatre shape, and had by the time of the *Oresteia* been using it to communicate with the Athenian audience for over forty years. In a living theatrical tradition,

'certain emotions become associated with certain spaces and

certain patterns of movement and can be evoked by them. Performance is then [. . .] expressive of specific thoughts and feelings; the physical reality of the stage becomes metaphorical as well as tangible, in the same way that words, in a literary work, become metaphorical as well as literal. This is how effective staging can proceed from the playtext, even when not found in the text surface. [. . .] Proper staging is in the text by implication. This does not mean that there is only one correct way of staging a script, but it does mean that, once variables of stage and actor are established, the script will suggest certain natural staging potentials.'[2]

The main aim of this edition is to help students and readers to imagine what the *Oresteia* was like for its original audience; and to supply theatre practitioners with an actable and accurate script, together with a conception of how that script originally worked in Aischylos' own performance space.[3] I hope that users of this series will create productions which will finally destroy the all-too-frequent picture of Greek tragedy as static, ritualized, obscure and hard to stage, and will re-create for today's audiences the dynamism, intensity and realism which lay at the heart of the dramatic experience for Aischylos, his acting company and his first audience.

Community and Festival at Athens

Tragedies were presented at the Great Dionysia, the main festival of the god Dionysos, each year from 501 BC.[4] At an unknown date early in the fifth century, the competitions for tragedy were transferred from the *agora* to a new purpose-built performance space beneath the south-western slope of the Akropolis, the Theatre of Dionysos. Modern estimates of the original seating capacity vary from 14,000 to 18,000; despite subsequent modifications to suit a very different style of drama, the sheer size of the fifth-century theatre is still evident from the ruins, and it remains extremely impressive.

---

[2] Hornby 1977, 171.

[3] Several divergences from traditional ways of presenting Greek tragedy in translation are designed to encourage readers to think of the tragedies within the framework of the ancient Athenian conception of drama.

[4] The traditional backdating (on weak evidence) to 534 BC was overset by Connor 1989.

The audiences for tragedy at the City Dionysia naturally comprised most of the (approximately) 6,000 citizens of Athens – enrolled freeborn adult males, who had a vote in the assembly and the right to act as elected officials and jurors – together with the *metoikoi* or resident aliens, and some foreign visitors. Athenian boys, women and girls,[5] and slaves were also present. This was therefore the largest and most inclusive gathering of the people of Attika.[6] The Great or City Festival of Dionysos, which included celebrations of civic greatness in the ceremonies prior to the tragic (and later comic) drama contests, was a central event in the life of the *polis*.[7]

There is no other known human culture in which a drama as serious and intense as ancient Athenian tragedy has commanded the close attention of virtually the entire community, and dramatized for their collective judgement playwrights' visions of major issues, situations and problems affecting their society.[8]

Performance Space and Performance Style

The *Oresteia* was first performed in the Theatre of Dionysos, which the Athenians had hollowed out of the slope under the south-east end of the Akropolis. The theatre consisted of a *theatron*, an *orchêstra* and a *skene* building. The *theatron* seated tiers of spectators rising from level with the performance area to far up the hillside; it surrounded almost three-quarters of a (probably) circular *orchêstra*[9] or dance floor – the performance

[5] Attendance by females (once a controversial topic) now seems settled by Henderson 1991.

[6] The total population of Attika in Aischylos' lifetime is unlikely to have exceeded 250,000; cf. Baldry 1971, 14.

[7] The Festival of Dionysos, and other festivals at which less important drama competitions were conducted, are well described in Baldry 1971, ch. 4 and Rehm 1992, 16–30. For a description which locates tragedy more precisely in its functional setting in the *polis* see Goldhill 1986, 75–7 (cf. *idem* 1990, 13–16).

[8] The origin and early form of tragedy, and Aischylos' relationship to the politics and social values of his time, are discussed in the Introduction to Ewans 1996.

[9] The circular shape has been questioned, by archaeologists who have noted that early assembly places elsewhere in Greece are frequently almost rectangular in form. Carlo Anti (1947; cf. Gebhard 1972), challenged the traditional belief that the Theatre of Dionysos in the fifth century had the circular orchestral shape seen in the later theatres at Epidauros and elsewhere. Like Melchinger (1974), I am not convinced that the archaeological evidence at Athens establishes a trapezoidal *orchêstra* (cf. also Ashby 1987). However, the dynamics of the performance area

space used by both solo actors and choros. Behind the *orchêstra* lay the third component of the theatre, the *skene* – a long single-storey wooden building on a tangent to the rearmost part of the *orchêstra* circle, and extending across its full width. It was perhaps therefore twenty metres long, two to three metres high, but not more than four to five metres deep, as the ground fell away steeply behind the rear of the theatre precinct. The *skene* had a practicable roof, one set of double doors (with a device, the *ekkuklêma* or 'rolling-out machine', to exhibit to the audience tableaux prepared indoors), and a façade decorated in such a neutral way that it could suggest a palace, temple, house or tent without incongruity.

The festival audience surrounded the performance area on three sides, looking down into it from rows of wooden benches[10] which rose steeply up the hillside. The farthest spectators could be up to one-hundred metres away from the *orchêstra*. Though the acoustics were good, and anecdotes confirm that the audience paid close attention to the words of the tragic and comic performances, the Greeks termed the area in which the audience sat not auditorium – hearing-place – as did the Romans, but *theatron*; seeing-place.

What they saw was subject to the constraints imposed by size. Facial expressions could have been seen only from the front rows. Masks, larger than the natural face, were therefore worn. The Greek word for what we call a mask is *prosôpon* – literally 'face'; the *prosôpon* was designed not to mask or conceal anything, but to make sure that all the spectators could identify the gender, age and status of the characters represented.[11]

are not significantly affected by the precise shape of the *orchêstra*. The key fact is that the playing space, with the *skene* building behind it, was surrounded on three sides by the spectators in the *theatron*.

[10] In Aischylos' time the seats were probably not laid out in the curved rows familiar from later marble theatres. The archaeological evidence would appear to suggest three to five blocks of straight rows; see Pöhlmann 1981.

[11] There were other reasons for the use of *prosôpa* by the Athenians, going back to before the construction of the large theatre. In Aischylos' lifetime the invention of dramatic impersonation in the West lay less than two generations in the past, and it is probable that acting a part was not regarded as possible without wearing another face than the actor's own. An anecdote relayed in Plutarch's *Life of Solon* (ch. 29) attests that the very concept of playing a part or dramatic impersonation aroused suspicion and distrust in one of Greece's legendary wise men when Thespis invented drama, disguising his face – according to tradition – by smearing it with the lees of wine. Cf. Rehm 1992, 39–42 and Bibliography.

Although gesture was an important element in Greek drama, it is notable that in both tragedy and comedy moments to which detailed gestures are important are always narrated carefully in the spoken or sung text – presumably so that distant spectators, who might miss seeing them, could follow the action.[12] The size of the *theatron* makes it certain that the primary means of visual expression in Greek tragedy was not gesture but blocking – the grouping of actors and their patterns of movement. What kind of space did they move in?

The Greek theatre was wholly unlike the proscenium arch theatre which has predominated in European cultures since the eighteenth century; it was more akin to the modern 'theatre in the round'. Our custom of physically separating actors and audience, and the frequent seclusion of VIPs in boxes from other parts of the audience, would have been totally alien to the Athenians.[13]

So too would have been the separation of solo actors, playing the parts of named individuals, from the choros. However, modern proscenium-arch based conceptions of theatre have been very influential – with disastrous results for the understanding of Greek tragedy. Many scholars[14] have conjectured that there was a low raised stage behind the *orchêstra*, and the actors of the

[12] Arnott 1989, 74; cf. Aristophanes, *Thesmophoriazousai* 634–51 for a striking example. Arnott (1989) and Taplin (1978) both provide good discussions of the use of gesture in Greek tragedy – but isolated from the context of the overall pattern of movement in the *orchêstra*.

[13] Walcot 1976, 4–5; cf. Arnott 1989, 11. Baldry (1971, 15) draws an acute parallel with the *agora*, where tragedies were first performed at Athens, before the Theatre of Dionysos was constructed. He makes the vital point (see below) that Athens's political assembly lacked the customary modern practice of elevating and separating speakers from their audience to enhance their status as figures of authority. Speaking well did not require standing still in political or legal debate, or when reciting epic or iambic poetry. Why should this have been the case in tragedy? Cf. Pickard-Cambridge (1968, 171–6) against Taplin (1977a, 20); and for the central role of performance, and competition, in Athenian culture cf. Rehm 1992, 3–11.

[14] Most eloquently Arnott (1962), Hammond (1972), Hormouziades (1965, 58ff.) and Aylen (1985). See also more recently Gould (1985, 269) and Goldhill (1992, 18–19). The raised stage was comprehensively refuted by Pickard in 1893; but his articles were almost completely ignored. Ley and Ewans (1985) re-established that the action in Greek tragedy must have taken place not on a stage but in the *orchêstra*, with its centre point as the principal focus; our conclusions were independently confirmed in 1988 by Rehm – also a scholar with practical performance experience of Greek tragedy (cf. *idem* 1992, 36).

individual name parts almost always performed on it, separated from the choros.

There is no archaeological evidence for a raised stage in the fifth century, and the presumed advantages do not exist, once we abandon as inappropriate modern ideas of how theatre must work. In the Athenian performance space, a low raised stage would not give the solo actors any visual advantage in relation to the choros, since the vast majority of the spectators looked down on the action from high up in a steeply raked *theatron*. Nor is there reason to suppose that there would have been any acoustic advantage in speaking from a stage behind the *orchêstra*, to compensate for the extra distance from the majority of the audience.[15]

The decisive argument against a raised stage lies in the nature of Aischylos' dramas themselves. Unlike most subsequent western forms of drama, Aischylean tragedy is an art-form in which individual characters are seen not in isolation but in a political and social focus; their fortunes are bound up with those of a group – the fellow-inhabitants of their *oikos* (their household) or their *polis* (their city-state).[16] Poems as diverse as Homer's epics and Pindar's victory odes show us that the classical Greeks invariably saw individual triumph or catastrophe not in isolation, but in relationship to the wider focus of its impact on the *oikos* and the *polis*; Aischylos embodies this way of seeing human life in the constant interaction between the solo actors and the choros, who play the part of the social group most affected by the action.[17]

The interplay between solo actor and choros is at the centre of almost every scene, and the director's main task is to realize in the playing area the ebb and flow of the power relationships which are central to the subtleties of the dramas. Such sequences as Elektra's colloquy with the Libation Bearers as she first hesitates and then 'turns' Klytaimestra's offerings (*LB* Scene 2), or Apollo's confrontation with the Furies outside his temple (*Eu* Scene 2) are constricted almost to the point of being unrehearsable if the actor is up on a raised stage, marooned in a separate playing area

---

[15] The experiments conducted by Hunningher (1956) demonstrate that the visual focus of the theatre – the centre of the *orchêstra* – was also the acoustic focus.

[16] Jones 1962, 72–140.

[17] Cf. Macleod 1982, especially 142–4, on the social significance of individual misfortune in the *Oresteia*.

behind the choros; and even the scene where Klytaimestra appears in triumph, and begins her first speech standing over the bodies of Agamemnon and Kassandra just in front of the *skene* doors (*Ag* 1379f.; 'I stand just where I struck . . .') gains very greatly both in force and in pathos if she soon comes forward into the *orchêstra* to challenge the Elders. Workshopping scenes both with and without a raised stage has convinced me that when the *Oresteia* was first performed there was no raised stage. The double doors at the front of the *skene* gave directly onto the back centre extremity of the *orchêstra*; actors and choros both used the whole of the *orchêstra*, and it was the sole acting area.[18]

A total misunderstanding of the role of the choros in Greek tragedy began early in the nineteenth century, with Schlegel's influential nonsense about the 'chorus' as an 'ideal spectator' whose function is to mediate between an action performed by solo actors and the audience, bringing a detached wisdom to the contemplation of that action.[19] This misunderstanding goes so deep that it even affects the way in which the choros part invariably appears on the printed page —with their speeches and songs prefixed 'Chorus'.[20]

The twelve men who made up the choros in Aischylos' time dance as a choros, but play the part of, and represent in the drama, a character; in the *Oresteia* successively the Elders of Argos, the Libation Bearers, and the Furies. The only differences from named individual actors are that choros members collectively represent and play the part of a group, do not normally make long speeches, and must give the illusion that they are a more passive character than the individuals – but only the illusion (in *Libation Bearers* and *Eumenides* the choros character is actively involved); they dance and sing regularly on their own, whereas the individual actors sing only rarely, and then only in response to and in interaction with the choros.[21]

[18] Apart from brief, exceptional uses of the roof of the *skene*, as in *Ag* Scene 1.

[19] This view is also justly condemned by Rehm (1985, 242). It has never wholly died out; it had an extreme manifestation in J. Michael Walton's concept of a choros miming, out of character, as an accompaniment ('orchestral' in a quasi-operatic sense?) to the mood suggested by the speeches of the principals (1980, 182–3, and 1984, 69–70, 81, 90 and 92). The idea is developed from Baldry (1971, 65–6); for the evidence against see Pickard-Cambridge 1968, 252).

[20] The sole exception known to me is Postgate 1969.

[21] The solo actors were termed *hypokritai*, 'responders' – appropriately, in view of the central importance of the choros in Aischylean drama.

The choroses of the *Oresteia* do not mediate between actors and audience; together with the solo actors they are virtually surrounded by the audience. Their choral odes do provide moments of reflection on the course of the action, but this reflection is not vague metaphysical speculation; rather, it is a precise reaction to the dramatic situation as it evolves, by a group of people who experience that situation from the inside, as active participants in and passive sufferers from the events.

It is very often assumed that the members of the choros were normally silent (as well as motionless!) during the spoken scenes of Greek tragedy (except for one spokesman termed the *koryphaios*),[22] and that their songs were invariably sung in unison, except for a few obvious places where the action makes division into two hemichoroses a strong possibility. Both these assumptions richly deserve to be challenged.

I have not seen a single modern production of a Greek tragedy prepared to countenance the assumption which has become the scholarly orthodoxy. No director tolerates the visual and verbal incongruity of having eleven individuals totally silent except during the odes, while a twelfth is overburdened by having to act as their spokesman. The divorce between drama in the study and drama in the theatre could hardly be more marked. Which is right?

During Aischylos' lifetime, the Athenians were rapidly evolving an innovative, highly participatory democracy; the assumption that 'a group must have a leader' is alien to their thought. That is the reason why the choros character's speeches and songs alternate naturally between 'I', expressing an individual member's particular point of view, and 'we', spoken by an individual to express what he or she takes to be the overall view of the group. If we regard Aischylos' choroses as playing the parts of twelve individuals who collectively form a group, their lines can be assigned to the actors in the choros in such a way as to bring out a particular temperament or attitude to the action in each of them, which can be developed over the duration of a drama.

[22] This view has little foundation: the Greek word for a choros-leader in and before the fifth century is *chorêgos*, and in the two contexts where its usage is clear (Alkman, *Poem* 23.44 and Aristophanes, *Lysistrata* 1315) it refers not to a spokesman but to the person from whom the others take their lead in the choreography. So too with *koryphaios*, when the term appears in the fourth century; Aristotle, *Politics* 1277a11 etc.

This idea has been resisted because it disturbs the authoritarian assumption that the name-role solo actor is far more important and interesting than the anonymous group – just as the raised stage was imported into Aischylean tragedy to separate the solo actor off from that group, and the choros's responses to the action were misread as spectatorial reflections to deny them their true role as participants in that action. But under the test of production the orthodox scholarly view collapses. The effect of dividing between a number of individual choros members such moments as the edgy dialogue between the Elders and Klytaimestra which opens Scene 2 of *Agamemnon*, or the cross-examination of Orestes and Apollo by the Furies in the trial scene of *Eumenides*, has to be seen to be believed. At once a balance and an impetus to dramatic flow are given to an action which is lame and halting if only one person speaks for the choros. Hence in this edition all choral dialogue is assigned, e.g., to '1. Elder', with the expectation that directors and actors will decide which individual choros member will speak each line – just as Aischylos himself doubtless did.

The orthodox consensus about choral singing is even more vehement. We are told that all Greek choral music was normally sung in unison; so too therefore were the choral lyrics of Greek tragedy. There are however good reasons to challenge this doctrine as well. There are three places in the trilogy where the choral lyrics patently must have been divided between different singers.[23] There are also several places where, although it is not essential, it would be very advantageous to divide a choral lyric between the members' individual voices (e.g. the first four choroses in the Finale of *Eumenides*); and there is no choral ode in the trilogy where some subdivision, at the discretion of the director and company, is not valuable.[24] The resistance to the assumption that some parts of the choral lyrics were sung by individual choros members as solos springs (I suspect) less from a genuine evaluation of the scant evidence for Greek musical

[23] *Ag* 474f. (*pace* Fraenkel's attempt (1950, 245ff.) to bully his opponents into submission) and *Eu* Choroses 1 and 2, where if you accept that the choros members entered individually to begin the dance, you cannot sensibly deny that they sang at least the first few lines individually as they entered in ones and twos.

[24] Cf. especially *Ag* 782f. The four variations on 'I agree', in Agamemnon's response at 830f., make theatre sense only if directed to four different individual Elders who chanted 788f., 795f., 799f. and 805f.

practice than from an unstated picture of Greek tragedy as something like an eighteenth-century sacred oratorio, with soloists playing individual parts which are far more prominent than the anonymous unison or four-part harmony of the choros.

There has also been a persistent failure to acknowledge that Athenian dramas were set outdoors primarily because in classical Greece (unlike northern Europe and north America) significant action and interaction took place outdoors, and indoor events are pertinent only in their impact on the community outside. Vickers and Walcot[25] are totally convincing in their insistence that what we – with criteria for realism derived from Ibsen, Chekhov and Stanislavsky – might regard as a stylized, ceremonial theatre was nothing of the kind to the Athenians. Aischylos' works are immediate, precise dramas – not loose poetic meditations on themes or philosophical truths whose 'real' enactment is else-where.[26] Actors wearing everyday contemporary dress acted out before the audience events familiar from real life – homecomings, prayers and offerings, the arrival of messengers and suppliants, a new dawn at Delphi and a trial for homicide. These events happen, as they all did in Athens, outdoors, anchored in the context of a specific place and political and social situation.

Athenian society was defined by a fundamental set of parallel binary polarities: between the public life of an individual as a citizen and his private life; between the male-dominated outdoors and the female-dominated indoors; between the realm of logical, word-based reason and the realm of emotional persuasion; in short, between *polis* and *oikos*. Just before the production of the *Oresteia* (sometime between 463 and 458), the performance area was modified to reflect this division. The introduction of a practicable *skene* building behind the *orchêstra* enabled tragedians to change the dynamics of the playing area; if they chose to use it to represent a building – a palace or temple in front

[25] 1973, 53–4; 1976, 6–7. My practical experience has encouraged agreement with Walcot 1976, 51 that the acting style – though obviously very large scale – was fundamentally realistic and designed to involve the emotions of the audience (cf. Taplin 1977a, 28–39 and Seale 1982, 19–20). Arnott (1989, 10) correctly insists that the arena theatre shape is an intimate one; again, it is a modern, and false, assumption that a large *theatron* and 'masks' automatically imply a remote, distant actor–audience relationship.

[26] For example, inside the palace, with Page (1957; cf. e.g. 117) and Scott (1984, 101 etc.), or on Olympos with Kitto (1956, 69f., esp. 78) and others.

of which the drama is enacted – then the *skene* doors, when they are in use, pull the focus of the action back from the centre point of the *orchêstra*. This sets up a dialogue between the *orchêstra*, which represents a public arena – frequently (as in *Agamemnon*) the *agora* where the Council assembles for its meetings with the king – and the *skene*, which represents the often sinister indoors.[27]

Aischylos made powerful and effective use of this innovation in the *Oresteia*. The building is used for representational purposes in the whole of *Agamemnon*, the second half of *Libation Bearers* and the first third of *Eumenides*. (At all other times its presence is ignored, and a property set at the centre pulls focus forward into the *orchêstra*.)

The trilogy opens with a speech delivered from the *skene* roof. Aischylos then frequently makes use of the double doors, which for the first time permitted sudden entries – especially with Klytaimestra's role in *Agamemnon*; and the first two dramas both reach a climactic revelation exploiting the *ekkuklêma* (the wheeled platform which had been incorporated into the building to deliver indoor events into public view) when they are so serious that they have implications for the life of the *polis*.[28]

The threshold, with the double doors at the entrance to the *skene*,[29] is extremely important when the *skene* is used to represent a building, since it is the point of transition between the two worlds. Aischylos constantly exploits that fact in *Agamemnon* and the second half of *Libation Bearers*, and even extends this literal liminality to a metaphorical liminality in *Ag* Scene 6 and *Eu* Scene 1, where the dark interior becomes a metaphor for the endless night of Hades.

An *orchêstra*, surrounded on two thirds of its circumference by the audience, requires a way of interacting between characters which is wholly different from the upstage/downstage antithesis in the modern proscenium arch theatre. Actors predominantly face each other, and must not be grouped towards the back of the *orchêstra* facing the central block of the audience.[30] In an arena

[27] Arnott 1989, 133. See also Gould 1985, 48.

[28] See notes on *Ag* Scene 7 and *LB* Scene 6.

[29] Dale (1969, 103ff.) convincingly demonstrates that only one doorway is required for performances of all the surviving fifth-century tragedies and comedies; (cf. Taplin 1977a, 344 and 349–51). Their arguments are not damaged by Hammond (1972, 438), Walton (1980, 116–8) or Bain (1981, 56ff.).

[30] The proscenium arch theatre cultivates this acting style; but in a production

production, turning one's back on part of the audience is perfectly acceptable, provided there is frequent movement so all spectators are given a chance to relate to each of the individual faces.

This must have been the case in the original productions, since the Greek theatre shape positively invites movement,[31] and makes stillness a powerful statement – especially the stillness of the choros, who must be moved to the front perimeter of the *orchêstra*, and preferably made to kneel or lie down as well, on the rare occasions (e.g., *LB* Scene 3), on which they take absolutely no part in the action, and need to be withdrawn from focus. Athenian tragedy was a vital, intense and dynamic medium,[32] which Aischylos used primarily for the representation of emotional, social and psychological conflict and its resolution.

Form and Meaning in the Oresteia

Aischylos created this trilogy for an audience which was closely familiar, since childhood, with a number of previous versions of the 'myth', the old story of the house of Atreus. He did not of course expect them to clear their minds of all memory of those versions while watching the *Oresteia* – this would negate the whole purpose of basing new tragedies on old stories. The audience was to presume, in general, that the 'standard version' of each story was being followed, unless it was specifically contradicted. But they had to hold that knowledge in a special

of Greek tragedy the result is that the players rarely face each other, even during crucial scenes of confrontation. This was one of the problems with Sir Peter Hall's 1982 National Theatre production of the *Oresteia*.

[31] *Pace* Peter Hall, his controversial production of the trilogy provided very little movement, implying a fundamentally rhetorical and ritualistic vision of Greek tragedy. In *Ag* Scene 7 his Klytaimestra moved once; by contrast there were thirty-four main movements for Klytaimestra in the première production of this translation, to reflect the complex ebb and flow of the confrontation between her and the Elders. Hall's production is well and justly criticized by Rehm (1985).

[32] Even an excellent modern book (Arnott 1989), which places appropriate emphasis on the importance of gesture in the production of Greek tragedy, continues to cultivate an image of a static, predominantly verbal medium (65, 68 and 195 n. 36). Played (as they were) in loose costumes and light, low-heeled shoes, with a fluid physical interaction (and without interlude and mood-setting music, which the Greeks did not employ), the dramas do not move at the slow and solemn pace which is often regarded as appropriate for classical tragedy. The uncut first performances of this translation played for 97, 63 and 65 minutes respectively.

relationship to the new dramas. It must not be allowed to rush in actively and fill gaps with incidents deliberately omitted by the playwright; and it must never be allowed to obliterate new variants, even when they departed from central, near-canonical parts of the traditional version.

The audience's provisional knowledge of how the story is likely to turn out was a passive field, so to speak, for the Greek dramatist to play on. The audience 'knew' more than the characters; except Kassandra they are placed in our normal situation of having no certain knowledge about the future. Since the outlines of what would happen could be guessed from the tradition, the Athenian playwrights were largely saved the burden of exposition, and could concentrate primarily on showing the interactions of people and events which explain *why* they happen. Aischylos had of course to make plain what is going on where he innovates in the *Oresteia* – as for example with the new reason for the sacrifice of Iphigeneia.[33] But elsewhere, allusion sufficed to carry even the most central points.[34]

Some of Aischylos' changes to myth would appear to be very substantial, even making allowance for our scanty knowledge of previous versions of the story since Homer. For example, legend provided a wealth of past crimes in the house of Atreus: the reckless ambitions of Tantalos; the murders of Oinomaos and Myrtilos by Pelops; Thyestes' adultery and Atreus' appalling revenge for it – all provided ample material for a playwright who wished to see Agamemnon as accursed, doomed to disaster by the violence of his ancestors. And many of the early Greeks believed that the gods exact payment from the descendants of men whose misdeeds go unrequited in their own lifetime.[35]

Aischylos does not employ that belief in the *Oresteia*. Of these horrors from the past, he refers only to the Thyestean banquet – but not until *Ag* Scene 6, and only to explain the presence of Aigisthos as Klytaimestra's fellow-conspirator. By altering the traditional account of the motivation for Artemis's anger,

---

[33] In the main tradition, Artemis demanded the sacrifice because Agamemnon had shot a sacred stag and boasted that 'not even Artemis could shoot so well'. Apollodoros *Library, Epit.* 3.21.

[34] The special relationship between a Greek audience and myth is discussed, in contrast with nineteenth- and twentieth-century perspectives, in Ewans (1982b, ch. 2, esp. 56f.) *Contra* Arnott 1989, 118.

[35] Cf. Solon 13 and Theognis 731f.; explicitly opposed by the Elders at *Ag* 750f.

Aischylos ensured that Agamemnon's own situation explains both his self-dooming action at Aulis and his consent to walk on the tapestries.

There are other striking innovations. Aischylos was almost certainly the first dramatist to have placed the murders of their kindred by Klytaimestra and Orestes unequivocally at the centre of this story. His version replaces Homer's all-too-feminine Klytaimestra, chaste and at first unwilling, but seduced by a powerful, noble Aigisthos into complicity in his vengeance on Agamemnon, with a strong, masculine-spirited Klytaimestra who does the murder herself and so in turn invites personal vengeance on her by her own son. These changes enable Aischylos to use the story to confront the issue of matricide, and the prospect of endless bloodshed (both studiously avoided by Homer), head-on in *Libation Bearers*; they also place gender conflict and sex role reversal at the centre of the trilogy.[36]

However, Aischylos works all his alterations gently into the texture. For example, the portrait of Klytaimestra's masculine powers is elaborated gradually over the whole first half of *Agamemnon*, from the Watchman's hint (l. 11) through to her triumph over Agamemnon in persuading him to walk over the tapestries. The fact that Agamemnon (again in contrast to the epic tradition) is to return without his army is introduced and developed with equal care, from Klytaimestra's first fears for the safety of the returning fleet (l. 338f.) through the Herald's confirmation that the Greeks destroyed the shrines of the gods in the sack of Troy (l. 527) to the moment at which the king arrives alone in his chariot (but for Kassandra), and is therefore vulnerable to Klytaimestra.

Aischylos does not employ the sudden reversals of audience expectation which play so large a part in Euripides, in the late dramas of Sophokles and in Aristotle's theory of drama. There is surprise in *Agamemnon*, but it is carefully directed into two impressive *coups de théâtre* – Klytaimestra's use of the tapestries and Kassandra's prophecies – which themselves advance the action powerfully towards the climax.

Each of the three dramas of the *Oresteia* leads up to a moment of acute tension whose outcome, far from being a surprise, fulfils

[36] Aischylos' changes from Homer's use of the Orestes myth in the *Odyssey* are well-discussed in Goldhill (1992, 46ff.).

the audience's deepest expectations. The *moira* of the characters increasingly takes shape until the moment when Agamemnon must and will die; Orestes will succeed in his plan, and must kill Klytaimestra; the Athenians will acquit Orestes and yet escape retribution. The audience's knowledge of the legend makes each outcome a strong possibility from the earliest moments, and Aischylos organizes the subsequent action so that this possibility is slowly but inexorably converted into certainty.[37]

The act of violence at the climax of each of the first two dramas is elevated to tragic stature, simply because by the time it takes place Aischylos has shown it to be in retrospect inevitable.[38] For all their horror, the deaths of Agamemnon and Klytaimestra bring a profound sense of relief, together with the pity felt for characters who are trapped (literally and metaphorically) in the web of their unfolding *moira* when it has achieved its final, tragic form. The power of these dramas lies in the fact that their evergrowing suspense leads to a terrible climax which is a surprise in terms of the exact moment when it happens, but in every other way has grown to be deeply expected.

Aischylos concentrates constantly on the twin axes of expectation and fulfilment, hope and fear. Throughout the main action of *Agamemnon* there is a sustained dialogue between the growing fear that Agamemnon will die and the increasingly futile hope that good will prevail. This pattern is then continued by the development through the even bleaker world of the second drama to the climax of the third, the moment when the Furies accept Athena's offer, and the Athenians' hopes finally cease to be qualified by fears.

The ending does not imply that situations like those which caused the tragic events of the first two dramas will never recur. Neither the order of human society nor that of the universe

[37] Aristotle repeatedly notes that in tragedy the events should form a sequence which is 'either probable or necessary'. Aischylos always structures his plot so as to tend towards the latter, stricter requirement. This aspect of ancient Greek *tragoidia* is discussed, in relation to Renaissance and modern concepts of tragedy, in Ewans (1995).

[38] However, nothing in Aischylos is predetermined; his characters are not puppets of the gods or of any omnipotent Fate. On the unfolding revelation of expectation in the trilogy cf. Ewans (1971, *passim*). See also Neuburg (1981, esp. 102–3), noting how Aischylos uses metaphors from animal and plant growth (e.g. crop from seed) to describe sequences which we view as cause and effect, but which for the Greeks contain their completion innate within their initial conception.

evolves or changes its nature in the *Oresteia*.[39] To believe that they do is to deny *Agamemnon* and *Libation Bearers* their immediacy and relevance to audiences, both ancient and modern; but the impulse towards an 'evolutionary' reading, in which the trial and Finale in *Eumenides* initiate a new world-order, has been astonishingly widespread.[40] John Jones argued conclusively, over thirty years ago, against any evolutionary reading of the *Oresteia*, whether metaphysical, democratic or Marxist, that '[Aischylos] is not looking down from a position of superior enlightenment upon the urgencies of the *Oresteia*'.[41]

Aischylos was well aware that no law court could solve a dilemma like Orestes' or prevent such terrible acts of revenge as Klytaimestra's. Kindred murder still happened in fifth-century Athens, as it still does in our own even more 'civilized' societies – and for compelling reasons. Lloyd-Jones rightly noted the *Oresteia*'s place in the continuity of Greek social practice: 'the cliché we have heard repeated all our lives, that the *Eumenides* depicts the transition from the vendetta to the rule of law, is utterly misleading. Even in the *Iliad*, the blood feud is regulated by the justice of Zeus administered through kings; even in the law of the Athenian *polis* in the fifth century, the blood feud and the Erinyes (Furies) have their allotted place'.[42] This trilogy is not an allegory of the evolution of civilization, or of divinity,[43] but a paradigm of patterns of human conduct – true for all time, and anchored firmly in his own time by the hope (and the warnings) extended to his fellow Athenians in the trial scene and Finale.

---

[39] Nor in any other surviving drama by Aischylos. The different picture apparently presented in the Prometheus trilogy is one of the main arguments against its authenticity; cf. Ewans (1996).

[40] Cf. for example (most recently) Herington 1986, Conacher 1987 and Sommerstein 1989. Mnouchkine's 1993 production assumed that the trilogy shows the triumph of an institutionalized patriarchal society, and mounted a critique of this from a feminist perspective (cf. Bryant-Bertail 1994, *passim*). If Aischylos had intended to show the social evolution which some of his male interpreters have wished on him, her revisionist reading would have been fully justified.

[41] 1962, 112.

[42] 1971, 94–5. Cf. Neuburg 1981, 75ff. and 183f.

[43] The ascription to Aischylos of the Prometheus trilogy, during which – some critics conjecture – Zeus did change his nature (or at least his behaviour) has provided a misleading 'parallel'. See Ewans, 1996.

For his entry in at least five of the festivals at which he competed, Aischylos chose to create a connected sequence in which his three tragedies were linked together, and told three chronologically successive parts of one single myth.[44] Of these sequences, only the *Oresteia* survives intact.

The word 'trilogy' is often loosely applied to almost any work of drama or prose fiction which consists of one story together with two sequels which continue its narrative further. The *Oresteia* of course includes this basic design; but Aischylos goes much further. All three tragedies move singlemindedly from the opening situation towards one main event which occurs two-thirds of the way through the play; the remaining third of each drama is then devoted to exploring the consequences of that event, and its implications for the future of the principal character.

Each of the first two dramas is therefore linked closely to the events which open the action of its successor. Furthermore, *Libation Bearers* and *Eumenides* are not just sequels which explore the consequences of the events of *Agamemnon*; they are also parallel to it in action and in structure.

The sequence is set in motion by Agamemnon's sacrifice at Aulis, which the Elders relive in *Ag* Choros 1. Agamemnon found himself faced with a choice which is, from another perspective, no choice at all.[45] He must lead the expedition against Troy, since he goes as the agent of Zeus to avenge the abduction by Paris of Menelaos' wife Helen, which violated the ties of *xenia* between host and guest. But, in sacking Troy to avenge Paris' deed, the Greeks whom Agamemnon commands will destroy many innocent lives; for that action the goddess Artemis, protectress of the young and innocent, demands her price. Agamemnon must sacrifice to her his own innocent daughter – and by doing so he will bring about his own death.

Agamemnon's act at Aulis is the paradigmatic situation which underlies the action of the rest of the *Oresteia*. The main action portrays three different agents in parallel dilemmas, all of

---

[44] In those years Aischylos also apparently used the concluding satyr-drama, in which players and audience relaxed after the three serious dramas, to treat in farce and burlesque a related aspect of the same myth. *Proteus*, which followed *Eumenides*, dealt with an episode during Menelaos' delayed and roundabout return from Troy.

[45] This interpretation of Aulis is justified in detail in Ewans 1975. Cf. Winnington-Ingram (1983, 85) and Neuberg (1981, 36ff).

whom come to find, like Agamemnon at Aulis, that they have to choose between two alternatives. Either choice threatens disastrous consequences (and in the ethics of Aischylos' time responsibility for action is absolute; 'diminished responsibility' cannot successfully be pled because of external pressure, even from the gods); but each agent comes to realize that only one of the alternatives is truly possible.

The climaxes of the three dramas (the murder of Agamemnon, the death of Klytaimestra and the acquittal of Orestes) are to be seen in parallel as well as in sequence. Klytaimestra when she murders her husband, Orestes when he kills his mother, Athena and her fellow-Athenians when they judge Orestes are all 'remaking' Agamemnon's traumatic moment of decision and attempting to purge the world of its consequences. And it is the agent's degree of insight into past and future, their moral stance as they embrace the terrible action which they must inevitably take, which determines what will ultimately happen to them.

The pattern of the whole trilogy is conveyed through this parallelism: from the rich canvas of *Agamemnon* the fortunes of the characters are locked into the narrow, dark world of the second drama, but eventually emerge into the new and different richness of *Eumenides*, where the Athenians find the power to avoid the threatened reprisal for their actions. This finally breaks the chain of violence, and the Athenians are then able to create a perpetual bond of mutual renewal with the Furies. The Finale then celebrates the prospect of future prosperity which is now deserved by the city of Athens.[46]

Aischylos expressed his meaning not simply through imagery or ideas, which are – as Walcot correctly insists[47] – subordinate to and incorporated in the drama, but by unfolding the pattern[48] of the story through the action as it is shaped by the theatrical forms through which Aischylos chose to dramatise it.[49]

[46] See notes on the *Eu* Finale, and Macleod 1982.

[47] 1976, 3–4; cf. Baldry 1971, 78ff. Both imagery and ideas have been amply studied by the critical tradition, but all too often in isolation from the action; cf. e.g. Lebeck 1971 (imagery), Rosenmeyer 1982 (ideas) and Goldhill 1984 (language).

[48] For this concept cf. Lattimore (1964, cc. 1–2). I apply it to *Agamemnon* in Ewans (1982a), and develop it further in Ewans (1995).

[49] For this reason the Notes in this edition are framed around the formal component parts of Aischylos' dramatic structure: the unfolding sequence of alternating scenes and choroses, which are also the natural units of subdivision in rehearsal.

Aischylos unfolds a vision of our world as a place where people choose freely, but every act has far-reaching implications, and everyone ultimately receives his or her deserts. He offers us a fierce, tragic but ultimately affirmative view of mankind; the contrast is stark between this harsh but comforting assurance and the bleaker image presented by the pattern of action in most of the surviving dramas of Sophokles[50] and Euripides. In the often tortured vision of the later fifth century, gods and goddesses could no longer be imagined as interacting on Homeric or even Aischylean terms with human beings. For Aischylos, the gods and *daimones* are immanent forces in a universe which is completely animate, surrounding and interpenetrating human nature and accomplishing or fulfilling the implied consequences of human actions. The presence in early fifth-century belief of this element of *to theion* – the Greek term which means 'divine', but by the same token signifies all that is wonderful, marvellous, strange in us and our world – is the distinctive feature which made tragedy possible.[51]

Much cultural, political, philosophical and religious 'meaning' has been read into the *Oresteia*; it has, in the currently fashionable jargon, been 'appropriated' by critics ancient and modern, who often reinflect Aischylos' thematic preoccupations to reflect their own concerns. In some aspects each of these readings is demonstrably right; in others, demonstrably wrong. None of them focusses clearly on the dramatic power of the trilogy. The *Oresteia* is more complex than any literary 'reading'; it can only be appreciated when translated and performed.

Translation

Reading the *Oresteia* for the first time in 1816, Goethe described Aischylean drama as 'a primaevally gigantic form, of monstrous shape, which shocks and overwhelms us'.[52] Throughout the nineteenth century, Aischylos was read as a Gothic or Romantic artist, a poet of rugged, awe-inspiring grandeur and spectacular theatrical effects.[53] There is no justification for holding to this

---

[50] Traditional readings of Sophokles' world-view as 'comfortable' have come under sustained and justified attack in recent years; cf. especially Kells 1973, Winnington-Ingram 1980 and Segal 1981.

[51] Herington 1986, esp. ch 1; cf. Ewans 1993 and 1995, *passim*.

[52] Cf. Ewans 1982b, 26.

[53] In part this view is a result of Aristophanes' wicked caricatures of Aischylos and

view today. Aischylos' dramas may have seemed bombastic or obscure to some spectators and (increasingly) readers during and after the late fifth century; but they were not so to their original audience in 458, who were steeped in a tradition of popular entertainment by rich and complex dramatic and choral verse; accordingly, they must not be allowed to seem so to modern audiences.

Steiner's massive essay on language and translation, *After Babel*,[54] demands that good translation should attempt the impossible – a synthesis of literal fidelity to the source text, and literate expression in the target language. The challenge of these dramas is to be as accurate as possible, while also providing actable versions, which enable a verse drama to be played before audiences which possess no live tradition of verse drama. It is no service to Aischylos to mimic English verse styles from the past, nor to present free adaptations, implying that the content of the work is unimportant to the modern audience if the version is playable.[55]

For this translation, I attempted to find a language that would match the feel of the text as I experience it, and to communicate clearly with the audiences of today. I wanted to present Aischylos' meaning as clearly and lucidly as possible, responding closely to the tone of each subsection of the drama and to the flow and shape of the syntax and the rhetoric.[56] At times (e.g. *Ag* 1208, *LB* 423f.), this demanded a slight simplification; at others, a decision had to be made between different interpretations of the original (e.g., *LB* 583).

Aischylos' language has an extraordinary range – from the colloquial to the elevated, from clarity to complexity, from

Euripides in *Frogs*; the clear preference of Aristotle, and of Hellenistic and Roman critics, for whom the style and content of Euripides was more congenial, also played a part. The ascription to Aischylos of *Prometheus Bound* – dramatically static but scenically grandiose – is again relevant (see n. 42).

[54] Steiner 1975, ch. 4 *passim*, esp. 313–6 on Aischylos.

[55] Cf. Ewans 1989, 120–1.

[56] Translators often miss fundamental features of Aischylos' rhetoric (e.g., *enjambement*, which is a very powerful tool for actors in articulating the meaning of dramatic verse). I was astonished to find how many recent versions fail to preserve, for example, the sudden swerve into the historic present as Klytaimestra vividly relives the murder of Agamemnon (1382f.), or the seven-line sentence which forces the actress to build towards a powerful climax in her passionate denunciation of the death of Iphigeneia (1412f.).

simplicity and sometimes shocking directness to delicate under-statement. There is also the contrast between almost purely comic moments (the Priestess re-entering on all fours, the Nurse's musing on baby Orestes' nappies, and above all Orestes' need to knock three times on his own door before a grumbling servant answers him, then slams it in his face) and the high tragic mode which predominates, for example, in *Ag* Scenes 6 and 7[57] and *LB* Scenes 1–3. I have therefore not hesitated to use mild collo-quialisms, and to bring out the humour of the script, where the tone of the Greek justifies this.

Since rhyme was unknown to the Greeks, and has a distancing effect on modern audiences with no rhyming verse tradition, blank verse is employed. No attempt has been made to re-create in English the metrical forms or strophic responsion (see below) of the original; the source and target languages are too different from each other to justify such a procedure. A sharp differentia-tion is however made between the five- to seven-beat line into which the Greek iambic and tetrameter dialogue is rendered and the much shorter lines, matching those of the original, in most of the anapaestic (chanted) and lyric sections. Special care has also been taken to ensure that the lyric sections can be sung.

Particular care has also been taken in the handling of the lesser deities known as *daimones*, and of value-words. No translation can hope to bridge completely the gap between our culture and Aischylos', in which there was no distinction between upper- and lower-case letters – the powers whom I reluctantly capitalize (e.g., as Persuasion and Ruin) denoted living daimonic forces, personified as goddesses, what we would call abstract factors operating in a situation – or convey how the word *miasma*, 'pollution', denotes a single entity combining physical dirt and psychic taint. Nor can a translator express the ways in which even so simple a word as *agathos*, translated here (inevitably) as 'good', denoted for the Greeks a set of values and qualities wholly different from those denoted by the English word in our post-Judaeo-Christian culture.[58] However, this translation carefully avoids importing concepts for which there is no equivalent in Aischylean Greek; 'guilt' and 'sin', for example, both suggest a

---

[57] Even in these scenes we must be alert for humour. Translators and performers should not miss, for example, the tone of *Ag* 1312, a sick joke to enhance by contrast the pathos of Kassandra's death.

[58] Awareness of value-terms was initiated by Adkins (1960).

Hebraic world-order alien to the culture of fifth-century Athens.[59]

I have sometimes replaced a god's obscure alternative title by his or her more familiar name, or included in the translation the name of a person or god who is alluded to but not named in the original Greek; Aischylos naturally presumed in his audience a level of familiarity with myth and cult which few modern spectators possess.

The notations A1, A2 etc. beside the lyric portions of the choral odes denote groups of 'strophic' responding stanzas. Each new system inside an individual choral ode is lettered A, B etc.; within each system the 1 stanza was precisely matched in metre by the 2 stanza in the original and was choreographed identically to it. In some cases the pattern of first and second stanza, *strophe* and *antistrophe*, is completed by a third stanza, an *epode* of a related but not identical metrical pattern which concludes that portion of the dance.[60]

All translation necessarily involves some loss – and no wise translator could pretend to render all of Aischylos' richness into English; but at least we can choose, carefully, what to keep.[61] Let us learn to see and hear Aischylos as a poet of lucidity – though also of complexity and richness – and as a playwright whose action is filled with human depth and emotional vividness. All these qualities are easily discovered in rehearsal.

MICHAEL EWANS

[59] The translation also avoids the neo-classical mistranslation of *hubris* – the normal Greek word for violence committed against other human beings – as an 'arrogant pride' which angers the gods and explains a hero's *nemesis* or downfall.

[60] This version does not attempt to bring out exact responsion between corresponding parts of *strophe* and *antistrophe*, since this would constrict and distort the English. It has been heroically attempted in the quotations in Aylen (1985), and also in Matt Neuburg's as yet unpublished version of Euripides' *Bakchai* – in the original Greek metres! To my mind, the price is too high.

[61] Cf. Evans 1989 *passim*, esp. 138.

NOTE ON THE TEXT AND TRANSLATION

This edition is the fruit of work on Aischylos extending back over 25 years to the start of my Ph.D. thesis on the *Oresteia*. The Introduction and Notes are however based primarily on insights gained during many years of workshopping individual scenes, and from the production processes for three separate, uncut productions of these translations, in the Department of Drama at the University of Newcastle, NSW, in 1983, 1985 and 1986.

These translations were originally made from the Oxford Classical Text edited by Sir Denys Page. The few deviations will be readily apparent to classical scholars. I principally consulted for *Agamemnon* the editions by Fraenkel (1950) and Denniston-Page (1957). I have made minor revisions in the light of four editions which have appeared since the translations were first made: *Libation Bearers* edited (under its Greek title, *Choephoroi*) by Garvie (1986) and Bowen (1986); and *Eumenides* edited by Sommerstein (1989) and Podlecki (1989).

The attributions of speeches, and all stage-directions in any translation from Greek tragedy are modern – except possibly the noises from inside the *skene* in *Eu* Scene 1.[1] The directions in this edition are for the Greek theatre shape, and are based on experience gained while rehearsing for the premiere productions. Modern directors who need to modify these directions to suit a differently shaped performance space must still be aware of Aischylos' own practice. Only those directions which I regard as certain are printed in the text; further suggestions will be found in the Notes.

A sudden entry could be made only through the doors leading into the *skene*. All other entries were gradual, down one of the two *parodoi*.[2] A character entering down a *parodos* is in the sight

[1] Taplin 1977b, 122.
[2] Reflecting the actual topography of Athens, these represented entry either from the downtown district of the place in which the action is located (*skene*-left), or from the country and from other cities (*skene*-right). Rehm (1992, 154)

of some of the actors and audience, on the opposite side from where he is making his entry, long before he steps into the *orchêstra*. Presumably the convention was that the actor was in character from the moment he became visible to any of the audience, but engaged in interaction with the players already there only after he stepped into the *orchêstra*. Accordingly in these texts the direction *Enter X* is positioned at the moment where X enters the *orchêstra*, not when the actor first comes into the sight of some of the audience.

The text is divided into Scenes (predominantly consisting of spoken dialogue), and Choroses (passages sung and danced by the choros alone). These are numbered in separate consecutive series for each drama. Two non-strophic choral odes, which are too short to interrupt the development of a scene as a whole (Choros 2 in *Libation Bearers* and *Eumenides*), are numbered as new odes; but the number is placed in parentheses, and the scene is not ended when they begin.

Alternation between choroses and scenes is the basic structural feature of fifth-century tragedy; I have therefore not obscured it by importing the later technical terms found in the twelfth, probably interpolated, chapter of Aristotle's *Poetics*.[3]

These dramas were first performed, together with the lost satyr drama *Proteus*, in the Theatre of Dionysos at Athens in the spring of 458 BC, sponsored by Xenokles of Aphidna. Aischylos won the first prize for tragedy.

Transliteration

In this edition, following the practice of an increasing number of classical scholars, proper names are transliterated directly from the Greek original, and the traditional Latinized spellings (e.g., Aegisthus, Clytemnestra) are not employed.

---

questions whether this convention goes back to the fifth century, rightly noting that the evidence is late, but unduly influenced by the orthodox view that Aischylean tragedy was not specific in regard to the geographical location of action.

[3] *Prologos, parodos, stasimon, epeisodion* and *exodos*. I have also not accepted the over-ingenious theory of Act-dividing and non-Act-dividing odes with which Taplin (1977a, 49f.) sought to replace this terminology.

LYRIC AND SPOKEN VERSE

The interplay between lyric and spoken verse is marked in this edition by double-indenting all verses that were sung in the original Greek dramas.

Line Numbering

For uniformity in referencing, all scholars use the line numbering of one of the early editions of Aischylos. This numbering sometimes diverges from the actual line arrangement; the layout of this translation follows modern editions which incorporate recent insights into the shape of Aischylos' lyric stanzas.

Notation

Positions in the *orchêstra* are described in the Notes by a combination of letters denoting its parts as viewed by an actor emerging from the *skene*:
F = front; B = back; L = left; R = right; C = centre; E = extreme (i.e., at the perimeter).
   All directions for entry and exit, left and right, are from the actor's not the spectator's viewpoint.

THE ACTORS AND THEIR ROLES

Agamemnon

A Watchman	Actor 2
The Elders of Argos	Choros
Klytaimestra	Actor 1
A Herald	Actor 2
Agamemnon	Actor 2
Kassandra	Actor 3
Klytaimestra's maidservants	Silent Faces
Aigisthos	Actor 2
Aigisthos' bodyguards	Silent Faces

Libation Bearers

Orestes	Actor 1
Pylades (at first apparently a silent face)	Actor 4
Elektra (later a silent face)	Actor 3
The Libation Bearers	Choros
A Servant	Actor 2
Klytaimestra	Actor 3
Orestes' former wet-nurse	Actor 2 or 3
Aigisthos	Actor 1 or 2

Eumenides

A Priestess	Actor 1
Phoibos Apollo	Actor 2
Orestes	Actor 3
A dream-image of Klytaimestra	Actor 1
Klytaimestra's Furies	Choros
Pallas Athena	Actor 1
A Herald	Silent Face
Citizens of Athens	Silent Faces
Women and Girls of Athens	Supplementary Choros

ORESTEIA

AGAMEMNON

Agamemnon

Preset the Watchman on the roof of the skene.

WATCHMAN   I beg the gods; release me from these sufferings,
    this year-long watch that I have lain
    huddled upon the house of Atreus' sons, just like a dog.
    I've come to know the mass of stars assembled in the night
    and those bright overlords, who bring to mortal men
    winter and summer – stars that shine clear in the sky
    both when they set and when they rise.
    So now I'm watching for the torch signal,
    a beam of fire to bring from Troy the news
    the city's fallen: that is how she's used her power –   10
    the waiting, hopeful woman who plans like a man.
    And when I try to rest at night, now here, now there,
    covered in dew, no dreams watch over me:
    instead of sleep, Fear stands beside my bed
    and stops my eyes from closing safely into sleep;
    but if I feel I'd like to sing or hum a tune,
    pricking myself with song as antidote for sleep,
    then I cry out in mourning for this household, once
    tended with care and labour – now no more.

But I still long for good luck, for release from suffering –   20
fire, shining out of darkness as the messenger of joy.

Flame in the night, I greet you! You bring us
the light of day, and you command
that all of Argos sing and dance to celebrate.
Hey! Hey!
By this shrill cry I signal Agamemnon's wife to rise
quick as she can, and raise a cry of greeting for this light
throughout the household, since the Trojan citadel of Ilion

has fallen, as the beacon tells so vividly.   30
And I myself will dance the prelude to their song;
for I shall place the pieces for my master's lucky throw,
since this my beacon-watch has landed triple six.
But . . . may it only happen: may he come home, and let me
    clasp
my well-loved master's hand in mine.
I'll say no more; upon my tongue
a great ox sits. The house itself, could it take voice,
would tell most clearly. I prefer to speak only for those
who'll understand; to those who don't, I haven't said a word.

Exit Watchman, descending into the skene.

CHOROS I

Enter the Elders of Argos, left.

ELDERS   This is the tenth year since Priam's   40
            great opponents
          Menelaos the king and Agamemnon,
          two sons of Atreus,
          firm in their partnership of power,
          twin-throned, twin-sceptred by the gift of Zeus,
          put to sea from this land
          an Argive fleet of a thousand ships,
          an army of men to fight for their cause.
          And they cried out with all their hearts
          for mighty War,
          like vultures with their nestlings gone and suffering,
          who circle eddying   50
          on high above the nest,
          plying the air with wings like oars
          when they have lost
          the toil of nurturing their young;
          and on the heights above some god – Apollo, say,
          or Pan, or Zeus – hears these strange residents
          of Heaven crying shrill in mourning,
          and sends down on the victim's ruthless enemies

a late-avenging Fury.
Just so does Zeus, great god   60
who watches over guests and hosts, send out
the sons of Atreus against Paris
for a wanton woman's sake, and lays
many contests, wearying their limbs,
as the knee is bent in the dust
and the spear is snapped as the rites begin,
on Greeks and Trojans alike.
Whatever's happening will be fulfilled
right to the destined end:
not by burnt offerings, nor pouring
out libations can you soothe   70
the stubborn angers of the gods.
With our old muscles
we were judged unfit for service:
they left us behind
to wait, guiding our child-like strength
with walking-staffs; the marrow leaps
in the young breast like an old man's – Ares
is not yet in his place; advanced old age,
its leaves already withering, goes on its way   80
three-footed, and no stronger than a child
wanders, a dream-image by day.

But you, daughter
of Tyndareus, Queen Klytaimestra,
what need of us? What is the news? What
have you heard, what message has persuaded you
to send and order sacrifice?
For all the gods – the city guardians,
the gods above, those of the underworld, the household
and the market place –   90
the altars blaze with offerings;
the flare of torches rises everywhere
as high as heaven,
tended by the soft and harmless aid
of sacred unguents
taken from the royal store.
Tell what you can, and what is right to tell,
of this; consent, and be the healer

of my deep anxiety—
for now I'm sometimes full of desperate thoughts   100
and sometimes from the sacrificial offerings
that you have made to blaze comes Hope,
preventing me from utter misery,
the grief that wears away the heart.

(A1)   I have authority to tell the power of young men in
              their prime
that ruled with friendly omen when the troops set out;
Persuasion still breathes down on me from heaven, and
my age is suited to a song of courage—
how a fierce, warlike bird-omen sent
the twin-throned power of the Achaians,
the single-minded leaders of the youth of Greece   110
with spear and with avenging hand to Troy,
the king of birds for the king of ships,
the black-tailed eagle and the white,
appearing near the household on the spear-hand side,
perched in full view,
feasting upon a mother hare pregnant with young;
her race was over, she would never come to term.   120
Cry sorrow, sorrow—yet may good prevail!

(A2)   The army's prophet saw the portent, and the two
              devourers of the hare,
who sent the army on its way, his wisdom knew to be
the two Atreidai, diverse in their temperaments. He spoke,
    reading the omens:
'In time this expedition captures Priam's city-state,
and kills a throng
of people caught outside the citadel;
then Destiny will ravage them by force.   130
Only . . . may no god's anger darken this great curb on Troy
by striking it beforehand, as the troops assemble; Artemis the
    pure
is jealous of the winged hounds of Zeus
in pity for the wretched, cowering thing they sacrificed
with all its young before their birth;
she hates the eagles' feast.
Cry sorrow, sorrow—yet may good prevail!

(A3)   'For she, the fair one, even loves   140
the fierce cubs of the savage lion,
and she takes pleasure in the suckling young
of all the animals that roam the wild;
now she demands the portent be fulfilled.
I judge the omens are part good for us, part bad.
I call in grief upon the god of healing: beg your sister
not to stop the ships, not to delay us with contrary winds
in eagerness to bring about another sacrifice, bereft of flute
    and feast,   150
building strife inside the royal house, beyond
the fear of any man: for she awaits, and will arise
    — a terrifying, treacherous
house-guardian, an unforgetting Wrath which will avenge
    the child.'
Such were the fearful happenings Kalchas proclaimed (with
    many blessings too)
as fated by the roadside portent for the royal house;
in harmony with them,
Cry sorrow, sorrow — yet may good prevail!

(B1)   Zeus — whoever he is,   160
if this name pleases him,
I use it as I call on him:
when I take stock,
there's nothing to refer to
except Zeus, if I'm to cast away the burden of
these futile thoughts once and for all.

(B2)   The one who once was great,
bursting with never-conquered might,
men now forget that he once lived.   170
The next great power both came and went,
thrown to the floor by Zeus
the conquerer; if you shout gladly for him by this name
you'll hit the target of good sense —

(C1)   the god who keeps us on the road to wisdom,
he who made it law that men
learn from experience.
But still, in sleep the pain
of memory drips down inside the heart; the calm   180

of reason comes even to those who do not want it.
I think the favours of the gods who sit on sacred thrones
are gifts that hurt.

(C2)   Just so, then, was the elder leader
of the ships of Greece,
not blaming any prophet,
breathing along with the winds of fate
until the food ran out
and all the Greeks were suffering because they could not sail,
were forced to wait upon the shore
across the flowing tides from Chalkis, at a place   190
called Aulis.

(D1)   The gales blew in from Strymon, winds
of harmful idleness, of hunger, evil anchorage,
driving men mad,
wearing away both ships and cables,
doubling and re-doubling time –
and crushed the flower of Argos into pieces.
Then against the bitter weather Kalchas shouted out
another remedy, proclaiming Artemis –
a cure more heavy on the chieftains than
the cause itself, and one to make the sons of Atreus   200
strike with their royal sceptres at the earth and weep
beyond control.

(D2)   Then the elder king said this:
'Heavy my fate to disobey,
but heavy if I slaughter my own child,
the glory of our household,
and pollute with streams of virgin blood
my hands – a father's hands – beside   210
the altar. Which of these courses lacks its evil?
How can I desert the ships,
abandoning the expedition?
No; her demand, her utter and insensate rage
for sacrifice of virgin blood
to stop the winds
is right. May all be well.'

(E1)   And when he put upon himself the harness of necessity
his spirit veered into a course

impious and unholy and impure, then 220
he changed, and all his thoughts were reckless.
For shameful are the counsels of that wretched mania
which gives men courage to embark upon a chain of miseries.
And so he dared to sacrifice
his daughter for a war
fought to avenge one woman, as
a sending-off rite for the fleet.

(E2)   Thirsting for war, the chieftains set
at nothing all her prayers, her cries of 'Father',
or her youth and her virginity: 230
after the prayer, her father told
the servants, as she lay
clasping his robes with all her heart,
to lift her up above the altar like a goat,
with head inclined, and bind
her lovely mouth – so that she might
not make a sound and curse the royal house –

(F1)   by force, and with a bridle silence her.
She poured her saffron robe towards the earth,
and her eyes struck each minister of sacrifice 240
with piteous glance, her silhouette
just like a figure in a painting as she tried
to speak to them by name, since often in
her father's halls she'd sung a paean
for them, and with her pure voice she,
a maiden not yet brutalized by man,
had paid this honour to the last libation of the feast
for her dear father.

(F2)   What happened after that I did not see, nor will I speak
    of it;
but Kalchas' prophecies are never unfulfilled.
The scales of Justice tilt – and some men learn 250
from their experience. For the future –
when it happens, then you'll hear about it: till then, let it go;
don't weep before it's time;
all will come clear when the day breaks.
Only, may the outcome now be good;
such is our wish, the only present guardians
of Argos.

SCENE 2

Doors open. Enter Klytaimestra, from the skene.

1. ELDER   Klytaimestra, I come in reverence for your power;
    it is the custom to esteem the ruler's wife
    when he, the male, is absent from the throne.   260
    And if you've heard good news, or have not,
    but commanded sacrifice in hope of happiness, I would
    be glad to hear it – but could not protest if you refuse.

KLYTAIMESTRA   May this dawn, coming from its mother
    Night,
    break full of happiness just as the proverb says.
    Now learn of joy greater than all our hopes:
    the Argives occupy King Priam's citadel.

1. ELD   What did you say? Your words have lost me; I cannot
    believe.

KLYT   Troy is now Greek. Do I speak clear enough?

1. ELD   Joy starts to creep up on me, and evokes a tear.   270

KLYT   Yes, now your eyes give witness of your loyal heart.

1. ELD   What has convinced you? Have you proof of this?

KLYT   Of course, how could I not? – unless a god deceived me.

1. ELD   Has a mere image in a dream persuaded you?

KLYT   I would not trust the vision of a sleeping mind.

1. ELD   I hope no fledgling rumour's swollen up your hopes?

KLYT   You scoff at me as though my mind was still a child's.

1. ELD   And how long is it since the city's fall?

KLYT   I'll tell you – the same night that gave birth to this dawn.

1. ELD   What messenger could possibly have come so fast?   280

KLYT   The god of fire dispatched his blaze from Ida's peak:
    beacon sent beacon on to here; Hephaistos was
    my courier. He leapt from Ida to the rock of Hermes
    in Lemnos; from that island Zeus's peak, the Mount
    of Athos, was the third to take the mighty blaze:

then, rising up to skim the sea,
the travelling torch passed on;
the golden pine-tree gleaming like the sun
came and announced its radiant joy at Makistos.
The man on watch there was not lazy, nor did he neglect   290
his task as messenger, bemused by sleep: from far away
the beacon's light across the streams of Euripos
told of its coming to the guardsmen of Messapion.
They lit their pyre in answer, sent the message on
by lighting up a pile of aged brushwood.
The light did not grow dim, but full of strength
it leapt across the plain of Asopos, just like
the shining moon, to reach the rock of Kithairon
and wake a new relay of beacon-fire.
Nor did the men on duty there reject   300
the distant fire, but kindled even more than any yet:
the light then darted down across the lake of gorgon eyes
and reached the mountain of the roving goats,
rousing the guard there to respect the fire's command.
They did not stint their strength, but sent it further on,
igniting a great beard of flame, which passed
beyond the promontory that looks upon
the Gulf of Saron: then it darted ever on, and came
to Mount Arachneion, the lookout nearest to our city;
from there the fire leapt down to this, the house of Atreus—   310
a true descendant of the blaze on Ida.
So the commands I gave my light-bearers were all
fulfilled, as each took over from the one before;
and victory belongs to every one, the first as well as last.
Such is the proof and token which I give to you,
sent by my husband here to me from Troy.

1. ELD   Lady, I shall give thanks in due course to the gods:
        for now, I long to hear this story as a whole
        and marvel; would you tell it once again?

KLYT   Today the Greeks hold Troy. And I would say   320
        that in the city sounds are heard that do not blend.
        Put oil and vinegar in one bowl, and they fight
        so that you'd call them anything but friends:
        just so you'd hear the cries of conquerers
        and conquered, very different as befits their fates:

the women falling to embrace the bodies of their men—
husbands and brothers; children at the side
of aged fathers; throats that are no longer free
cry out in anguish for the fate of those they loved.
The others, weary from wandering after the battle stopped, 330
hunger drives them to breakfast on the city's food,
not billeted according to their rank,
but as each drew the lot of chance.
Now they are lodged in captured Trojan homes;
they've won release from frost and dew
under the open sky; like prosperous men
they sleep securely through the night.
And if they reverence the city gods
of their new-captured land, and the gods' shrines,
then they, the captors, won't be taken in their turn.   340
But still I fear; may no desire fall on the troops
to ravage sacred places, overcome by love of gain;
for they still need a voyage home,
a safe return along the course's second leg.
And if the army comes without offence against the gods,
the sufferings of the dead might still be roused from sleep—
unless some unexpected harm lands its blow first.

Well, there is all that I, a woman, have to say:
yet may the good prevail—and clearly, for us all to see;
for I would want to eat the fruit of many blessings now.   350

Exit Klytaimestra, into the skene. *Doors close.*

1. ELD   Lady, you've spoken graciously and wisely, like a man;
and I, since I have heard trustworthy proof from you,
will now prepare a fitting address to the gods;
great is the favour granted in return for pain.

CHOROS 2

ELDERS   Oh Zeus our lord
        and wonderfully ornamented Night,
        our friend because you cast
        over the towers of Troy your covering
        mesh, so that not one, however great or young,
        could overset it and escape from Ruin's

mighty, all-embracing net   360
of slavery;
I reverence Zeus, great god of guests and hosts,
who took this as his price, and aimed his bow
at Paris long ago, so that the shot would not
be wasted, falling below the mark
or far above the stars.

(A1)   They have been struck by Zeus –
that much we can track out;
he did as he decreed. Once someone said
the gods don't think it worth their while   370
to be concerned with men who trample on
the beauty of a sacred thing; but he was impious.
Suffering falls
for deeds beyond
all daring, done by men
proud past the bounds of Justice,
living in homes that teem with riches,
far beyond what's best. Let wealth
be free from pain; enough to satisfy
men of good sense.   380
For it is no defence
against excess, when once a man
has kicked into obscurity
the great altar of Justice.

(A2)   Fearful Persuasion forces him,
unbearable child of the plans of Ruin.
All cure is vain – his wound
cannot be hidden, but shines out with dreadful gleam:
and like bad bronze   390
that's rubbed away and knocked around
he has his blackness deep ingrained
when he is tested, since
he is a child chasing a bird upon the wing,
bringing unbearable affliction on his city.
None of the gods will hear his prayers:
the man familiar with such things,
the unjust man, a god destroys.
Just so was Paris, when he came
to the house of Atreus' sons   400

and shamed the table shared by guest and host,
stealing another's wife.

(B1)   Leaving her city's people
a tumult of shielded warriors,
ambush and sea-borne armament,
she brought to Troy instead of dowry
death and destruction, as
swiftly she passed between the gates
daring to do what nobody should dare.
The palace seers
loudly cried out, and said:
'Disaster for the rulers of the house,   410
disaster in the marriage-bed and everywhere she used to go
loving her husband. You can see him sitting there
dishonoured, silent, unable to curse or pray:
in his desire for her beyond the sea
Helen's ghost will seem to rule the house,
and now the husband hates the beauty of
her graceful statues;
in their empty eyes
all his desire is lost.

(B2)   'Repentant images of her appear   420
in his dream-visions, and they bring
an unreal joy:
unreal because when someone sees a promised good
the vision swerves and slips
out of his hands, and never afterwards
accompanies on wings the paths of sleep.'
These were the griefs at home, beside the hearth
– these, and much more;
and all through Greece a woman waits at home
with patient sorrow in her heart   430
for each of those who went to Troy.
Many things touch their feelings:
each one knows the person she sent out;
instead of him
a pot of ashes comes back home.

(C1)   The god of War's a money-changer, dealing in bodies;
he lifts his scales in the combat of spears

and from the funeral fires of Ilion   440
he sends the relatives
the heavy dust for which they'll weep
cramming the urns with ashes
easy stowed
in place of men.
Then they lament: this one
they praise – he was well skilled in fighting;
this one died nobly, as the battle raged
– but all for someone else's wife:
that's what they murmur quietly,
and jealous anger creeps up on   450
the leaders of this cause, the sons of Atreus,
while Greeks in all their beauty
lie around the walls,
in Trojan graves; a hostile soil
covers the men who won it.

(C2)   The city's angry words are dangerous;
they pay the debt due for the people's curse.
I'm waiting anxiously to hear
the truth the murky night conceals: 460
the gods unfailingly mark out
those who've killed many, and the black
Furies in time cast into darkness anyone
who's built success by unjust means;
they turn his fortune round and wear his life away;
and then when he has gone among the shades
there is no help. To be praised very much
is dangerous; a thunderbolt from Zeus
is cast down on the house.   470
I seek prosperity with no such jealousy;
may I not be a sacker of cities,
nor eat away my life
slave to another.

1. ELD   The beacon's good news sent
swift Rumour through
the city; but who knows if
it's true, or a deception sent us by the gods?

1. ELD   Who'd be so childlike or crazed
to let his heart be set on fire   480

by the new message from the beacon-flare, and then
be upset when the tale is changed?

1. ELD   It's typical of female leadership
to praise the favour of the gods before it's come.

1. ELD   The borders of a woman's mind are easy crossed
by quick invading thoughts:
she's far too credulous; a rumour trumpeted
by woman's quick to die.

SCENE 3

1. ELDER   We'll soon know now about the torches bearing light,
relays of beacon-watching and of fire –   490
whether they're true, or like a dream
this joyful light has robbed us of our wits:
I see a Herald coming from the shore, his forehead crowned
with olive branches; and the thirsty dust,
sister and closest relative of mud, assures me that
he will not make signs to us by the smoke of fire,
voicelessly kindling flames from mountain wood;
he'll either tell us clearly that we can rejoice,
or else . . . but I do not desire to hear the opposite.
Good things have come to us so far; let's have more good.   500
If anyone prays for the city otherwise than us,
may he himself reap all the fruit of his perverted thoughts.

Enter Herald, right.

HERALD   Land of our fathers, soil of Argos!
I've come to you in this, the tenth year's light.
One hope has stayed intact when many hopes were broken:
I never did believe that I would die
back in this land of Argos, and be buried here.
I greet the earth, I greet the sunlight,
Zeus, our lord on high, and the great god of Delphi.
Do not shoot your arrows at us any more: 510
you were our enemy more than enough at Troy;
now change your aspect, and become our saviour and our
   healer,

Lord Apollo. And I now address the gods
of the assembly-place, especially my own protector,
Hermes the herald-god, whom heralds love and honour most,
and all the heroes who once sent the army out; I pray to you
welcome back kindly all that's left of us.

Halls of our kings, dearest dwelling-place,
and sacred thrones and gods who face the sun,
if ever you did once, with gladness shining in your eyes,   520
receive the king with honour fitting after all this time –
for he returns, bearer of light in darkness
for you and all those here to share, Agamemnon the king.
Welcome him truly, as he well deserves,
who dug down Priam's city to the ground
with Zeus' pick-axe. Nothing stands upon the plain of Troy;
the altars and the shrines of gods are all destroyed,
and all the seed has perished from the land.
Such is the yoke he's cast on Troy – and now
the elder king, the son of Atreus, comes home   530
a man blessed by the gods: of all those living on the earth
most worthy of esteem. Paris and Troy
must now admit that what they did
is less than what they've suffered. He was convicted both of
     rape
and theft: he's forfeited his booty, and has reaped the harvest in
total destruction of his fathers' house and land.
So Priam's sons have paid a double penalty for crime.

1. ELD   I greet you, Herald of the army of the Greeks.

HER   I'm happy, but I would consent now if the gods demand
     my death.

1. ELD   Did longing for your native land exhaust you so?   540

HER   Yes, my eyes are filled with tears of joy.

1. ELD   You were then struck by a most pleasant malady.

HER   What do you mean? Teach me, so I may master what you
     mean.

1. ELD   You longed for those who longed for all of you.

HER   You mean they missed the army here, as we missed them?

1. ELD   So that I often groaned, my mind clouded by darkness.

HER   How did this gloomy misery attack your heart?

1. ELD   Since long ago silence has been my remedy for grief.

HER   What? While the kings were absent was there someone
       whom you feared?

1. ELD   So much that now – to use your words – death would be
       joy.   550

HER   Yes. The outcome has been good. Over a span of time
       you'd say some things have fallen well –
       and others badly. Who except the gods
       lives through his lifetime free of pain?
       Suppose I told you of our sufferings – bad quarters,
       narrow gangways, lousy bedding – what did we not
       complain about? Each day brought every form of misery.
       Then when we landed things were even worse:
       we had to sleep close under hostile walls;
       and from the heavens and the meadowland   560
       dew drizzled down on us, a constant plague
       making our woollen garments verminous.
       And then the winter, death to all bird life,
       intolerable cold brought by the snows of Ida –
       or scorching heat, when the sea fell into sleep,
       a noon siesta without wind or wave.
       What reason to lament all that? The pain has gone!
       It's gone for us, and for the dead
       there is no fear they'll ever have to rise again,
       while for what's left of all the Argive troops   570
       the gains are won, and not outweighed by sufferings.
       Why should we count the number of the dead like votes,
       why should the living grieve that Fortune wounded them?
       Myself, I want to bid a fond farewell to misery,
       since we can rightly boast here, in the sun's bright gleam,
       words that will soar on wings above both land and sea:
       'We are the Argive force that once took Troy;
       these are the spoils we nailed, throughout the length of Greece,
       upon their temple walls as everlasting glory for the gods.'
       When men hear that, their duty is to honour both   580
       this city and its generals; so will we pay our debt to Zeus,
       whose favour gave this prize to us. That's all I have to say.

1. ELD   Your words have won me over – that I won't deny;
old men are always young enough to learn.
But this is news which should especially concern the house
and Klytaimestra – though I also gain.

Doors open. Enter Klytaimestra, from the skene.

KLYTAIMESTRA   I raised my cry of joy some time ago,
when the first messenger of fire by night
came telling of the capture and the sack of Troy.
Then some reproached me, saying 'D'you believe   590
just from these beacons in the fall of Ilion?
How typical of female empty hopes.'
Such speeches made me seem a lunatic;
but still I sacrificed, and as we women do
we raised a cry of ecstasy through all
of Argos, lulling at the altars of the gods
the incense-laden, fragrant flames.
So now, why should you tell me any more?
I'll hear the story whole, from my own lord.
I must be active now, to welcome back   600
as best I can the husband I revere; can you
imagine any sweeter light for woman to behold
than that of opening the doors, after the gods have brought
her man safe back from war? This is my message: tell my
    husband he
must come quick as he can – the darling of his city;
here he will find a faithful wife
just as he left her, watchdog of the house,
loyal to him, an enemy to those who wish
him harm, and as she was in every way; through all
this time she's broken not one seal.   610
Of pleasure from another man, or rumoured scandal,
I know less than how to temper bronze.
Such is my boast; brimful of truth –
and one a noble woman may proclaim without disgrace.

Exit Klytaimestra, into the skene. *Doors close.*

1. ELD   That speech was pleasing to the ear, but for
a clear interpreter her words have only surface charm.

Tell me, Herald, I now want to learn
of Menelaos; is he safe and on his way
back here with you, the much-loved ruler of this land?

HER   There's no way I can tell a fair false tale of which   620
my friends could reap the harvest for a good long time.

1. ELD   Then why not tell the exact truth?
When truth and good are torn apart, it cannot be concealed.

HER   The man is missing from the fleet—
he and his ship. That is not false.

1. ELD   Did he set off from Troy in plain sight, or
did stormy weather hit the whole fleet, tearing him from you?

HER   You've hit the mark just like a master of the bow—
expressed a length of suffering in one short phrase.

1. ELD   What was the rumour spoken of his fate   630
by other sailors – dead, or still alive?

HER   No one knows enough to say with truth,
except the Sun, who nurtures all the life on earth.

1. ELD   Then tell us how the storm came on the fleet—
and how it ended – by the anger of the gods.

HER   It is not right to mar a glorious day
with words so bad. The honour due the gods stands far apart.
But when a grim-faced herald brings the city news
long prayed against, their army's loss,
then it's a wound for the community   640
– so many men, dragged out from many homes
as sacrificial victims by the double whip
the War-god loves, the murderous double spear . . .
When one is loaded down with cares like that
it's right to sing a paean to the Furies;
but when one comes with messages that all is safe
back to a city which rejoices in its fortune, how
can I mix good things in with evil, telling you
about the storm of anger from the gods against the Greeks?
Two bitter, ancient enemies became allies—   650
water and fire; they made a pledge
between them to destroy the wretched Argive force.
Evil, hostile waves rose in the night;

the wind from Thrace made ship collide
with ship; and they, ramming each other in the violence
of storm and hurricane and driving rain, sank out
of sight, rough-handled as by some vindictive shepherd.
When bright daylight came,
we saw the whole Aigeian sea blossom with shipwreck
fragments and the corpses of the Greeks.   660
Our ship escaped untouched —
some god (it was no mortal man) stole us
or begged us off, guiding our helm,
and saving Fortune graciously sat on the ship;
we did not have to anchor and risk being swamped,
nor were we run aground on rocky land.

So we escaped a watery grave, and in
the white daylight, scarcely believing in our luck,
we ruminated on our recent sufferings —
the wreck and miserable pounding of the fleet.   670
And now, if any of them still remains alive,
they'll speak of us, of course, as dead;
we think the same fate's theirs.
May all turn out as best it can: you must
most certainly assume Menelaos is coming here;
and if some sunbeam's found that he
is still alive and well, by Zeus' will
who does not yet want to destroy our royal house,
there is some likelihood he'll get back home.
Know all you've heard is truth.   680

Exit Herald, left.

CHOROS 3

ELDERS (A1)   Who can it be who once named you
        so perfectly in every way —
    was it not one we cannot see
    guiding his voice successfully
    who saw into her destiny,
        and called the woman married by the spear
        and fought for — Helen? Fittingly, for Helen means
        destruction: she destroyed men, ships and cities

when she left her delicately curtained bed   690
to sail away upon the giant
West wind breeze;
a hunting pack of many men with shields
chasing the vanished track of oars
beached on the leafy bank
of Simois,
drawn after her by bloody Strife.

(A2)   For Ilion the goddess Wrath
began the marriage-bond   700
which was a sorrow, and in later time
exacted vengeance for the outrage to
the guest-table and Zeus
god of the common hearth, from those
who loudly celebrated with a song
of honour to the bride,
the marriage-hymn which then
the bridegroom's kinsmen had to sing.
In its place, the ancient citadel
of Priam had to learn a different song   710
of bitter lamentation, and it called
in agony on Paris of the fatal marriage
as it died for ever, drenched
in pitiable bloodshed of its citizens.

(B1)   Just so a man once reared
a lion's cub inside his house,
robbed of its mother's milk and longing for the breast;
and as its life began it was   720
so tame it loved to play
with children, and delighted all
the elders.
It got many treats, held in their arms
just like a nursling child,
glancing bright-eyed towards the hand,
fawning in hunger.

(B2)   But in time it showed
its parents' temper: it repaid
thanks to the fosterers
by slaughtering their flocks;   730

it made a feast unasked.
The house was fouled with blood,
an anguish that the household could not fight,
a murderous great wound;
the gods had reared inside their halls
a sacrificial priest of Ruin.

(C1)   And at that time I'd say there came
to Ilion the spirit of
a windless calm,
a delicate adornment to their wealth,   740
a soft dart from the eyes,
a flower of sex to pierce the heart.
She turned aside, and made
a bitter ending to the marriage-rites,
an evil and unbearable companion
whirling onto Priam's children,
sent by Zeus the lord of hosts and guests,
a Fury to bring bridal tears.

(C2)   There is an aged saying,   750
long-established, that a man's
prosperity full-grown
gives birth – it does not die
without a child; and from good fortune for a race
is bred insatiable misery.
I'm separate from others, isolated in
my own belief; impiety
gives birth to still more impious deeds
in its own likeness, while the destiny   760
of straight, just houses always is
a handsome child.

(D1)   Among the worst of men
an ancient Violence always breeds
a new, young Violence at some time
or other, when the day comes round
appointed for its birth;
the goddess who cannot be fought,
unholy daring of black Ruin on the halls,   770
the very image of its parents.

(D2)   Justice shines clear

in smoky homes, and she respects
a man who lives inside his destiny;
she leaves the houses decked in gold
where there is filth upon the hands
with eyes averted, and she goes
to holy places — she cannot respect
the power of wealth when falsely stamped
with praise. And she steers everything   780
right to its end.

SCENE 4

Enter Agamemnon and Kassandra in a chariot, right.

1. ELDER   My king, sacker of Troy,
             Son of Atreus,
             how shall I greet you? How honour you,
             not shooting over or below the mark
             of favour due?
1. ELD   Many cross the boundaries
             of Justice, valuing appearances;
             and there are always people ready to lament   790
             together with a victim, though the sting
             of grief misses their hearts.
1. ELD   They also force unsmiling faces into grins
             which seem to share
             another's joy.
             But if a man's a good judge of his flock,
             he cannot be deceived by eyes
             whose look seems to come from a loyal mind
             but fawns with friendship weak as water.
1. ELD   Then, when you started with the army off to Troy
             because of Helen, you (I won't deny   800
             the fact) were very ugly pictured, as
             a man who'd lost his judgement,
             giving courage by a sacrifice
             to dying men.
1. ELD   But now in deep, true friendship I
             am well disposed, since you have triumphed over suffering;
             by inquiry you'll come to know in time

which of the citizens who stayed at home
has acted justly, and which has misused his time.

AGAMEMNON   First it is just that I address   810
this city, Argos, and its gods, who are responsible with me
both for my homecoming and for the Justice I exacted from
King Priam's city: for the gods heard pleas
uttered by force of arms, and they unanimously cast their votes
into the urn for murder and the sack of Troy; towards the urn
of mercy, Hope only came near – it was not filled.
Still now the rising smoke marks captured Troy;
gusts of destruction thrive, and embers dying hard
send on their way rich breaths of wealth.   820
This favour of the gods must never be forgotten:
we must pay them thanks, because we have exacted price
for reckless theft, and for a woman's sake
the Argive beast has ground the city into dust –
the offspring of the Horse, the force of shield-bearers
which made its rushing leap around the setting of the Pleiades;
springing across the battlements the ravening lion
licked up its fill of princely blood.

That was my prelude, drawn out to the gods:
as for your thought, I've heard, I will remember,   830
I agree – I'd say the same;
for there aren't many men who find it in their hearts
to reverence unjealously a friend's success;
the arrow of his discontent attacks the heart
redoubling the sufferer's pain;
he is himself weighed down by his own burdens, and
weeps at the sight of all his neighbour's wealth.
I speak from knowledge – well I understand
the mirror of society, image of a shadow,
men who seem to be my most devoted friends.   840
Only Odysseus, one who sailed against his will,
when harnessed proved a ready trace-horse for me;
though I don't know if I speak of a man alive
or dead. For all the other matters that concern
the city and the gods, I shall have open meetings, and decide
in full assembly. Then we must determine how
to make the good things last,
and where there is a need for healing remedies,

we will use sensibly burning or surgery,
in an attempt to turn away disease's harm.   850

Now I will go into my house,

Doors open. Enter Klytaimestra from the skene, *followed by
Maidservants with tapestries.*

and make beside the hearth first greeting to the gods,
who sent me out so far and led me back again.
Since victory has followed me, may it remain secure.

KLYTAIMESTRA   Men of the city, Elders of Argos, I
am not ashamed to speak of how I love
my husband. Time erodes
all reticence. I have not learned from others —
I shall tell you of my wretched life
for all the time this man was camped before the walls of
    Troy.   860
First, for a woman to remain at home
alone, without a man — that is unbearable:
she has to hear so many fresh and wounding rumours —
one herald comes, and then another brings a tale of woe
worse than the last, crying sorrow for the house;
indeed, if this man here had suffered from
as many wounds as rumours said
which reached us, he'd have more holes in him than a net.
And if he'd died as many deaths as stories claimed
he'd be a second Geryon with three bodies   870
and he could boast that he had got a triple cloak
of earth, a death for each of his three shapes.
Because of all these stories that came back,
they often had to hold me forcibly
and free my neck from nooses I had strung from up above.
That's why your son's not standing here
as he should be, the guardian of the pledges made
by me and you, Orestes; do not be amazed;
our faithful ally's looking after him,   880
Strophios the Phokian. He alerted me
to dangers on two sides: first, your peril in the war
at Troy, and then the chance that popular
revolt might overthrow the Council,

since men often give a further kick when one is down.
So this excuse of mine bears no deceit.

But as for me, the gushing fountain of my tears
have now run dry, and not one drop is left.
With waiting late at night my eyes are sore
as I cried bitterly because the beacons for your victory   890
always refused to light; and in my dreams
I was awakened by the gentle rushing of a gnat
buzzing aloud, since I saw you suffering more
than could have happened in the time sleep shared with me.

Now I've endured all that, with joyful heart
I would proclaim this man the watchdog of a farm,
the saving forestay of a ship, a high-roofed house's
solid pillar, or a father's only son,
to thirsty travellers a flowing spring,
and land for sailors suddenly in sight beyond   900
their hopes, a fair day dawning after storm.

*Klytaimestra prostrates herself full-length on the ground before
him in homage. After a few moments she rises to her feet again.*

These are the words in which I think it right to honour him:
may Jealousy stand far away; we have endured so much
before. And now, my dear beloved, step
out of this chariot – but don't permit your foot
to touch the ground, my king, the foot that conquered Troy.
Women, why do you wait? I have instructed you
to clothe the area with fabrics where he has to walk.

The Maidservants strew tapestries between the skene *door and
the chariot.*

Create at once a crimson path, where Justice may   910
lead him into a house he never thought to see.
All else a mind not overcome by sleep
will justly make, with gods' help, reach the fated end.

AG   Daughter of Leda, guardian of my home,
      you matched your speech quite closely to my absence;
      it was very long. And modest praise would be
      a gift I should receive from other mouths than yours.

As for all this, you must not treat me softly
like a woman, nor as if I were an oriental king
gape grovelling upon the ground to cry my praise.   920
Nor should you make my path into the house subject to
  jealousy
by strewing it with tapestries: the gods alone deserve such
  honour;
I, a mortal man, can't walk upon such beautiful
and finely woven robes without evoking fear.
I tell you, pay me the reverence due a man, and not a god.
My fame shouts out aloud: it does not need the aid
of beautiful foot-wiping cloths; and the gods' greatest gifts
are sense and judgement. Count only that man fortunate
who ends his life in peace and happiness.
If I can always act in such a way, I can be confident.   930

KLYT   Now tell me this, and tell me what you judge to be the
   truth.

AG   Know that I never will destroy my judgement.

KLYT   In a time of danger would you vow before the gods to do
   this thing?

AG   Yes, if a wise man told me this is what I have to do.

KLYT   If Priam had achieved all you have, what would he have
   done?

AG   I think he certainly would walk upon the tapestries.

KLYT   In that case do not fear the censure of mere men.

AG   The people murmur, and their voice is full of strength.

KLYT   But no one can be praised who is not envied too.

AG   All this desire for combat is unwomanly.   940

KLYT   Yet for the prosperous even defeat shows grace.

AG   So do you really value victory in this?

KLYT   Give way; you win if you have yielded of your own free
   will.

AG   Well, if it is your wish, let someone quickly take
from me these boots, the gear that's subject to my feet;

A Maidservant removes his boots.

> and as I walk upon these sea-dyed crimson garments of the
>   gods,
> may jealousy not strike me from a distant eye.
> I feel great awe as I destroy part of my house; my feet
> ruin the wealth of this rich, silver-purchased web.

Agamemnon steps from the chariot.

> Enough of that: as for this stranger,   950
> welcome her into our house; the god looks kindly from afar
> on those who conquer, but do not abuse their power.
> No one wears the yoke of slavery with willingness;
> and she has come back here with me, the flower chosen
> by the army as my gift from all our wealth.
> But since I've been subdued into obeying you in this,
> I trample crimson as I go into my house.

*Agamemnon moves to the edge of the tapestries, but then
hesitates.*

> KLYT   There is the sea, and who shall drain it dry?
>   It breeds an ever self-renewing stream
>   of crimson dye for clothing, worth its weight in silver ore: 960
>   thanks to the gods the house is rich in goods
>   like these; my king, your house has never suffered poverty.
>   I would have vowed the trampling down of many vestments, if
>   we had been told in oracles it was
>   the only way to bring this man back here alive:
>   for when the root is there, the leafage comes over a house
>   extending shade above to shield us from the dog-star heat;
>   now you have come back to your hearth and home,
>   that signals warmth has come back in the winter-time;
>   and when Zeus makes the wine from bitter, unripe grapes   970
>   then there is coolness in the house
>   when he, the man, fulfils his role and roams around his halls.

Exit Agamemnon, into the skene. *The Maidservants remove the
tapestries and exeunt into the skene.*

Zeus, Zeus, fulfiller: now fulfil my prayers;
take care to fulfil all of this that you intend.

Exit Klytaimestra, into the skene. *Doors close.*

CHOROS 4

ELDERS (A1)   Tell me, why does this
    persistent fear
    hover in front of my prophetic heart?
    My song is full of prophecies,
    unbidden and unpaid,
    and my heart doesn't have the daring and the trust   980
    to spit away their meaning like
    a dream of doubtful outcome.
    Ruin passed its prime when mooring-ropes
    were cast back on the sand, and our fleet sailed
    for Ilion.

  (A2)   I have seen him return – I've witnessed it
    with my own eyes;
    but still my spirit sings   990
    self-taught within a tuneless dirge,
    fit for the Furies, since it is bereft of all
    the welcome confidence of hope.
    The innards of a man
    do not tell idle tales;
    my heart throbs ominously close
    beside a mind which knows that Justice comes;
    I pray that this may fall
    out of my expectation, false
    and unfulfilled.   1000

  (B1)   The moment where great health reaches its end
    is all-destroying; for disease, its neighbour, shares
    the party-wall and presses hard.
    So too the destiny of one
    who travels straight can strike a reef
    that was invisible.
    Then caution can defend
    his property, by casting out

the right amount of goods—   1010
the whole house will not founder, over-
burdened with excess of agony;
he does not sink the ship.
A large gift from Zeus,
springing abundantly from ploughing every year,
wards off the plague of famine.

(B2)   Once the black blood of death
has fallen from a man into the ground,   1020
who could recall it singing any spell?
The one who truly knew
to bring back men from death—
Zeus stopped him savagely.
And had the gods not set
each human fate so it prevents
the next from taking more,
my heart would overcome my tongue
and pour out all it feels;
but as things are it murmurs in the dark,   1030
sick-spirited, and not expecting to bring anything
through to the end while my mind burns.

SCENE 5

Doors open. Enter Klytaimestra, from the skene.

KLYTAIMESTRA   You, go inside as well, Kassandra. Since
   Zeus brought you in kindliness to share
   this household's purifying rites, standing among
   our many slaves beside his altar as the god of property,
   get down from this chariot: do not be proud;
   they say once even Herakles was sold   1040
   and forced to eat the bread of slavery.
   And if Necessity bears down and brings one to this fate,
   it is worth much to be the slave of masters who have long been
      rich.
   Those who have reaped fine harvests suddenly,
   beyond their expectations: they are cruel to slaves,
   and treat them worse than proper rules require.
   You've heard from me just what our customs are.

1. ELDER It's you she spoke to — very clearly, too;
　　since you are caught inside the net of fate
　　obey, if you are going to; perhaps you won't.

KLYT Unless she's like a swallow, speaking only　　　　1050
　　unintelligible foreign sounds, I'll reach
　　inside her mind and win her over with my words.

1. ELD Follow; for as things stand she says what's best.
　　Obey, and leave your place here on the chariot.

KLYT I have no leisure now to waste time out of doors.
　　Beside the central hearth already stand
　　the sheep prepared for sacrifice —
　　a pleasure which we never hoped to see.
　　If you will do at all what I say, don't waste time;
　　but if you cannot fully understand my words　　　　1060
　　then answer with the hand, as all barbarians do, instead of
　　　　speech.

1. ELD I think the stranger needs a clear interpreter;
　　she's like an animal just taken in a trap.

KLYT She must be mad, sent crazy signals by her mind,
　　to come here from a city newly sacked,
　　and not learn how to bear the bit, until
　　she's had her spirit broken in a foam of blood.
　　I will not waste more words on her and be disdained.

Exit Klytaimestra, into the skene. *The doors remain open.*

SCENE 6

1. ELDER Well, I will not be angry — for I pity her.
　　Unhappy woman, leave the chariot, and willingly　　　1070
　　yield to Necessity; accept this unaccustomed yoke.

*Kassandra leaps from the chariot, which is then removed by the
left* parodos. *She bursts into agonized, energetic dance and song.*

KASSANDRA (A1)　　　(*Shrieks*)
　　Oh Apollo, Apollo!

1. ELD   Why do you cry in agony and name Apollo?
    He's not a god whom anyone lamenting should approach.

KASS (A2)   (*Shrieks*)
    Oh Apollo, Apollo!

1. ELD   Now once again she cries out ominously to
    the god who cannot listen to a plaintive song.

KASS (B1)   Oh Apollo, Apollo,   1080
    God of the Ways, and my destroyer;
    once again you have destroyed me easily.

1. ELD   I think she's going to prophesy about her miseries;
    the god's gift stays with her, although she's a slave.

KASS (B2)   Oh Apollo, Apollo,
    God of the Ways, and my destroyer.
    Ah! Where have you led me? To what house?

1. ELD   The house of the Atreidai: if you don't know that
    I can inform you; then you will not speak it false.

KASS (C1)   Ah! Ah!
    A house that hates the gods, and knows   1090
    inside its heart murder of kindred, eaten flesh—
    a slaughterhouse, a floor sprinkled with blood.

1. ELD   The foreign girl is like a hunting dog, keen on the scent.
    She searches for the track of murder; she will find it, too.

KASS (C2)   Yes, I believe this evidence
    about the baby children who lament
    their slaughter, and their roasted flesh their father ate.

1. ELD   We certainly have heard of your prophetic gifts;
    but we want no predictions here today.

KASS (D1)   Oh god, what's being plotted? What   1100
    is this new grief? Great
    evil's planned here in this house,
    unbearable to all its friends, impossible to cure; and help
    stands far away.

1. ELD   I cannot understand this prophecy; as for the others,
    I knew them: the whole of Argos cries them out.

KASS (D2)   Oh wretched woman, is this your design?
                 To wash your husband in a ritual bath,
                 then – how shall I speak the end?
                 It will come quickly – look, she reaches out,   1110
                 stretches each hand in turn.

1. ELD   I don't yet understand: for now after her riddles
          I'm bewildered by these obscure oracles.

KASS (E1)   Oh God, oh God, what's this?
                 A net of Death?
                 But no, the snare's the partner in his bed
                 and in his murder; in this family insatiable strife
                 must cry a victory-song for sacrifice to be avenged.

1. ELD   What kind of Fury do you ask to raise her cry
          over this house? Your words bring me no joy.   1120

ELDERS   But to the heart the saffron drop
              runs fast, the blood which for men speared
              reaches its end as life's sun sets.
              Destruction quickly comes.

KASS (E2)   Ah! Ah! Look! Keep the bull
                 from the cow! She's tangled him
                 in robes, and with a black-horned thing
                 she strikes; he falls into the water.
                 I tell you the treachery that happens in the bath.

1. ELD   I would not boast that I am really good   1130
          at understanding prophecies; but this I do not like.

ELD   What happy word for mankind
           ever came from oracles? Only through misfortune
           do the wordy crafts of prophets bring
           their tales of terror for us all to learn.

KASS (F1)   Oh! What about my miserable, evil fate?
                 I cry aloud, pouring out my own sufferings as well.
                 Why did you bring me here in all my misery,
                 except to die with you? What else?

ELD   You're frenzied, carried from us by the gods,   1140
           as you cry your own tuneless elegy,
           just like the tawny nightingale whose miserable heart

      laments unendingly for her dead son
      slaughtered by both his parents.

KASS (F2)   I wish my fate were like
      the tuneful nightingale's: the gods gave her
      a feathered shape and sweet life free from pain;
      I will be cloven by a double-sided spear.

ELD   What god impels these rushing stabs   1150
      of useless inspiration; why do you
      mould to a melody of dissonant and piercing strain
      such fearful things?
      Who marked for you the limits of this path
      of evil-omened prophecy?

KASS (G1)   Oh Paris, Paris, when you married you destroyed
      your family!
      Skamander, river of my native land —
      beside your banks I once was nursed and grew
      unhappy;
      now I know I soon will prophesy   1160
      around the rivers Acheron and Kokytos.

ELD   This is all too clear! Why do you say
      such things a baby child could understand?
      A deadly sting attacks me as you cry
      so pitiably for your dreadful fate,
      it breaks my heart to hear.

KASS (G2)   Oh pain, pain of my city utterly destroyed,
      and sacrifice my father made before the walls
      recklessly rich in slaughter of the grazing flocks;
      there was no cure to save   1170
      my city from its fate,
      and I will swiftly fall warm-blooded to the ground.

Kassandra collapses.

ELD   This follows what you said before:
      and some malignant daimon weighs so heavily
      he forces you to sing of miserable suffering and death;
      I cannot see how this will end.

KASS   (*slowly rises to her feet*)
Now my oracle will no more peek
from under veils like some new-married bride –
no, it will come in radiance, as does the wind   1180
at sunrise, so that miseries far greater than
our present woes will surge like waves towards
the light. I will teach you now in no
more riddles; witness how I run close and scent out
the trail of the crimes that happened here.
A chorus lives inside this house, and sings
in unison a tuneless melody that does not tell of good.
To gain more courage they have drunk their fill
of human blood, and stay to celebrate an orgy in the house,
impossible to send away – the Furies of this family.   1190
The song they sing as they beseige this house
tells of the first-beginning crime, and turn by turn they spit
    upon
the brother's marriage-bed in hatred of the man who
    trampled it.
Well, have I missed – or do I shoot and hit my prey?
Or am I just a phoney prophet peddling nonsense door to door?
You, be my witness and swear on oath that I know all
the ancient crimes committed in this house.

1. ELD   But how could any oath, though truly taken, heal
this wound? I am amazed that you,
grown up across the sea, can speak about a foreign city
    with   1200
as much authority as if you had been here yourself.

KASS   The prophet-god Apollo gave this power to me.

1. ELD   Was he – although a god – struck by desire for you?

KASS   Before now I was too ashamed to speak of it.

1. ELD   Yes, anyone can have that luxury when prosperous.

KASS   He was a wrestler who breathed favour strongly onto me.

1. ELD   And did you come together to the work of making
    children?

KASS   No, I pledged my body to him, and then broke my word.

1. ELD   After you'd been possessed by the gods' skill of
          prophecy?

KASS   I had already told the Trojans of their future
        sufferings.   1210

1. ELD   How were you not harmed by the anger of the god?

KASS   Since this offence, no one believes a word I say.

1. ELD   To us, at least, all that you prophesy seems true.

KASS   Ah, Ah! Agony!
        Once more the fearful pain of true prophetic sight
        whirls me around inside and vexes me; the prelude to a trance.
        Look, can you see these young ones sitting close
        beside the house, like in their shape to dreams?
        Children, it seems, whom their own relatives have killed;
        their hands are full of meat – their own flesh served as
            food,   1220
        a pitiable burden! I can see them holding up
        the vitals and the entrails, which their father tasted.
        I tell you someone plans to be avenged for this –
        a lion-coward, wallowing in the marriage-bed,
        a stay-at-home takes vengeance on the man who has returned,
        the master who is mine – for I must bear the yoke of slavery.
        Commander of the fleet, sacker of Ilion,
        he does not see that soon the hateful bitch's tongue
        which spoke at length to welcome him with joy
        will strike by evil fortune at its target – hidden death.   1230
        Such is her daring – she, the woman, is the slayer of
        her man; what fearful monster can I call her,
        and be right? An amphisbaina, or a Skylla lurking
        in the rocks, to bring destruction down on sailors,
        raging, hellish mainad who breathes out relentless War
        against her kindred! How she trumpeted her victory,
        all-daring, just as if she'd turned the tide in battle –
        while she seemed to be rejoicing at his safe return.
        And if you don't believe me – well, so what? It's all the same.
        The future comes, and very soon, if you stay here, you'll
            see,   1240
        and pity me, and call me all too true a prophetess.

1. ELD   The feasting of Thyestes on his children's flesh

I understand, and shudder at it — fear grips me
to hear these things told truly, not in flights of fantasy.
As for the rest, I've fallen far outside the track.

KASS   I tell you that you'll witness Agamemnon's death.

1. ELD   Silence, unhappy woman; do not speak ill-omened
words.

KASS   The god of healing does not govern what I say.

1. ELD   No, not if that's to happen; but I beg it won't.

KASS   While you say prayers, they're planning how to kill. 1250

1. ELD   Who is the man preparing for this crime?

KASS   You've really lost the path of all my prophecies.

1. ELD   Yes, for I cannot see what means the murderer could
use.

KASS   And yet I can speak Greek — perhaps too well.

1. ELD   The oracles at Delphi, though they're Greek, are hard to
understand.

KASS   Ah! The fire again! It's coming at me!
Oh Apollo, wolf-god, let me go!
A double-footed lioness beds down beside
the wolf, during the absence of the noble lion.
She's the one who'll kill him! Like someone preparing
drugs   1260
she'll add my quittance to her brew of hate;
and as she sharpens up her sword upon the man
she'll boast that she is paying him for bringing me back here.
Why do I still wear all these things that mock at me —
this sceptre, and a prophetess's woollen bands around my
neck?
I will destroy you now, before I die myself!

Kassandra throws off the emblems of prophecy.

Just go to hell. There, drop; that's how I pay you back.
Enrich some other girl with misery instead of me.
Look now, Apollo, no-one else, is stripping me

of my prophetic garments. He has seen me mocked   1270
most terribly by 'friends' who were my enemies.
As if I were a wanderer in search of alms from door to door
I was called beggar, wretch, and starveling—
that is what I had to suffer. Now the prophet-god has finished
     with
his prophetess, and brought me here to meet my death.
Instead of our ancestral shrine, a butcher's block waits here for
     me;
my warm red blood will furnish the preliminary sacrifice.

But yet we will not die dishonoured by the gods;
for there will come another, one who will requite our
     fates—   1280
an offspring who will kill his mother, to avenge his father's
     death.
An exile, wanderer, a stranger to this land
he will return to put the coping-stone on all these kindred deeds
     of hate.
For there has been a mighty oath sworn by the gods
that his dead father's corpse will bring him back.
Why do I still lament so piteously?
Since I have seen my native city, Ilion,
suffer the way it did, and those who captured Troy
ending like this under the verdict of the gods,
I'll go; I will begin the rite; I can endure my death.   1290
Now I address these doors as those that lead to Hades;
May I meet one lethal stroke
so I may close my eyes without a struggle,
as my blood streams from me in an easy death.

1. ELD   You are a lady greatly to be pitied; wise as well,
in your long speech. But if you truly know
that you yourself will die, how can you tread the path
towards the altar with the courage of an ox driven by gods?

KASS   Strangers, there's no escape for any further time.

1. ELD   Last moments are the highest valued.   1300

KASS   This day has come. I gain nothing by flight.

1. ELD   Your constancy's the mark of a courageous soul.

KASS   Fortunate people never have to hear such words.

1. ELD   Still, a glorious death brings fame.

KASS   Oh, my father, and your noble children!

1. ELD   What is it? What fear turns you back again?

KASS   Oh! Oh!

1. ELD   Why d'you cry out? Some horror in your mind?

KASS   This house breathes out a bloody stench of murder.

1. ELD   That's the smell of sacrifices at the hearth.   1310

KASS   The reek is putrid like that from a grave.

1. ELD   You certainly aren't speaking of a Syrian incense in the
          house.

KASS   Well I will go, and in the house I will lament
        my own and Agamemnon's fate; I've had enough of life.

        Oh, strangers,
        do not think I'm trembling, like a bird scared of the trap;
        I simply beg you be my witnesses after my death,
        when one more woman dies in recompense for me,
        and for the man so badly married yet another falls in turn.
        I ask this of you as a stranger who's about to die.   1320

1. ELD   Unhappy one, I pity you the fate you have foreseen.

KASS   I want to utter one more speech – or dirge –
        my very own; I pray to this, the last
        sunlight that I will ever see, that those who come
        to kill in vengeance for my master take revenge as well
        for me, a slave who died, an easy thing to kill.

        Oh, the fate of human beings! When prosperous
        they're like a shadow; if misfortune strikes,
        one stroke of a wet sponge destroys the picture.
        I pity this more even than our pitiable fate.   1330

Exit Kassandra, into the skene. *Doors close.*

CHOROS 5

ELDERS   Success is an insatiable danger for
            mankind; but no one bars it from the halls
            that all men point at, saying
            'Do not come here any more'.
            The blessed ones gave this man the great gift
            of sacking Troy, and he returned
            home honoured by the gods;
            so if he now must pay for blood
            shed long ago, and by his death pay back the dead
            a complete recompense for other deaths,   1340
            what mortal man could boast aloud that he
            was born under a daimon who protects from harm?

SCENE 7

AGAMEMNON   (*inside the* skene) Oh god, I'm struck a deep
    and mortal wound.

1. ELDER   Silence! Who cries that he is struck a deadly blow?

AG   Oh god, I'm struck again.

1. ELD   From the king's cries I think the deed is done:
    let us take common counsel; is there some safe plan?

1. ELD   I'll tell you what I think; let's have a herald tell
    the citizens to come and bring help to the royal house.

1. ELD   No! I think we had better break in there at once   1350
    and prove the deed while the sword flows fresh blood.

1. ELD   I share his views completely, and I vote
    that we do something; it's a time for no delay.

1. ELD   It is quite clear: this is the work of people who
    intend imposing tyranny upon the city-state.

1. ELD   Yes, we are wasting time, while they tread underfoot
    gracious Delay; their hands are not asleep.

1. ELD   I haven't got a plan to offer; and
    no one should act unless he has already planned.

1. ELD   I agree; I do not know how any words   1360
    could bring the dead man back to life again.

1. ELD   Shall we then yield, and just drag out our lives
    subjected to these people who've defiled the house?

1. ELD   It is insufferable; I'd rather be dead.
    That is a gentler fate than tyranny.

1. ELD   But are we just presuming he is dead
    upon the evidence of those two cries?

1. ELD   We really shouldn't talk about this till we know,
    for guessing is a very different thing from certainty.

1. ELD   I'm filled from every side with votes for this: 1370
    that we must know exactly what has happened to the king.

Doors open. Enter Klytaimestra, with bloodstained sword, on the
ekkuklêma *over the bodies of Agamemnon (covered by a net-like
robe) and Kassandra.*

KLYTAIMESTRA   Much I have said before to suit the
        moment, and
    I'm not ashamed to contradict it all;
    how else could anyone contrive hostilities against an enemy
    who seemed to be a friend, and fence the hunting-nets
    of pain up to a height beyond escape?
    This conflict is the climax of an ancient feud—
    it's been long in my mind, but still at last it came.
    I stand just where I struck; the deed's been done.
    And I will not deny that I made sure   1380
    he had no chance to escape or ward off his fate.
    I cast an endless mesh around him, like
    a net for fish—a rich and evil robe.
    I strike him twice, and with two cries
    his limbs went slack, and when he'd fallen
    I give him a third, a votive offering
    of thanks to Pluto, saviour of the dead.
    And as he lies he breathes his life away,
    and blowing out a rapid spurt of blood
    he strikes me with black showers of murderous dew,   1390
    and I rejoice no less than does the growing corn
    in Zeus' rain during the birth-pangs of the sheaf.

Elders of Argos, this is how things are;
be glad, if that's your will, and I will glory openly.
If it were right to pour libations now
upon this corpse, it would be just, it would be more than just;
such was the bowl of cursed evils this man filled
inside our house, and drains it now on his return.

1. ELD   We marvel at your tongue, the boldness of your speech,
for you to make a boast like this over your husband's
corpse.   1400

KLYT   You try me like a woman of no sense,
but I speak out to you, who know it well,
with fearless heart; whether you wish to praise me or to blame,
it's all the same. This is Agamemnon, my husband,
now a corpse, the work of this right hand,
a just executant. And that is all.

ELDERS (A1)   Woman, what evil drug
grown in the earth, or drink
sprung from the sea did you consume
to give the daring for this act of murder? You
reject and cut away the people's curses; you will be   1410
cast out, a hateful burden on the citizens.

KLYT   So now you judge it right that I be exiled from this land
and have the hatred of the citizens and people's curses,
who never showed the slightest opposition to this man
when he, not caring much about it, just as if an animal was dead
out of abundant flocks of fleecy sheep,
killed his own daughter, dearest fruit sprung from
my labour-pangs, to charm away the winds from Thrace.
Should you not rather then have driven him out of this land
to expiate that crime? But when you come to look   1420
into my deeds, you are a savage judge. I tell you this:
if you make threats, know I'm prepared
on equal terms: if someone conquers me by force
then he may rule; but if the god ordains my victory,
you'll learn discretion, late although the lesson comes.

ELD (A2)   You aim too high,
your words are over-proud; your mind
is maddened by your murderous deed,

      your eyes are flecked with blood.
      Bereft of friends, you will one day pay for this crime
      with blow in turn for blow.   1430

KLYT   Now hear my solemn, righteous oath:
   by the fulfilling Justice of my child, and by
   Destruction and the Furies, goddesses to whom I sacrificed this
      man,
   my expectations do not tread the house of fear
   so long as fire is kindled at my hearth
   by Aigisthos, who now, as always, cares for me;
   he is my mighty shield of confidence.
   Here lies the man who has defiled my womanhood,
   the one who charmed each golden girl he saw outside the walls
      of Troy,
   and here's the captive, portent-reading   1440
   concubine who gave him oracles—
   his faithful mistress, who wore out the benches of the ships
   beside him. They have both received what they deserve:
   he died as I have told, while she sang her last song,
   her funeral lament, just like a swan, and lies
   beside him as his lover; she has given me
   a dainty side-dish for my feast of sexual ecstasy.

ELD (B1)   Oh, if only sudden death—not fraught
   with agony or lengthy pain—
   could come, and bring to us   1450
   eternal, everlasting sleep, now that
   our kind protector's been struck down;
   after enduring much for one woman,
   another woman took his life.

   Demented Helen,
   you alone destroyed those many,
   many lives at Troy; and now
   you've crowned yourself with this last, perfect
   ornament through ineradicable blood. Surely there
      then   1460
   was in this house a Strife, the sorrow that destroys mankind.

KLYT   Do not pray for death
   weighed down by this,
   and do not turn your anger onto Helen,

calling her a man-destroyer, claiming she
alone destroyed the lives of many Greeks,
creating pain beyond our power to heal.

ELD (B2)   Oh daimon, as you fall upon this house
          and on Tantalos' two descendants,
          you show your power that bites my heart   1470
          through women who are kindred souls; look,
          like a hostile crow she stands
          over the body, and she glories
          in her tuneless, bitter song.

KLYT   Now you have mended what you say, invoking him,
      the
          thrice-gorged daimon of this race;
          through him the lust for lapping blood
          is nurtured in the belly; before an ancient sore
          is healed, new pus breaks out.   1480

ELD (C1)   The daimon whom you praise
          is truly great, and heavy in his wrath
          against this house: an evil song of praise,
          full of insatiable disaster,
          all through Zeus,
          the cause and the contriver of it all;
          for what's fulfilled for mankind without Zeus?
          Is any of this not ordained by gods?

          Oh, my king, my king,
          how shall I weep for you?   1490
          What can my loving heart tell you?
          You lie here in this woven spider's web
          breathing your life away murdered outrageously,
          trapped like a slave,
          tamed to a treacherous death,
          struck by her double-sided sword.

KLYT   You claim the deed was mine?
          Then do not think of me
          as Agamemnon's wife.
          The sharp avenging spirit born   1500
          from Atreus' cruel feast
          took the shape of this man's woman,

giving him, full-grown,
as crowning sacrificial payment to the young.

ELD (C2)   Who will say that you
are not at fault in this man's death?
How? How? But still, the spirit sprung
for vengeance from his father might have taken part;
the black War-god forces his way
with streams of kindred blood,   1510
until his path brings payment for
the eaten children's clotted gore.

Oh, my king, my king,
how shall I weep for you?
What can my loving heart tell you?
You lie here in this woven spider's web,
breathing your life away murdered outrageously,
trapped like a slave,
tamed to a treacherous death,
struck by her double-sided sword.   1520

KLYT   I do not think his death
was slavish, nor can you reproach
me for my treachery;
did not this man lay deceit
and ruin on our house?
He took my own child I brought up,
my much-lamented Iphigeneia, and for what
he did unjustly to her he now suffers
justice; let him not
talk big in Hades, since death by the sword
took payment from him for what he began.

ELD (D1)   I am bereft of thought's   1530
resourceful care; the house
is falling, and I do not know
which way to turn.
I fear the drumming of this stream of blood
that shakes the house; it is no drizzle now.
Justice is being sharpened for another deed
of harm, at other sharpening-stones of Destiny.

Oh Earth, Earth, if only you
had taken me before I saw him in

this wretched resting-place, the silver-sided bath.   1540
Who will lament him? Who will bury him?
Will you dare to kill
your husband and bewail him too,
unjustly pay his shade a tribute that is no
true tribute for his mighty deeds?
Who will speak the funeral praise
over this godlike man,
and do the task sincerely, tearfully?   1550

KLYT   It's not your business to concern yourself
with this: he fell and died
at my hands, and I'll bury him—
not with laments by people from his home;
no. At the swiftly flowing crossing
of the stream of tears
his daughter, as is right,
Iphigeneia, will
embrace and kiss her father lovingly.

ELD (D2)   Now taunt meets counter-taunt,   1560
and it is hard to judge.
The robber's robbed, the killer pays,
and this remains as long as Zeus sits on his throne:
he who does, shall suffer; that is law.
Who could cast the seed of curses from the house?
This family is welded to destruction.

KLYT   Your words of prophecy are filled
with truth; but I for my part want
to swear a bargain with the daimon
of this house, to tolerate what's happened   1570
(though it's hard to bear); and for the future,
he must leave this house, to wear away
another family with kindred murders.
Keeping just a small amount of all
my wealth's enough, and would content me, if
I've rid these halls of mania for murder.

SCENE 8

Enter Aigisthos with armed Bodyguards, left.

AIGISTHOS   Oh welcome light! This is the day of justice!
   I would say at last the gods avenge mankind
   as they look down from high upon the sorrows of this earth,
   now I can see this man lie here in woven robes devised   1580
   by Furies, a delight to me, as he pays us in turn
   for all the fearful guile his father's hand contrived.
   For Atreus, when ruler of this land, the father of this man,
   expelled Thyestes from the city and his house
   (Thyestes was my father, let me tell the story
   lucidly) – when there was dispute about his right to power.
   Later, unfortunate Thyestes came back here as suppliant,
   took refuge at the hearth, and so obtained a safe retreat:
   he did not die and pour blood on his native soil –
   at least not his; to welcome him the godless father of this
      man,   1590
   Atreus, more in eagerness than friendship, entertained
   my father under pretext of a splendid feast,
   and served a meal made of his children's flesh.
   The feet and fingertips he cut up small,
   concealed them under flesh so they could not be seen, then gave
   this dish to Thyestes, who sat alone; he took and ate
   in ignorance the meal that's brought destruction, as you see,
      upon this race.
   And when he realized the ghastly thing that he had done,
   he cried aloud and fell back spewing out the bitter meat,
   and vowed intolerable death for all the sons of Pelops,   1600
   kicking the banquet-table over as he laid his curse,
   'So perish the whole race of the Pleisthenidai'.
   That is the reason you can see this man lie here;
   and it is just that I contrived this act of murder.
   He drove me, the thirteenth child, together with
   my wretched father into exile, still a babe in swaddling clothes;
   but when I had grown up Justice led me back home,
   and I laid hold of this man – though I was not actually here –
   when I devised the many details of this plan of treachery.
   Indeed, even my death would be a joy to me,   1610
   now I have seen him in the net that Justice wove.

1. ELDER   Aigisthos, I have no respect for one who gloats
     among
misfortunes. You say you killed this man
of your free will, and you alone contrived his pitiable death;
then I say in the hour of justice you will not escape
curses that threaten death by stoning at the people's hands.

AIG   So this is how you talk, as you sit down below
upon the lower deck, while we, the masters of the ship, are on
     the bridge?
In your old age, you'll see how hard it is
to learn at such a time of life, when calm discretion is
     imperative;   1620
imprisonment and hunger-pangs are two most excellent
prophets and healers for the mind, even of senile men.
Have you got eyes, and yet cannot see this?
Don't kick against sharp spikes, or you will suffer pain.

1. ELD   You woman, did you wait for them to come back from
     the war,
and while you stayed at home defiled a husband's bed
as well as plotting death against our army's general?

AIG   Here are yet more words bound to end in tears!
Your tongue is just the opposite of Orpheus':
for he seduced all creatures by the pleasure that his singing
     gave,   1630
while you stir up my anger by your childish barking; you'll
be led away, and when you're mastered we will see you much
     more tame.

1. ELD   So you will really be our tyrant here in Argos,
you who planned the murder of the king,
but did not dare to do the deed yourself?

AIG   Well, the deceit was clearly woman's work,
while I was suspect as an enemy from long ago.
I shall attempt to use the wealth of this man's house
to rule the citizens; if anyone does not obey,
I'll place a heavy yoke on him—he won't be   1640
a barley-fattened trace-horse! Darkness has
a fearful housemate, Hunger, and she'll make him powerless.

1. ELD   Given your evil purpose, why did you

not slaughter him yourself? Why allow the woman
to pollute this country and its gods, in killing him
with you? Oh, if Orestes somewhere sees the light,
that he may come back here, and with good fortune win
the victory by killing both of them.

AIG   If that's the way you talk and act, you'll soon know better.

1. ELD   Hey! On guard, my friends; action is coming now. 1650

AIG   Hey! Everyone, sword ready, hilt forward!

1. ELD   I too am hilt-forward; and I do not refuse to die.

AIG   We accept your talk of death, and welcome it.

KLYTAIMESTRA   No, dearest man; let us do no more harm.
So many grievous things have now been done that they will be a
    bitter harvest.
There has been enough torment already; let us not be stained
    with blood.
Elders, please go back to your homes; it's better to take thought
before you act and suffer; we must all accept what has been
    done.
If only we could say 'Here is the end of all our troubles';
we have been mangled terribly by the god's heavy claw.   1660
These are a woman's words, if anyone thinks them worth
    learning from.

AIG   No. They are aiming empty threats at me,
and risk their lives by throwing out such words.
You lack all self-restraint and sense, to heap abuse upon your
    master.

*The Elders begin to exit left, some individually and some in small
groups.*

1. ELD   It would not be the Argive way to fawn upon so base a
    man.

AIG   I'll persecute you later on, and be revenged for this.

1. ELD   Not if the god decides to bring Orestes back.

AIG   I know it well: all exiles feed on hope.

1. ELD   Go on, grow fat, soil Justice – while you can.

AIG   You will pay me amends, be sure, for all this
foolishness.   1670

1. ELD   Boast and be confident, just like a cock beside his hen.

The last Elders exeunt.

KLYT   Take no account of all these idle barkings; you and I
shall rule this house and order all things well.

Exeunt Klytaimestra, Aigisthos and Bodyguards into the skene.
Withdraw ekkuklema. Doors close.

LIBATION BEARERS

Libation Bearers

SCENE I

Preset Agamemnon's grave.

Enter Orestes and Pylades right, in travelling clothes.

ORESTES   Hermes! God below the earth, protector of my
    father's power,
become my saviour, fight beside me as I ask you now.
For I have come back to this land; I'm home once more;
and here upon his burial mound I call out to my father:
hear me! Listen!

Orestes cuts two locks of his hair, and places them on the grave.

This is a lock of hair for Inachos, where I grew up;
and this, a second lock, a token of my grief.
For I was not here, father, to lament your death,
nor could I raise my hands in tribute when they carried out your
    corpse.

What do I see? Who are those women, all together, clothed in
    black   10
and coming here? What misfortune could this be?
Has some new torment fallen on our house,
or would I be right if I guess that they have brought
libations for my father, offerings to soothe the dead?
It's that and nothing else! I'm sure one of them is
my sister, Elektra, marked out by her special grief.

Zeus, grant that I avenge my father's death;
become my ally of your own free will.

Pylades, let's stand out of the way, so I may clearly learn   20
Just why this group of women has come here.

Orestes and Pylades withdraw out of the orchêstra *into the right*
parodos.

Enter Elektra and the Libation Bearers, left.

CHOROS I

LIBATION BEARERS (A1)   We have come from the house,
          sent here
      to bring libations. Sharp blows rained on us.
      Look at these gashes on my cheek —
      they're new; but for a long time now
      my heart has fed itself on misery.
      We've rent the fabric of our clothes in grief,
      we've torn and crushed the veils around our breasts.   30
      These are disasters which bring no one joy.

   (A2)   A piercing cry rang out,
      it made our hair stand up!
      At dead of night shrill Fear, the dream-interpreter,
      roared out its anger from her sleep
      deep in the house,
      and fell in fury on the women's rooms.
      Then those who judge the meaning of such dreams
      swore oaths before the gods to tell the truth
      and said it meant the dead below the earth
      were furiously angry, held us all to blame   40
      and raged against their murderers.

   (B1)   Oh Mother Earth! This is no real service to the dead!
      That godless woman sent me here
      to ward off torment from herself.
      And I'm afraid to speak the words she wants.
      How can the house be purified, once blood's been shed?
      Oh hearth of utter misery!
      Oh ruined house!   50
      Sunless, hateful mists of darkness shroud these halls
      where the true kings are dead.

   (B2)   Their glory once could not be fought or tamed.
      It found its place in every Argive heart.
      And now it's gone. We're all afraid. Success —

for everyone that is a god, more than a god.   60
But Justice holds her scales,
and suddenly strikes down those in the light,
while other criminals live on – yet in the twilight of their life
they suffer pain. Unfathomable night holds more.

(C1)   The Earth our mother's soaked up too much blood;
the gore of vengeance clots, and cannot be dissolved.
A painful Ruin keeps the murderer alive until
diseases bloom.   70

(C1)   There is no going back for anyone who takes
a girl's virginity, and just the same
if every river in the world ran through a single stream,
even they could never purify
the man whose hands the blood of murder has defiled.

The gods imposed their yoke upon my city.
I was led out from my father's house
to suffer, fated evermore to be a slave.
We must approve of everything they do,
just and unjust; we are compelled   80
to overcome our bitter hatred.
So, I weep beneath my cloak
for the misfortune of the rightful kings.
My hidden grief has chilled my heart.

SCENE 2

ELEKTRA   Slave-women, keepers of the house,
since you are here as my attendants
for this ceremony, please advise me now:
what shall I say, as I pour these libations at his grave?
How can I please him? What should I ask of my father?
Am I to tell him that I bring these offerings from a loving wife
to her beloved husband – when the gift is from my mother?   90
I dare not lie like that; I don't know what to say
as I present this offering at my father's tomb.
Should I use the old form of words that starts
'To those who've sent these garlands, grant their just
    rewards . . .'

– in this case, that would mean a payment worthy of their evil
   deeds.
Or should I just pour out this stream of liquid for the earth to
   drink
in silence just as deep as when my father died,
pay him no honour, then creep off
like one disposing of the residue from sacrifice,
and throw away the pot with eyes averted?
Friends, help me in this quandary,   100
for we all share a common hatred in our home.
Don't hide your thoughts inside your hearts through fear.
If something's fated no one can escape it, whether he
be free as he was born, or someone else's slave.
Please tell me: have you thought of anything?

1. LIBATION BEARER   I reverence your father's tomb as if it
   were
a sacred altar; here, as you ask, I'll tell you what I really feel.

EL   Please tell me, since you reverence my father's grave.

1. LB   You must say words which show you care for all your friends.

EL   Who in this household can I call my friends?   110

1. LB   First, yourself, and all who hate Aigisthos.

EL   So this should be a prayer for you and me?

1. LB   You've realized what you should do; go on.

EL   Should I add anybody else?

1. LB   Do not forget Orestes, even though he is no longer in the
   house.

EL   That is good; you are right to remind me.

1. LB   Now, when you get to Agamemnon's murderers . . .

EL   What shall I say? Teach me, lead me – I must know.

1. LB   . . . pray that some god or mortal man may come . . .

EL   To judge them, or to be the instrument of Justice?   120

1. LB   Simply say; to kill them in their turn.

EL   Would the gods see this as a pious prayer?

1. LB How could they not? It's right to pay your enemies for
       what they've done to you.

*Elektra kneels, places the garlands on the grave, and takes the
mixing bowl.*

EL   Hermes, great herald of the gods above us and below,
     help me! Lord of the earth, I beg you be my messenger
     and take my prayers to the gods beneath the earth,
     the guardians of my father's house,
     and Earth herself, she who gives birth to every living thing
     and nurtures it, and takes their offspring back again.

*One or two Libation Bearers mix wine with milk and honey in
Elektra's bowl.*

     Now, as I pour out this libation to the dead,
     I say this, calling on my father: 'Pity me   130
     and your dear son Orestes; bring the light back to this house.
     For as it is we wander, just as if we had been sold,
     and in exchange for us our mother took a man,
     Aigisthos, who was with her when she murdered you.
     I live like a slave; Orestes is in exile, and bereft
     of all his property, while they rejoice
     exultantly at all your sufferings.
     Father, I pray to you that by some turn of fate
     Orestes may come here – I charge you, hear me!
     For myself, make me a better woman than my mother,   140
     self-controlled, and reverent in everything I do.
     These are my prayers for us; but for our enemies
     I say that you must be avenged;
     the murderers must die, in just reprisal for their deeds.
     This I place among my prayers for good;
     I have pronounced a curse on them alone.
     For us, send up your blessings; with the aid
     of all the gods, and Mother Earth, may justice bring us victory!'

     These are my prayers; to follow them, I will pour out these
       offerings;

Elektra pours the libations.

custom demands that you must help their power to bloom   150
by crying out in lamentation; sing a song of victory for the
  dead!

(CHOROS 2)

LIBATION BEARERS   Let out a tear! It drops, it dies
        just like the king it's shed for
        as it falls upon this mound,
        defender of good, and enemy of evil.
        When these offerings are poured
        may all pollution be removed.
        Hear me, great majesty! Hear me, great king
        although your senses are now dimmed.
        Oh . . . !

Elektra sees – and moves to – the lock of hair.

        A man must come and liberate this house,   160
        a strong man with a spear,
        a War-god brandishing his bow
        in combat, ready for the work,
        or fighting hand to hand and sword with sword.

ELEKTRA   My father has his offerings; they've soaked into the
    earth.
  But now, share something new with me.

1. LB   What is it? My heart leaps with fear.

EL   I see a lock of hair that someone's cut and laid upon the
    grave.

1. LB   Who could it be? What man or girl would do that?

EL   Easy; anyone could guess.   170

1. LB   You must teach me, even though I'm older and you're
    young.

EL   No one else but me could have cut off this lock.

1. LB   Yes; those who should be mourning for him are all
    enemies.

EL   Still, it's here, and if you look it's very like . . .

1. LB   What kind of hair? That's what I want to know.

EL   It has a close resemblance to my own.

1. LB   Could it be a secret gift from Orestes?

EL   It does look very like his hair.

1. LB   But how would he dare to come here?

EL   He hasn't; he's just sent a cut-off lock, in homage to his
      father.   180

1. LB   We have then no less cause to weep,
      if this means he will never set foot in this land again.

EL   Now a wave of bitter bile has surged up to my heart,
      and it's as if a dart had pierced right through me.
      From my eyes thirsty tears pour down
      like winter floods against my will, when I
      look at this lock of hair. How could I think
      that any ordinary citizen could be the owner of such tresses?
      Nor would she, the murderess, have ever dared to offer it,
      my so-called mother, who does not deserve the name   190
      because she's filled her heart with godless hatred for her
         children.
      But then, how can I simply welcome it, and be sure
      this is a token from the dearest of all men to me,
      Orestes? I am fawned upon by hope.
      If only it had sense and voice, just like a messenger,
      then I would not be so distracted and confused;
      it could tell me plainly whether I should spit away the hair
      — if it has come from enemies of ours —
      or if it is a kindred lock, and so could grieve with me,
      a true adornment for this grave, an honour given to my
         father.   200
      We call upon the gods, who know
      that great waves toss us all around
      like men at sea; but when we're fated to survive,
      a small seed often grows into a great tree-root.

Elektra sees, and moves to, some footprints near the grave.

Here is a second sign – some footprints! Look.
They match each other – and are similar in shape to mine.
These are the outlines of two pairs of feet,
those of the man himself and of some friend.
And as I measure them, the heels, the contours of the tendons,
   all
are in proportion with the prints I made!   210
Oh, this is anguish, and my senses are destroyed.

Orestes and Pylades advance into the orchêstra.

ORESTES   Tell the gods your prayers have been fulfilled;
   now you can pray your future will be prosperous as well.

EL   What is it that I've now been given by the gods?

OR   You see at last the sight you've long desired.

EL   Whom do you think I've prayed for?

OR   I know that you have often missed Orestes.

EL   But how have I an answer to my prayer?

OR   I'm he; do not seek any closer relative than me.

EL   Stranger, is this some trap that you are casting round
   me?   220

OR   If I did that, I would be weaving snares to catch myself.

EL   Do you just want to mock me in my misery?

OR   I would be mocking my own misery, if I mocked yours.

EL   So I must really call you by his name?

OR   You are so slow to realize – now you see me in the flesh;
   but when you saw this offering of hair,
   and when you followed in my footsteps like a hunter,
   your heart flew like a bird, as if Orestes was before your eyes.
   Look! Place that lock of hair where it was cut –   230
   it is your brother's hair, and much resembles yours –
   now see this piece of weaving, done by your own hands;
   here are the strokes of your own needle, this is your design –
     wild animals.
   No, no – do not go mad with joy;

for I am well aware our so-called family
are bitter enemies to us.

EL   My dearest, darling of your father's house,
beloved hope, seed of salvation,
trust in your strength; you will regain your father's house.
Eye of delight! You have four parts to play for me;
I must now turn to you in place of my dead father,
all my mother-love is turned to you   240
because I hate her utterly; and then, my sister-love for her
who was so mercilessly slaughtered – all is yours.
You are my faithful brother, bringing glory back into my life;
may Strength be with us now, and Justice, with the third,
the greatest god of all – lord Zeus!

OR   Zeus! Zeus! Look down and witness this!
You see the orphaned offspring of the eagle who has died –
a fearful serpent's trapped him in its coils. They are bereft
of father-love, and suffer pangs of hunger; they're not strong
    enough   250
to hunt food like their father, bring it to the nest.
That's how we are. Here you can see Orestes and Elektra,
children who no longer have a father,
both of us in exile from our home.
And yet our father sacrificed, and paid great services to you;
if you let his young children be destroyed, where will you find
such rich and splendid gifts from other hands?
If you were to destroy the eagle's brood, you could not send
back any sign of hope to mortal men;
and if this tree of kingship shrivels up and dies   260
we will not be your ministers upon the festive days of sacrifice.
So keep it safe! From such a little start you can raise up once
    more
a great house, which men now believe
has fallen utterly.

1. LB   Dear children! Saviours of your father's house!
Do not say more; let no one overhear and,
just because he wants to talk, tell all you've said
to those who now command us. How I want to see
them dying, plunged in oozing, boiling pitch!

OR   Apollo's great and mighty oracle will not forsake me.

He ordered me to pass through all these dangers,   270
shrieking out his prophecies; he told
of vile and frosty torments that would chill my heart
if I did not pursue those who contrived my father's death
in just the same way — meaning I must kill them in return.
He said that I would pay with my dear life — but first
would suffer ghastly tortures; I would lose my heritage,
and this would drive me mad and violent as a bull.
There are — he told me — things men can do, which will
placate the anger of the dead; but there are also terrible
   diseases,
creatures which invade the flesh with vicious teeth,   280
cankers which eat at healthy skin,
and leprosy, whose ulcers blossom with white hair!
Then Apollo spoke of other enemies; it would not matter
whether I were still alive, or in the underworld,
the Furies would pursue me, springing from my father's blood.
The long dark arrows of the gods below
are sent by suppliants — fathers and grandfathers who died
an unjust death, and cry for vengeance; madness, empty
   terrors in the night
attack, harass and drive the coward son
out of his city, beaten with a lash of bronze.   290
A man like that is not allowed to share
the common bowl of wine, nor may he drink the pure fresh
   water
which men use to make libations to the gods.
His father's anger comes unseen to drive him back
from altars; he cannot be welcomed in
to take his rest under another's roof. He'll die at last
unloved, uncared for; he will shrivel up
and end his life in fearful pain.

Should I not trust such oracles as these?
And even if I don't, this still remains a deed that must be done.
Here many different needs fall into one;
the god's command, my father's suffering,   300
and also I am weighed down by my need for my inheritance —
it is not right that citizens of Argos, noble-hearted men
who gained eternal glory from the sack of Troy
should be the subjects of this pair of women.
For his heart's a woman's; if it isn't, we'll soon see.

LIBATION BEARERS   You mighty Powers of Destiny,
    may Zeus grant us the outcome we desire,
    as Justice turns our way.
    They speak in words of hatred;
    let our words of hatred answer them.
    Justice cries out aloud as she exacts her debt;   310
    'for bloody blows let bloody blows
    take vengeance'. 'He who does, must suffer';
    that is the wisdom of the ages.

OR (A1)   Oh my father, my terrible, dead father,
    What can I say or do to bring
    you from the far place where you lie?
    The light is very different from the dark;
    but still perhaps a noble act of lamentation   320
    may bring some joy to you, great son of Atreus.

LB (B1)   Dear son, the ravening jaws of flame
    cannot subdue a dead man's powers of thought.
    He shows his anger, even after death.
    We sing his dirge,
    he comes for his revenge.
    If we can raise up loud and strong
    the due lament for a dead father   330
    it will hunt down his murderers.

EL (A2)   Now, father, hear in turn
    the sorrows which have made me weep.
    Here are your children standing at your grave
    to chant the song of lamentation.
    Exile and suppliant, this tomb welcomes us.
    Is my life nothing but suffering?
    Can we never conquer misfortune?

LB   The god may still lead us to sing a sweeter song   340
    if that is his desire.
    Now we are chanting dirges at a tomb—
    but soon a song of victory
    will welcome back the new-mixed cup of wine
    to celebrate the king's return.

OR (C1)   If only you had died at Troy,
    my father, cut down by a warrior's spear;
    you would have been revered throughout your halls,

held in high regard
because your children flourished.   350
Your grave would be a noble mound
beyond the sea,
no burden for your relatives to bear.

LB (B2)   His fellow warriors have welcomed him
who died with glory in the Trojan War;
he is an honoured leader of the dead,
the servant only of the highest kings,
the gods who rule the underworld.
For while you lived you were a king   360
and in your mighty hands
the sceptre held the power of life and death.

EL (C2)   No! My father, you should not even have died
under the walls of Troy!
And not be buried there, beside the waters of
Skamander, with the other warriors.
His murderers should meet
their share of death
in just the way he did;
a kind of death so terrible
that far and wide
men who know nothing of our suffering   370
would hear about it.

LB   What you are asking is better
than gold, or great good luck.
And you can ask.
But look! Your ceremony is a double lash,
its blows strike home;
our allies are here, below the earth.
The rulers' hands are stained with hatred;
you are gaining power!

OR (D1)   This goes straight to his ears   380
like a javelin.
Zeus, send up vengeance, all too long delayed,
for the reckless heart and the daring hand;
the debt I owe my parents
will be paid!

LB (E1)   May it only be my right
             to sing the blazing song of victory
             when he is speared and she has been destroyed;
             why should I hide the thought
             which always flutters in my heart?
             Anger blows right through us,   390
             long-felt, bitter hatred.

EL (D2)   When will Zeus, in his abundant power,
             bring down his hands upon them,
             smash their heads?
             Fulfil your pledges to this land!
             I ask for Justice to reverse injustice.
             Hear me, Earth, and hear me, powers below.

LB   When drops of murdered blood   400
        fall to the earth, they call for yet more blood;
        that is the law. Havoc brings out the Fury
        from the bodies of the dead
        to pile disaster on disaster.

OR (F1)   Hear me, lords of the underworld;
             See us, mighty Curses of the dead,
             see the last survivors of the house of Atreus
             helpless, cast out from our halls.
             Oh Zeus, where can we turn?

LB (E2)   My heart is shaken   410
             as I hear this bitter lament.
             Sometimes my hope is dim
             and I go black inside
             listening to your words;
             but when I see you strong again
             hope easily drives out my anguish;
             all will turn out well.

EL (F2)   What should we say to get through to him?
             Just tell of the anguish we have suffered?
             She can fawn on us if she wants; it will not soften us.
             We are savage, just like wolves: 420
             we have our mother's spirit,
             it cannot be tamed.

LB (G1)   I beat my breast and sang the dirge

of Asiatic wailing women.
You could see my hands—
they struck, they clutched, they pressed
spattered with blood,
stretched out from high, from high above
until my head resounded with the blows.

EL (H1)   Oh, my cruel,
        all-daring Mother, how did you dare   430
        to take him out and bury him?
        No citizen went with the king,
        no one was there to sorrow for him
        or cry lament for him. A cruel funeral!

OR (I1)   All that you've said humiliated him!
        Shall she not pay for my father's shame?
        The gods will help
        my hands will help
        when I have killed her I can die.

LB (I2)   Know this: he was mutilated.   440
        She did it when she buried him
        to make his fate unbearable for you.
        Now you have heard the outrages they did your father.

EL (G2)   You tell of how my father died.
        I stood apart, humiliated, worthless,
        shut off in my bedroom like some savage dog.
        I needed to conceal my grief; I could not try
        to laugh; instead I swamped it in a flood of tears.
        Father, listen to this and carve it on your heart.   450

LB (H2)   Yes, carve it! Let this story pierce
        your ears and come with gentle step
        to soothe your heart. We've told you how things are;
        now burn to know how they will be!
        If you would win, you must not lose your strength.

OR (J1)   Father, I beg you. Help your children.

EL   Through my tears I ask this too.

LB   We all echo them;
        listen, come into the light,
        help us against your enemies.   460

OR (J2)   War-god will clash with War-god, right with right.

EL   Oh gods, fulfil our rights; bring justice.

LB   I shiver as I hear them pray.
           The hour of destiny has waited long;
           it will come now they plead for it!

   (K1)   Oh suffering innate within the race
           and bloody, hideous, discordant stroke
           of utter ruin,
           moaning weight of grief,
           unbearable disease.   470

   (K2)   The house must find
           the dressing for this wound,
           and not from others from outside
           but only from its own,
           through savage, bloody strife.
           This hymn is for the gods below the earth.

           But hear us, blessed powers of the underworld;
           answer this prayer by sending help.
           Be eager for the children's victory; let them prevail.

OR   Father, you did not die a kingly death;
       give me the power I ask for in your house.   480

EL   Father, I have this need of you;
       let me contrive Aigisthos' death, and find a man.

OR   If you do this, you will receive the banquets
       due to you from us; but if you don't, when other dead feast
           joyfully
       on rich burnt-offerings, you won't receive your share.

EL   And I will give you offerings, when I inherit all that is my
           due,
       libations on my wedding day from our ancestral store.
       This is the tomb which I will honour more than any other one.

OR   Oh Earth, release my father, let him watch me fight.

EL   Oh goddess of the underworld, grant us the beauty of
       victory.   490

OR   Think of the bath in which she murdered you.

EL   Think how they made a net to trap you.

OR   They hunted you with fetters that no blacksmith made.

EL   They planned to trap you in a cloak of shame.

OR   Are you not moved by these reproaches?

EL   Won't you raise up your head, my dearest father?

OR   Send Justice up to be an ally for your children
or else help us to bind them fast, the same as they did you.
They beat you; don't you want to throw them down in turn?

EL   Hear one more cry from me.   500
Look at your offspring as they nestle at this grave.
Pity us both, the man and woman joined together by their grief.
Do not destroy us, offspring of the house
of Pelops; while we live, you live.
Children preserve a hero's glory past his death,
just like the corks that hold a net afloat
and stop the meshes sinking out of reach.
So hear us. All of this lament has been for you,
and you'll be saved forever if you honour what we've said.

1. LB   No one could blame you for these many words;   510
you've given honour to a grave — and to a fate — no one has ever
   mourned.
But now, since you're resolved, you can proceed;
test if the god is still with you.

OR   I shall. But it will not deflect me from my course to ask
why she sent these libations, what persuaded her to try
too late to make up for irreparable suffering.
This was a paltry act of honour for a king
who's dead and hates her. I can't understand.
Her gifts are so much smaller than her crime.
You could pour all you have in recompense   520
for bloodshed, and your labour would be wasted. So I think.
Please tell me why she did it, if you know.

1. LB   I do know — I was there. She was terrified
by dreams and roving horrors which attacked her in the night.
That's why the godless woman sent these offerings.

OR   Do you know her dream enough to tell it right?

1. LB   She told us herself: she dreamt she gave birth to a snake.

OR   Go on. What was the end of the story?

1. LB   It nestled in its swaddling-clothes just like a human child.

OR   This newborn viper, did it want to eat?   530

1. LB   She dreamt that she herself gave it her teat to suck.

OR   How could a deadly thing like that not wound her breast?

1. LB   It did – a clot of blood poured out into the milk.

OR   This is no empty vision.

1. LB   Screaming in terror, she woke up.
The braziers were blazing up around the house
to soothe our mistress – but the darkness blinded them.
Then she sent these offerings,
hoping to find a cure that would cut through her torments.

OR   But I pray now to Earth and to my father's grave   540
that this dream may be fulfilled for me.
For if this snake emerged from that same place as I
and then was wrapped in swaddling-clothes
and put its fangs around the breast that nurtured me
and made a clot of blood mix with the milk of life
so that she cried aloud in fright and pain,
then she, because she nurtured such a terrifying portent,
must die by violence; I become the snake
and kill her. That's what this dream says.   550

1. LB   I choose you as my dream-interpreter;
may you be right! Now tell your friends
what they must do; for some, this means what not to do.

OR   My plan is simple. Elektra is to go inside the house.
I charge you to keep secret all our plans,
so they, who killed a noble man by treachery,
shall die by treachery in turn, and die
in that same net – for so has Loxias ordained,
the lord Apollo, prophet who has never lied.
I shall disguise myself in travelling-clothes   560
and go with this man, Pylades, right to the outer gates,
pretend to be a friend and ally of the house.

We'll both assume a dialect – Parnassian –
and talk the way they do in Phokis.
It's possible the doorkeepers won't welcome us
with open hearts, because the gods have filled the house
with evil fortune. Then we'll stay, so anyone who walks along
beside the palace will be quite amazed, and say,
'Why does Aigisthos not receive the suppliant at once,
if he is somewhere in the city and has been informed?'   570

But should I cross the threshold of the outer gates
and find him sitting on my father's throne,
or if he comes back home to speak to me
– you may be sure he'll meet me man to man –
before he says 'Where is the stranger from?', he'll be a corpse,
impaled upon my sword so fast you'll hardly see.
And so the Fury of our house, who is not starved of deaths,
will drain the third and final cup of undiluted blood.

Elektra, you must supervise with care inside the house,
so that this plan of ours may hold together,   580
while you must watch your words almost religiously:
be silent when need be, speak only what will help our cause.
All else, I call on Agamemnon here to oversee:
guide me, let my sword win the contest!

Exeunt Orestes, Pylades, Elektra and the Libation Bearers, left.

Strike Agamemnon's grave.

Enter Elektra, right: she knocks and is admitted at the skene door.

CHOROS 3

Enter the Libation Bearers, right.

LIBATION BEARERS (A1)   The earth
       breeds terrifying beasts.
       In her embrace the sea
       encompasses a multitude
       of monsters that can kill a man.
       Up in the sky are comets, meteors –

like flying torches which descend 590
to harm us. Then think of the hurricane,
the anger of the stormwind.

(A2)   But who can find words to speak
of the ever-daring mind of man
or woman's love that dares all,
wedded to disaster?
When passion overcomes
the female, it destroys
the unions of animals, 600
the marriages of men and women.

(B1)   So listen! If your thoughts do not fly too high,
learn from Althaia, who destroyed her child.
She lit a bloody torch
the day he came out, crying,
from his mother's womb.
It followed him throughout his life; 610
when it blew out, he died.

(B2)   There is another one to hate in the old tales,
a bloodstained girl.
She killed her father for her city's enemies,
bribed by a necklace wrought of gold,
the gift of Minos, king of Crete.
Her father, Nisos, did not know;
the bitch cut off the lock of hair
that gave him everlasting life 620
as he lay unsuspecting in his sleep.
Death has him now.

(C1)   Since I've remembered cruelties
which cannot be assuaged, should I not speak
about the bitter marriage here
that's hateful to the house,
the evil plans which took shape in this woman's heart
against a warrior, a man of glory whom
his enemies had all too much good cause to hate?
May the hearth not be warmed by civil strife,
may woman's strength not turn to outrage. 630

(C2)   Of all the crimes in legend
the Lemnian is the worst, most hated and most feared.

The name of Lemnos is a proverb for
the ultimate in horror.
Polluted, hated by the gods,
their race is cast out by mankind.
No one helps those the gods reject.
Am I not right to tell these stories?

Enter Orestes and Pylades, right.

(D1)   The sword strikes near the lungs;
it's sharp, it goes straight through;   640
Right's driving it!
They trampled Justice to the ground;
they broke with everything that's good
and went against the majesty of Zeus.

(D2)   The anvil of Justice is planted in the ground.
Destiny's the blacksmith, she forges the sword.
The glorious Fury's planned both long and well,
and now she brings back to this house
a child to make return   650
for all the bloodstains of the past.

SCENE 3

ORESTES   (*Knocks*)
Hey, slave, do you not hear me knocking on the courtyard
door?

(*Knocks*)
Is anyone at home? Slave, I'm calling you a second time!

(*Pause. Knocks again.*)
This is my third demand for someone to come out
if Aigisthos allows this house to welcome travellers.

SERVANT   (*in the* skene.)
All right, I can hear you. (*enters*) Who's the stranger? Where's
he from?

OR   Announce me to the masters of this household; say
I've come to see them, and I bring some news.

Be quick, though, since the night's dark chariot   660
is speeding on, (*exit Servant, into the* skene) and it's the time
    when travellers need to find
a friendly house, where they can drop anchor and feel safe.
Someone should come who has authority –
the woman who is mistress? Better still, perhaps, a man.

Doors open. Enter Klytaimestra from the skene, *attended by
Elektra.*

For reticence in conversation makes one's words
obscure. A man can speak with confidence
before another man, and will convey quite clearly what he
    means.

KLYTAIMESTRA   Strangers, you can tell me what you need;
    for here we have
all that you would expect in such a house as this –
warm baths, soft beds to charm away   670
your aches and pains, and people round you who will do no
    harm.
But if you want to transact business of importance, then
that is the work of men, and I must share it with them.

OR   I am a Daulian; I've come from Phokis.
This is all the luggage that I own, and I was on my way
to this place, Argos, which I've reached at last.
I met a man I did not know, and he did not know me;
but when he'd asked my destination and had told me his,
I learnt his name – Strophios the Phokian; here is what he said.
'My friend, since you are bound for Argos anyway,   680
whatever else you do, remember this: tell his parents that
Orestes is dead – please don't forget!
I don't know if his relatives will want to bring him home
or if they would prefer to have him buried here, an alien, as our
    guest
for all eternity. We mourned him well, and now
his ashes wait, surrounded by the bronze sides of an urn.
Bring their instructions back to me.'
I've said all that I heard. But I don't know
if you're the people I should really say this to.
I think his father should be told.   690

KLYT   How utterly we are beseiged!
Oh Curse upon this house, so hard to wrestle with,
so many things attract your eye — even those we tried to place
out of your way. You bring us down with deadly arrow-shots,
you strip me of my relatives, and I have nothing left.
Orestes now! He was no fool; he kept his feet
far distant from this deadly swamp.
But now the Hope is gone, which was the cure
for those foul Furies' orgy in this house.
Mark down that it's betrayed us.

OR   When a host is prosperous like you,   700
I would have liked to introduce myself by giving joyful news
and earn your hospitality. A friendly guest
likes nothing more than to deserve his entertainment.
But I felt it would be almost impious
if I had not informed Orestes' relatives
when I had pledged to do so and was welcomed here.

KLYT   You will not be received less worthily than you deserve,
nor are you any less this house's friend.
This news would have come anyway; it's all the same.
But now it is the time when those who've spent all day   710
upon the road should be supplied with what they need.
Take him to the apartment for male visitors,
together with his fellow-traveller here,
and let them receive whatever we can give.
I tell you, do this well: you are responsible to me.
I shall report this news to those in power.
We do not lack for friends; we will take their advice about this
    new disaster.

Exeunt Klytaimestra, Orestes, Pylades and Elektra into the skene.
Doors close.

CHOROS 4

LIBATION BEARERS   Now, dear friends, servants of this
        house,
    when will we show that our lips have the power   720
    to help Orestes' cause?

Oh sacred earth, sacred mound
that now lies piled
upon the body of our king, the lord of ships,
hear us now! Help us now!
This is the time; now sly
Persuasion must come down
to help us; and Hermes, ruler of the dark,
must guide them as
they draw their swords and fight.

SCENE 4

Doors open. Enter the Nurse, from the skene. *Doors close.*

1. LIBATION BEARER   I think the stranger's up to
    something.   730
  Look – here's Orestes' nurse, in tears.
  Kilissa, why are you leaving the house?
  Where are you going? Grief goes with you, like
  a fellow-traveller you do not want.

NURSE   That woman – our mistress – has ordered me to fetch
    Aigisthos
  as fast as possible to see the strangers, so he may learn this news
  more clearly, man from man. In front of us
  her eyes were sad and full of grief; but it was all a sham
  to hide her joy at news which is so good
  for her, but utterly disastrous for this house,   740
  if what the strangers said so clearly is not false.
  Aigisthos will be overjoyed the moment he is told.
  But as for me – all the old miseries mixed in together
  here in the house of Atreus – they're so hard to bear
  my heart is nearly broken.

  Never have I suffered a grief like this.
  I drained the others dry without complaint,
  but – dear Orestes! I wore myself out for him.
  His mother gave him to me and I brought him up.   750
  He used to cry out in the night and get me out of bed,
  and I did so much work for him – now gone for nothing.

Babies are just like animals: they never think, and you have got
to bring them up the way you want.
When he is still in swaddling clothes a baby doesn't tell you
if he is in need of food, or drink,
or making water – boys' young bladders have a will of their
    own.
I had to guess when that was, and I know
I often got it wrong – which meant I had to wash his clothes,
since I was nurse and laundrywoman too.   760
I was skilled at both these jobs,
that's why Orestes' father gave me him to mind.
Now I'm sad. I have been told that he is dead,
and I must go to see a man who has defiled
this house, and will be glad to learn the news.

1. LB   How did she say he should equip himself?

N   What do you mean? Say that again, so I may understand.

1. LB   Is he to bring his bodyguard, or come alone?

N   She says he should bring armed men to attend him.

1. LB   Don't tell our hated master that!   770
Tell him to come as soon as he can – and say it cheerfully,
so he will listen without taking fright.
The messenger can make a bent word straight.

N   Are you pleased with what I've told you?

1. LB   Just suppose that Zeus might free us from our misery.

N   But how? Our only hope, Orestes, is now dead.

1. LB   Not yet. He would be a poor prophet who said that.

N   What do you mean? Do you know something different?

1. LB   Take your message, do what you've been told.
This is the gods' concern, and they will handle it.

N   Well, I will go, and I will do what you have asked.   780
May the gods grant it turn out for the best.

Exit, left.

CHOROS 5

LIBATION BEARERS (A1)   Now I ask you, Zeus,
    father of the gods,
    grant success to those who strive for it,
    the rightful owners of this house.
    All I have said is just;
    Zeus, fulfil my words.

(A1a)   Now he is in the house;
    let him confront his enemies;
    he will repay you willingly   790
    twice over, three times over,
    when he is raised to greatness.

(A2)   Know this! The orphaned colt
    of one who was once dear to you
    is harnessed to a chariot of pain.
    He has begun the race.
    Grant he not lose his pace.
    Let him finish the course.

(B1)   You household gods, who live   800
    near to our secret store of wealth,
    be on our side!
    Reach a new verdict,
    dispel the bloodshed of the past.
    May the old massacres no more
    give birth within this house.

(B1a)   Great god Apollo,
    lord of a vast and sacred place,
    grant that Orestes' house may raise its head,
    and make the light of freedom come
    clear for his eyes to see,   810
    released from the veils of darkness.

(B2)   Hermes may justly lend his hand,
    the god who is most apt
    to bring a favourable outcome.
    His eyes can penetrate the night,
    he can cast darkness on our sight
    and he is never seen.

(C1)   Then we shall sing at last!
            Loud and clear, the noble song   820
            of a house set free:
            'For this city, all is well'.
            That will be our glory, ours alone;
            disaster will be far from those we love.

(C1a)   But you! When the moment comes
            take courage.
            If she cries, 'Child!', shout back,
            'Truly I am my father's child.'
            Go through with it; you may kill her
            and never suffer blame.   830

(C2)   Remember that your deed is the desire
            both of your loved ones now beneath the earth
            and of the gods above.
            Be brave as Perseus;
            give bloody murder to the dreaded Gorgon in this house,
            and when you see the man
            who is the cause of all our grief
            destroy him!

                        SCENE 5

Enter Aigisthos, left.

AIGISTHOS   I come not of my own accord, but summoned by a
        messenger.
    I understand that certain strangers have arrived
    and bring some news that gives me no delight—   840
    Orestes' death. This would be a bloodstained burden
    for the house to bear, already wounded as it is,
    poisoned by bitter murders long ago.
    How can I think it is a living truth?
    Are these perhaps just fearful, women's words
    which leap high in the air, then die in vain?
    What can you tell of this to clear my mind?

1. LIBATION BEARER   We've heard. But you must go inside
    and find out from the strangers. It's nowhere near as good

to let a woman tell you as to hear yourself, from man to
   man.   850

AIG   I want to see this messenger and question him carefully,
   to learn if he was there and saw Orestes die,
   or just reports a rumour he has heard.
   My mind has eyes; it cannot be deceived.

Doors open. Exit Aigisthos, into the skene. *Doors close.*

CHOROS 6

LIBATION BEARERS   Zeus, Zeus, what shall I say?
   How should I call on you?
   I wish him well, but how
   can my words be enough
   to bring him help?
   Now bloody chopping-knives will kill   860
   and either utterly destroy
   the house of Agamemnon for eternity
   or else the son will kindle fire and light
   for freedom, rule his city and
   inherit all the riches of his ancestors.
   Such is the contest that godlike Orestes joins,
   one against two, his father's only champion.
   May victory be his!

SCENE 6

Aigisthos' prolonged death-cry is heard from inside the skene.

1. LIBATION BEARER   That's it!   870
   (*pause*)
   What's happened? What's the fate of the house?

1. LB   The end is near; let us stand back,
   so we may seem not to have played a part
   in causing evil things. The battle's finished now.

Doors open. Enter Servant, from the skene.

SERVANT   Cry out in sorrow for our stricken lord,
cry sorrow yet again,
Aigisthos is no more. But open up
as fast as you can, undo the bolts
upon the women's doors. It needs a younger man,
and not to help Aigisthos; he is dead. What can I do?   880
Hey!
I'm shouting to the deaf; I'm babbling while they
waste time asleep. Where's Klytaimestra? What's she doing?
Her neck is right upon the chopping block
with Justice poised to strike.

Enter Klytaimestra, from the skene.

KLYTAIMESTRA   What is it? Why this cry for help to the
    house?

SERV   I tell you that the living die, killed by the dead.

KLYT   Oh god, I understand the riddle. Now
we die by treachery, just as we killed.
Get me an axe at once; (*Exit Servant, into the* skene.)
Let's see if we are finished, or still have a chance;   890
this terrible affair has gone that far.

Enter Orestes and Pylades from the skene; *Orestes with drawn,
bloodstained sword.*

ORESTES   It's you I'm looking for; he's had enough.

KLYT   Oh god, you're dead, my darling, strong Aigisthos.

OR   You love the man? Then you shall lie
together in the grave; he is dead, and you
will never be unfaithful to him.

KLYT   Stop, my son; show awe, my child
before this breast, at which you often drowsily
sucked with your lips the milk that gave you life.

OR   Pylades, what shall I do? Should I not fear to kill my
    mother?

PYLADES   Would you destroy the standing of Apollo's
    oracles
                                                            900

for all the rest of time, and of his solemn oath?
Count all men hateful to you rather than the gods.

OR   I judge that you have won, and your advice is good.
Follow me: I mean to kill you at Aigisthos' side.
In life you thought him greater than my father.
Now sleep with him in death:
you chose this man, and hated him you ought to love.

KLYT   I brought you up; let me grow old with you.

OR   You killed my father, and you want to share my house?

KLYT   Fate had a certain share in that, my son.   910

OR   Well then, it's Fate that brings death to you now.

KLYT   Do you not fear the Furies of a mother?

OR   No. You gave me birth, but threw me out to suffer pain.

KLYT   Not so, I sent you out to live with friends.

OR   I was a free man's son, sold like a slave.

KLYT   Then where's the price I got for you?

OR   I am ashamed to name it clearly – you would be disgraced.

KLYT   Your father strayed as well – why don't you mention
that?

OR   Don't blame the man. He laboured while you sat at home.

KLYT   It hurts a woman not to have a man, my child.   920

OR   The man's hard work supports the women who remain at
home.

KLYT   I see, my son, you mean to kill your mother.

OR   It's you who kill yourself, not I.

KLYT   Watch out! Beware your mother's angry, hounding
Furies.

OR   But how should I escape my father's Furies, if I do not do
this deed?

KLYT   It seems as if I'm weeping uselessly, while still alive,
before my tomb.

OR   Yes, now my father's fate wafts death towards you.

KLYT   Oh god, this is the snake I bore, and nurtured at my
      breast.

OR   How true a prophet was that fearful dream.
      You killed, and it was wrong; now suffer wrong.   930

Exeunt Klytaimestra, Orestes and Pylades into the skene. *Doors
close.*

1. LB   I even mourn for these two, and their fate;
         but now, now that our poor Orestes sets
         the coping-stone upon these many streams of blood,
         we just want this: may he, the eye of the house,
         not fall and be destroyed.

                         CHOROS 7

LIBATION BEARERS (A1)   Justice came!
      The Trojans suffered
      heavy punishment.
      Orestes came!
      to the house of Agamemnon
      like a lion or a god of war.
      The exile guided by the god of Delphi   940
      and protected by the wisdom of the gods
      has won!

   (A1a)   Cry out in joy!
      Our masters' house
      is freed from all its suffering, and from
      the wasting of its riches by those murderers,
      a lamentable fate.

   (A2)   He came! His duty was a secret war
      and stealthy punishment.
      And the daughter of Zeus, the faithful one,
      guided him in battle—
      we call her Justice   950
      when we name her right—
      breathing destructive anger on her enemies.

(B1)   Great Apollo, Loxias,
     the ruler of the navel of the earth,
     he gave her victory with guile that is no guile.
     Justice was wounded here
     in time long past
     but she has come back now.
     The will of the gods prevails!
     I do not serve the wicked.
     It is right to worship the lords of heaven.   960

(B1a)   The light is here to see, and the vast yoke
     is lifted from these halls.
     Oh house, rise up! For too much time
     you have lain tumbled on the ground.

(B2)   And now great Time, fulfiller of all things,
     will pass between our entrance doors,
     when all the stain has vanished from the hearth,
     and we have purified it, driven all disaster out.
     Our fortune's turned: it will be fair of face
     and welcome back the rightful lord   970
     into the house.

SCENE 7

*Doors open. Enter Orestes, sword in hand, Pylades, holding a
wreath and an olive branch decorated with wool and Elektra on
the* ekkuklêma, *with the corpses of Aigisthos and Klytaimestra
covered by Agamemnon's net-like deathrobe.*

ORESTES   Look! Here are the tyrants of our land;
     they killed my father and they sacked this house.
     Then they seemed very grand, both seated on their thrones;
     and I would guess that they are lovers even now.
     They've died together, faithful to their vows—
     for they once took an oath to kill my wretched father
     and die together. That's turned out all right; they've kept their
          pledge.
     Now, as you listen to these evil things, just look at this,   980
     the horrible device with which they bound my wretched father,
     shackled him both hand and foot.

Stretch it out! Stand round in a circle,
show this thing with which they overcame a man,
so that the father, Sun who looks down on us all,
may view the monstrous actions of my mother,
come, when I am brought to trial,
and be my witness that it was with justice I pursued
this murder of my mother. I don't count Aigisthos' death –
he met the usual fate of all adulterers.   990
But she! – who plotted this foul deed against the very man
whose children she had carried once inside her womb.
Then she was glad to bear us as her burden, now we are
her deadly enemies, as you can see . . . what do you think?
If she had been a seasnake, or a viper, she could make men's
     flesh dissolve
without a bite, so great her daring
and the power of her evil mind.
What shall I call her, and be right?
A huntsman's net, or else a shroud-like
bather's wrap? You surely could well say
a trap, a net, a cloth that hems men in.   1000
She is the sort of lure a thief might use
to trap a traveller and rob him of his silver.
That's a way to make a living! He would warm his heart
by killing many victims with a trap like this.
May such a woman never come to share my house;
far better dead, struck childless by the gods.

LIBATION BEARERS   Ah! Miserable deed!
     It is a hateful death you have given them.
     Pain blossoms for the living too.

OR   Did she do it or not? This robe bears witness for me   1010
     how she stained Aigisthos' sword with gore.
     The spurt of blood conspires with Time
     and they've defeated every dye put on the finely woven cloth.
     Now I can praise him, now I am here to mourn him properly,
     as I speak here before this web in which my father died;
     I grieve for what I've done, this suffering, and all our family.
     I've won; but my victory is tainted, and no one would envy me.

LB   Ah!
     No mortal ever lives his life right through

free both from honour and from harm.
There has been pain already; more will come.   1020

OR   You must know now I do not know how this will end;
I'm like a charioteer who's forced to drive
outside the course; I am beaten, and cannot control
my senses. Terror comes prepared to sing its song of hate
beside my heart, and join the dance.
While I still have my sanity, I want to tell my friends
I killed my mother not without some justice:
she was polluted by my father's death and hated by the gods.
And for the drug which gave me courage for this deed
I name in chief Apollo, seer of Delphi; for he prophesied   1030
that if I did this I would be beyond the charge
of wickedness; but if I let it go . . . I will not speak the penalty,
for no one's bow could hit the mark of such an agony.

Pylades hands him the olive branch and wreath.

That's why you see me now, prepared.
With this young olive branch and wreath of flowers
I shall approach the navel of the earth,
the shrine, Apollo's sacred place
and the bright blaze of fire that we are told
is everlasting. Then I will escape this stain
of kindred blood. For Loxias instructed me
that I should turn to no other hearth than his.
And now I bid all Argives, in the time to come,   1040
remember how these evil things were done,
and testify for me to Menelaos, if he should return.
I am a wanderer, an exile banished from my native land;
living or dead, I leave behind me nothing else but this appeal to
    you.

1. LIBATION BEARER   No. You have done well; do not let
    your mouth be forced
to speak unworthy words; do not let evil touch your lips.
You liberated our whole city-state of Argos when
you cut with ease the heads off those two snakes!

OR   Ah! Ah!
These evil women! Gorgons

robed in black, and intertwined with myriads
of snakes. I can no longer stay.   1050

1. LB   What are these visions spinning you around,
Orestes, dearest to his father of all men?
Be strong, do not give way to fear; you've won so much.

OR   These are no fantasies of evil; I can see
they are the enraged hunting Furies of my mother.

1. LB   The blood is fresh still on your hands;
that's why your senses are confused.

OR   Oh lord Apollo! There are more and more of them,
and blood is dripping from their eyes.

1. LB   There is one cure: if Loxias can touch you with his hands
he will release you from these sufferings.   1060

OR   You do not see these creatures; I see them.
They drive me from this place; I cannot stay.

Exit Orestes, right.

1. LB   May you find good fortune! May the god
look kindly on you, and protect you, grant you happiness.

CHOROS 8

LIBATION BEARERS   This is the third storm
to vent its rage
in the royal house.
First was the pitiable torment of
the eating of the children;
then, the death of a king,   1070
when Agamemnon, leader of the Greeks in war,
was slaughtered in his bath.
Now he has come, the third, the saviour—
or should I call this death?
Where will it end? When will it be sated,
lulled to sleep, the force of destruction?

Exeunt left.

Withdraw tableau of Pylades, Elektra and the bodies on the ekkuklêma. *Doors close.*

EUMENIDES

Eumenides

SCENE 1(a)

Enter Priestess, left.

PRIESTESS   First of the gods I honour in this prayer
the Earth, first prophetess. And then Themis,
goddess of Right, the second – so one story tells –
to sit here on her mother's throne of prophecy. The third
– and by consent; there was no use of force –
was yet another Titan daughter of the Earth,
Phoibe, who gave this oracle, the day that he was born,
to lord Apollo, who inherited from her his other name,
      Phoibos.
He left the marshy lake and hog's back ridge of Delos,
beached his ship on Pallas' busy shores,   10
then came up to this land, where Mount Parnassos lies.
He was escorted with great reverence by Athenians,
who tamed a savage land and smoothed the way for him.
When he came here, the people greatly honoured him;
so did the king, Delphos, the helmsman of this state.
Zeus breathed the heavenly skill of prophecy
into Apollo's mind, and set him as fourth prophet on this
      throne.
He is called Loxias – the prophet of the Father, Zeus.
These are the gods I honour now, in my first prayer.   20

Pallas Athena, she whose shrine is near this oracle,
deserves my reverence; and the nymphs, whose cave of Korykis,
beloved of birds, the gods frequent.
Dionysos also rules this place – I don't forget –
since he led out an army of Bakchantes, and contrived
the death of Pentheus, ripped to pieces like a hare.
I call upon the springs of Pleistos and on lord

Poseidon; last I pray to Zeus, the great accomplisher,
and now I go, to sit as prophetess upon the throne.
May the gods grant this session be my best   30
by far; if any Greeks are here, they may come in—
draw lots first for your places, as the custom is.
All that I utter will be as the god directs.

Doors open. Exit, into the skene.

Re-enter Priestess from the skene, *on all fours.*

A sight too terrible to see or speak about
has sent me back out of Apollo's hall;
I have no strength, I cannot stand—
I run, but on my hands and knees, not on my feet.
When frightened an old woman's nothing, just a child.
As I was going to the inner shrine, where flowers wreathe
the temple, I saw on the very navel of the earth   40
a man abominated by the gods, posed as a suppliant.
His hands were dripping blood; he held a new-drawn sword,
   also a
branch of olive, bound up reverently by a long band
of shining wool; about this I can speak with clarity.
But all around this man there slept
a terrifying crowd of women resting on our seats.
Not really women—they were more like Gorgons;
but I cannot truly liken them to Gorgons
nor Harpies—for I saw a picture once
of Harpies stealing Phineus' feast, and they   50
had wings; but these have none, and they are black
and horrible in every way. They're snoring,
and the stench around them is unbearable.
Disgusting streams of filth
pour from their eyes. Their garments are unfit
to be worn near the images of gods or in the homes of mortal
   men.
I've never seen the tribe from which this band of predators
has come, nor can I guess how any land could nurture them
and live unscathed to tell the tale without regret.

What happens now will have to be the care   60
of Loxias himself, the mighty master of these halls;

he is a lord of healing, he can read prophetic signs,
and he has often purified the homes of other gods and men.

Exit, left.

SCENE 1(b)

Enter Orestes from the skene *in anxiety and haste, followed by Apollo.*

APOLLO I will not betray you; I will guard you to the end,
   both when I stand near by you, and when far away,
   I never will grow soft towards your enemies.
   So now you see these rabid creatures overcome;
   they've fallen into sleep, the loathsome virgins—
   haggard, aged children, whom none of the gods,
   no man nor beast, has ever coupled with.   70
   For evil they were made, and evil is that gloomy
   Tartaros where they hold sway beneath the earth;
   they're hated by mankind and by the gods.
   So much for them. You must escape, and not grow weak;
   for they will drive you through the length of Greece.
   You must stride on across the earth, your wanderings will tread
     it down
   beyond the sea, beyond the island cities which the sea
     surrounds.
   Do not grow weary; tend this labour
   like a herdsman—only rest when you have come
   to Pallas' city; clasp her ancient image in your arms.   80
   There we will have men who can judge this case,
   and words to charm them; we will find a way
   to free you utterly from all these sufferings.
   For I persuaded you to take your mother's life.

ORESTES Lord Apollo, you know better than to harm your
     suppliant;
   with all your knowledge, do not wrong him by neglect.
   Your strength for doing good is worthy of men's trust.

AP Remember that; do not let terror conquer you.

Exit Orestes, right.

> Now, brother, son of my own father;
> Hermes, guard him! Answer to your name;   90
> be his escort, tend my suppliant as if you were
> his shepherd, as you return him to the world of men;
> for Zeus reveres an outcast's sanctity.

Exit Apollo, into the skene.

SCENE I(C)

Enter a dream-image of Klytaimestra, right.

KLYTAIMESTRA   You wish to sleep? What use are you
        asleep?
    Because I get no help from you, among the other dead the
        shades
    of those I killed reproach me ceaselessly:
    I wander in disgrace! I tell you that
    I bear a heavy burden for their deaths.
    These grievous torments were inflicted by my own
        blood-kin   100
    and yet no god is angered by my fate,
    though I was slaughtered by the hands of my own son!
    Look at these wounds, and let them strike your heart;
    for when it sleeps the mind has eyes!

    You have lapped up my many offerings,
    wineless libations, soothing draughts.
    I've given many solemn feasts for you
    beside the fiery hearth at dead of night, the hour that's yours
        alone.
    And now all this is trampled underfoot;   110
    he sprang into the air and vanished like a fawn.
    How easily he leapt out from the middle of
    your tightest nets and made great fools of you!

    Now you have heard me speak about the very life-blood
    of my soul; awake to wisdom, goddesses of Earth below;
    I am Klytaimestra, and in your dream I summon you.

FURIES   (*from inside the* skene; *moaning*)

KLYT   You may well moan – but he has now fled far away.
The suppliant is not devoid of friends.

F   (*moaning*)   120

KLYT   You sleep too much, you have no pity for my suffering;
I am the mother murdered by Orestes, and he has escaped.

F   (*groaning*)

KLYT   You groan, you sleep; get up at once!
What other duty have you but to cause him pain?

F   (*groaning*)

KLYT   Hard work and sleep are powerful conspirators;
they've drained off all the deadly venom from the snake.

F   (*moaning, twice as loud*)
Get him, get him, get him. There!   130

KLYT   You're hunting in a dream! You're barking like a
sleeping dog
that can't forget its need to kill.
What are you doing? Up! Do not succumb to toil;
sleep's made you weak and ignorant of what's been done to
you.
Let my complaint torment your hearts; the honest soul
is spurred to action by a justified reproach.
Blow out your bloody breath against that man,
waste him away with blasts of inner fire,
pursue him once again until he drops!

Exit, right.

1. FURY   (*in the* skene) Wake up! And now wake her as I have
woken you.   140
Do you still sleep? Get up, and kick away your slumber –
let's find out if that dream was false.

CHOROS I

Enter Furies in ones and twos, from the skene.

FURIES (A1)   Oh . . . ! Oh . . . ! We have been wounded,
      friends.
      How many wounds we've suffered, all unjustified.
      Now we've been wounded terribly;
      this is unbearable.
      The quarry's leapt out from the trap and gone;
      sleep conquered me and I have lost my prey.

(A2)   Great son of Zeus, you are a thief!
      You are still young, and you have ridden roughshod over
         ancient goddesses   150
      by rescuing the godless suppliant
      who was his mother's bitter enemy.
      You are a god, and yet you stole the matricide away.
      Would anybody say that this is just?

(B1)   While I still slept, reproaches came in dreams
      and struck me like a horseman with his whip
      in the belly, down below the liver.
      Here, the chill, the heavy chill,   160
      the dreadful whip-lash of the executioner!

(B2)   This is the sort of thing the younger gods all do,
      ignoring justice, lording it around
      a throne that reeks of slaughter
      head to foot!
      Here, on the navel of the earth,
      the dreadful curse of kindred blood!

(C1)   Prophet, you have defiled the shrine
      at your own hearth, and brought pollution on yourself;   170
      by helping him you have destroyed the gods' own laws
      and all the ancient ways of Destiny.

(C2)   I hate Apollo, and he will not help that man escape.
      Orestes never will be free, even beneath the earth.
      He is a murderer, and even there
      he'll bring a new avenger down upon his head.

SCENE 2

Enter Apollo, from the skene, *armed with a golden bow and arrows.*

APOLLO   Get out, I tell you, leave my house at once;
     you must be gone from this prophetic shrine   180
     or you will feel a gleaming, poisoned arrow's bite
     winged on its way by my bow's golden cord.
     The pain will make you spit black foam
     and puke up all the clotted human gore you've quaffed.

     It is not fit that you draw near these halls;
     your home's the slaughterhouse where heads are lopped,
     eyes are gouged out for vengeance, boys' young manhood is
        destroyed
     by cutting off their testicles; where men are mutilated, stoned
     to death, and groan with piteous cries
     impaled on stakes. Do you not realize   190
     it is because you love such hideous feasts
     that all the gods spit you away? The way you look
     tells the whole story; creatures such as you
     should live inside the lairs of lions that feast on blood,
     rather than grind pollution into soil as pure as this.
     Get out, you flock without a shepherd, there's no god
     who would delight in herding you.

1. FURY   Lord Apollo, listen to us in return;
     you are yourself not just a part-conspirator in these events;
     in every way your actions show you are their cause.   200

AP   How? You may speak long enough to tell me that.

1. F   Did you not give an oracle that he should kill his mother?

AP   That he should punish those who killed his father; what of
     that?

1. F   You then stood ready to receive him with the blood fresh on
     his hands?

AP   I did, and told him he must turn towards this house.

1. F   And now you slander us because we follow him?

AP   Yes, you're not fit to enter such a shrine.

1. F   But this has been ordained; it is our task.

AP   Oh, really? Let me hear it; boast about your sacred privilege.

1. F   It is our duty to pursue a matricide from house and
         home.   210

AP   Well, what about a woman who has killed her husband?

1. F   She would not have killed a true blood-relative.

AP   Then you reduce to nothing and despise
     the sacred vows of marriage, sanctified by Zeus
     and Hera the fulfiller; you dishonour and reject Kupris,
     the goddess who gives humankind their closest bond.
     The bed, where man and woman are united by their destiny –
     Justice defends that even more than sacred oaths.
     And so, if you are less than strict in your pursuit of murderers,
     and don't exact a penalty or visit them with all your anger,
        then   220
     I say you have no right to persecute this man;
     for now I find that some misdeeds enrage you, while
     on others it is obvious you take a softer line.
     The goddess Pallas will watch over how this case comes out.

1. F   I will not ever let him go.

AP   Well then, pursue him. Give yourself more toil.

1. F   Don't try to cut my privileges down by words.

AP   I wouldn't want to have your privileges.

1. F   No; whatever happens you are held in high regard beside
         the throne of Zeus.
       But I – since I am driven on by mother-blood –   230
       will go in search of justice. I will hunt Orestes to the end!

Exeunt, right.

AP   And I will give protection, and will save my suppliant;
     the anger of a man who turned to me for refuge would be
        terrible,
     among both men and gods, if I could help, and failed.

Exit, into the skene. *Doors close.*

Orchêstra *empty. Preset an image of Athena.*

SCENE 3

Enter Orestes, right.

ORESTES   Lady Athena, I have come at Loxias' command;
    receive this wanderer with kindness.
    I am not now a suppliant with unclean hands;
    no – my pollution's lost its edge; it has been worn away
    in other houses, other paths of men.
    I've crossed both land and sea, and all the way I've kept   240
    Apollo's orders in my mind; goddess, I now approach
    your temple and your holy image. I will stand guard here
    and wait until the outcome of my trial.

Enter Furies, right.

1. FURY   Look! Here's a clear sign of the man,
    a silent accuser; follow where it leads!
    We'll hunt him out the way a dog tracks down
    a wounded fawn – by following the trail of dripping blood.

1. F   This manhunt has exhausted us – our guts
    are heaving. We have roamed the earth,
    and flown across the ocean fast as ships, although   250
    we have no wings. I know he's lurking somewhere here;
    the smell of human blood smiles on me now.

(CHOROS 2)

FURIES   Look, look here!
    Everyone fix your eyes on him, don't let
    the mother-killer flee unharmed.
    Here he is – in safety!
    Wrapped around the image of the goddess, now
    he wants a trial to free him from his deed.   260

But that can never be. His mother's blood upon the ground
can never be recalled.
It soaked into the earth and vanished. In return
I will demand red clots to gulp
of your own living blood: you are to be
my food and drink;
and when I've sucked you dry I'll take you to the underworld
where you will pay with agony for all your mother's pain.
There you will meet the other criminals
who've shown no reverence to the gods,   270
to travellers or parents —
all receive the treatment that their deeds deserve.
Below the earth Hades the great accountant calls
all human beings to their final reckoning.
Nothing escapes his eye; it's all engraved
upon the tablets of his mind.

ORESTES   My sufferings have taught me, and I know
what's best to do in many things, including when
to speak and to be silent. Now in this affair
a wise instructor's told me I must speak.
The blood I shed is drowsy now; it dies away and leaves my
    hand.   280
A matricide's pollution can be washed away.
For it was driven from me, while still fresh,
at the god's hearth; Apollo purified me by the ritual sacrifice
    of swine.
The story would be long, if I spoke now of all
the people I approached without inflicting harm —
for Time can heal all wounds, while he and they grow old as
    one.
And now from a pure mouth I solemnly entreat
Pallas Athena, ruler of this land, to come
and be my helper; she will gain without a war
me, my country, and my citizens   290
as just and faithful allies for the rest of time.
She may be far away — perhaps in Libya,
her birthplace by the streams of Triton;
then, she may be marching, or advancing cautiously,
to help her friends; perhaps, bold general that she is,
her eye is turned upon the plain of Phlegra.

Goddess, come! For you can hear me, even far away;
become my saviour, free me from these torments!

1. FURY   Neither Apollo nor Athena's strength
will save you; you will be forgotten, when you fall   300
into the place where you will know no joy —
a bloodless shadow, feast for demons.

1. F   Nothing to say? You spit away my words,
you who were nurtured for me, consecrated as my sacrifice?
No slaughter at the altar; I will feast on you
while you still live. Now, victim, hear
this song that binds you fast.

CHOROS 3

FURIES   Come, let us form the circle and dance;
we are resolved
to show you all our fearful power of song,
and tell you how we carry out   310
our tasks among mankind.
We say that we are fair;
when a man can show pure hands
none of our anger chases him,
he lives his life unharmed;
but if someone offends us like this man,
and tries to hide his murderous hands,
then we appear! We are the victim's ever-truthful witnesses;
we are there to help her; we exact
the final penalty for blood.   320

(A1)   Oh mother who gave birth to me, oh mother
Night, hear this! Chastiser
of the living and the dead;
Leto's whelp has cheated me —
he stole away this prey,
my sacred, consecrated offering
because he shed his mother's blood.

(A1a)   This is a song
for the one who is doomed,
a blow to the heart that smashes the mind,   330

a song of the Furies to bind his wits,
a horrible sound to parch the brain.

(A2)   Destiny spun this from her thread
as my unchanging duty, fixed for evermore;
if any man should use his hands
for deeds of violence, then
we follow him until he goes
beneath the earth; and even dead
he is not free of us.   340

(A2a)   This is a song
for the one who is doomed,
a blow to the heart that smashes the mind,
a song of the Furies to bind his wits,
a horrible sound to parch the brain.

(B1)   These duties were ordained for us when we were born.
The gods must keep their hands away; we have
no fellow-banqueters to join our feast.   350
I do not share in their white robes
or in their joyous company.

(B1a)   For I have chosen overthrow of houses!
When War becomes innate within a family, and kin
strike down their kin,
then we pursue the murderer;
however strong he is, we spring up from the new-shed blood
to cast our shadow over him.

(B2)   I speedily remove these troubles from the world.   360
My labours keep the gods immune
from worry; they don't even have
to start inquiries. Zeus has ruled
that we are bloodstained, hateful, and
may not approach his meeting-places.

(C1)   In human life even most solemn dreams
of glory melt and vanish underground, discredited,
when our black forms advance   370
and our feet dance vindictively.

(C1a)   I spring high up;
I bring my foot right down with crashing force.
My limbs are dangerous; I'll trip

the fastest runner, and his fate is death.

(C2)   He doesn't know he's falling – his pollution maddens
       him,
    such is the cloud of filth that hovers round;
    and Rumour weeps to tell
    of the dark mist upon his house.   380

(D1)   This stands forever; we are skilful,
    and complete our task.
    We do not forget the wicked, we are awesome,
    we cannot be bribed.
    We do the work the gods disdain,
    that no one gives us credit for,
    in sunless darkness; we are sheer and hard
    for both the living and the dead.

(D2)   So! Is there anyone who does not feel respect
    and fear of what we do   390
    when he has heard the final rights that destiny decreed
    and that the gods conceded us?
    I still retain
    my ancient privileges;
    no one has yet dishonoured me
    although I live beneath the earth
    in darkness where the sunlight never falls.

SCENE 4

Enter Athena, right.

ATHENA   I heard your call for help, though I was far away,
    taking possession of the land beside Skamander, which
    the leaders and the chieftains of the Greeks
    made over to me roots and all for evermore –   400
    by far the greatest part of all the wealth won by their spears,
    a special gift to the Athenians.
    My feet cannot be wearied; I flew here
    without the use of wings, by brandishing my aigis.

    These people here are new to me;
    I have no fear, but wonder strikes my eyes.

Who are you? I am speaking now to all of you—
both to the stranger sitting at my image
and you—you do not look like any other race,   410
not kin to any goddesses the gods have seen,
nor are you similar in shape to mortal women . . .
But to speak ill of guests who've done no harm,
that is not right; it would be far from just.

1. FURY   Daughter of Zeus, you will learn all at once;
we are the children of the everlasting Night;
we are called Curses in our home beneath the earth.

ATH   I know about your ancestry, the names and titles that you
bear.

1. F   Now you will quickly learn our role in life.

ATH   I would learn that if someone tells me clearly.   420

1. F   We hunt down murderers and drive them from their homes.

ATH   Is there a limit to the killer's flight?

1. F   A place where there is never any thought of joy.

ATH   And now you're driving him to such a fate?

1. F   Yes, for he thought he had the right to be his mother's
executioner.

ATH   Was he forced to do it? Did he fear the anger of some god?

1. F   Where is the goad sufficient to compel the crime of
matricide?

ATH   Here are two sides but only half an argument.

1. F   He won't affirm on oath that he is innocent.

ATH   You'd rather be renowned for justice than be just in all
you do.   430

1. F   What do you mean? Show me. For you are wise.

ATH   I say injustice must not win by oaths.

1. F   Well, you look into it; find out which case is right.

ATH   Would you trust me with how your accusation ends?

1. F   Why not? We hold you to be worthy in yourself and in your
           parentage.

ATH   Stranger, what do you want to say against this, in your
           turn?
   Tell me your fatherland, your ancestry, and all your sufferings,
   and then defend yourself against the charge they bring,
   if you sit there and guard the image near my hearth   440
   because you trust in justice, if you are
   a solemn suppliant like Ixion.
   Respond to all these points with clarity.

ORESTES   Lady Athena, first I will remove
   the great concern expressed in your last words.
   I do not come unpurified; I did not take my place
   beside your image with pollution on my hands.
   And I will tell you a great proof of this:
   it is the custom for a murderer to stay
   in silence till a man with power to purify
   has cleansed him of the blood, by slaughtering a new-born
           animal.   450
   This sacred rite was done for me in other places, long ago,
   with other animals than yours, and other flowing streams.
   So I tell you that fear is not in our way.
   And now you'll swiftly learn my parentage.
   I am an Argive, and you do well to inquire
   about my father, Agamemnon, gatherer of men of war,
   with whom you made the city of the Trojans, Ilion,
   into a desert. But when he came home
   he died ingloriously: my black-hearted mother murdered him –
   she trapped him in a many-coloured hunter's net   460
   which still remains as witness of the slaughter in the bath.
   When I returned (I had been long in exile), I
   killed my own mother – I will not deny the deed –
   to punish her with death for my own, dearest father's death.
   And Loxias is equally responsible with me:
   he spoke of torments which would be like lashes to my heart,
   if I did not do something to my father's murderers.
   Now you decide the case – if I was right or not;
   whatever happens to me here, I will be satisfied.

ATH   This matter is too large, if any human beings thinks   470
   that he could try it; even I have not the right

to judge the issue in a case of murder where hot tempers rage—
especially since you have come here to my halls
schooled by your sufferings, a pure and harmless suppliant;
while they . . . they have a duty which we cannot simply
   disregard,
and if they do not win the victory
the arrows of their pride will come back afterwards
and fall upon our soil, a horrible, unbearable disease.
So that is how it is; to let you stay, or make you go—   480
either alternative is hard for me, and will bring harm.
But now, since this affair has fallen onto us,
I will choose blameless men of Athens,
judges of murder, faithful servants of the law
which I will found for all time as the bedrock of their plighted
   oaths.
Then you must call your witnesses, and show your proof—
sworn testimony which will aid your case.
I shall select the best of all my citizens,
and then return to give true judgement here.

Exit Athena, left.

CHOROS 4

FURIES (A1)   Now it would be the overthrow   490
      of her new laws
      if his outrageous case
      for mother-murder won.
      Mankind would then unite
      in a new harmony of hands
      ready for crime.
      It's true!
      Parents must then expect
      that wounds will be inflicted by their offspring
      evermore.

  (A2)   We are the watching mainads;
      but our wrath will cease to fall
      on those who do vile deeds.   500
      I will let every kind of death run wild!
      As he cries out about their suffering

each man will ask the next
if this torment will ever ease, or end;
his wretched friend will then console him – but in vain,
with remedies that do not work.

(B1)   Let no man call on us
when he is beaten down by suffering, and cry out loud
'Oh Justice,   510
Sacred Furies'
– as perhaps a father
or a mother who has just been hurt
cries in agony, because
the house of Justice has collapsed.

(B2)   There is a place where Fear is good,
and needs to stand as silent guardian
on watch over the mind;
it's right that pain should teach good conduct.   520
How could any man or city that does not
nurture an element of fear inside the heart
still worship Justice?

(C1)   It is wrong to praise
the life of anarchy
or that subject to tyranny.
In all things God has given victory
– whatever end they reach –   530
to those who take the middle path.
Let me tell you a word that matches this:
Violence is the true child of Impiety;
a healthy mind will lead
to that prosperity which all adore
and long for.

(C2)   We tell you this:
worship the altar of Justice,
don't kick it down with godless feet   540
and recklessly dishonour it for gain.
A penalty will come;
the end is final, and it waits for you.
Reverence your parents,
welcome strangers, wait on them;
so should you live.

(D1)   The man who willingly serves justice
          will not lack prosperity!   550
          He will not be destroyed.
          But anyone who dares to stand against us, carrying
          the spoils of wickedness piled high –
          sooner or later he will lose his sails,
          the moment that disaster strikes
          and breaks his mast.

(D2)   There he is, struggling in the middle of the whirlpool –
          no one hears him!
          Then the god laughs, to see the man   560
          of fiery blood – who never thought he could be trapped –
          beyond escape, and so exhausted by his peril that
          he can't get clear.
          His lifelong wealth has foundered on the reef
          of Justice, and he perishes
          unseen and unlamented.

                              SCENE 5

Enter Athena, left.

ATHENA   Herald, gather my people;
          let the shrill Etruscan trumpet
          filled with human breath
          give out its piercing cry to summon them.
          Then, when the court is filled, there must be silence.   570
          I shall state laws which everyone must learn,
          both my whole city for the rest of time
          and those here now, so that this case may be tried well.

*Fanfare. Enter eleven citizens of Athens, left. They bring benches
and two large urns. Enter Apollo, right.*

1. FURY   Lord Apollo, use your power only over what is yours.
          Tell us what part you play in this affair.

APOLLO   I come to testify – for this man is my suppliant,
          he came to Delphi, took the ritual place before my hearth,
          and he was purified of murder at my hands –

also to stand trial by him. For I am the cause
of this man's murder of his mother. You, bring on the case;   580
decide the outcome, as you best know how.

ATH   I now bring on the case; it is your turn to speak.
For if the prosecutor speaks first at the start
then he can teach us truly what the issues are.

1. F   Though we are many, we shall not say much.
You must now answer word for word.
First tell us if you killed your mother.

ORESTES   Yes, I killed her. No one can deny the fact.

1. F   Here is the first of the three wrestling throws.

OR   Don't boast; I'm not yet down.   590

1. F   But you must still tell us just how you killed her.

OR   Yes, I shall; with sword in hand I cut her throat.

1. F   Who then persuaded and advised you to do that?

OR   Apollo's oracle. And he bears witness for me.

1. F   The prophet counselled you to kill your mother?

OR   Yes, and till now I have not blamed my luck.

1. F   When the vote catches you, you'll tell another tale.

OR   I have faith: from his grave, my father sends me help.

1. F   So you put faith in corpses, mother-murderer?

OR   Yes, deep pollution touched her twice.   600

1. F   How? You had better tell the jurors what you think.

OR   She killed her husband, and she killed my father.

1. F   So what? You're still alive, while death frees her from
punishment.

OR   Why did you not pursue her into exile while she was alive?

1. F   The man she murdered was not her blood-kindred.

OR   Am I then kindred to my mother's blood?

1. F   You murderer, did she not nurture you

within her womb? Do you renounce the life-blood given by
    your mother?

OR   Now you must testify, Apollo; give your counsel and
    explain
    if I had Justice with me when I took her life.   610
    I did it; that is true, and cannot be denied;
    but was the bloodshed just or not? What do you think?
    Give me your judgement, so that I can tell the court.

AP   You are Athena's mighty court of law; all I will tell you now
    shall be with justice. Then, I am a prophet, and I never lie.
    Not one word have I spoken from my throne of prophecy
    about a man's, a woman's or a city's fate
    that is not by Zeus' order – Zeus, the father of the gods.
    Well now, think what a powerful point of law that is.
    I do advise you to follow my father's will;   620
    there is no oath which has more strength than Zeus.

1. F   So it was Zeus, you say, who granted you this oracle
    to tell Orestes that he could avenge his father's death
    with no account at all paid to his mother's rights?

AP   Yes. For it's not the same as when a man has died –
    a noble man, with royal sceptre granted by the gods –
    this at a woman's hands, and not at all heroically.
    She did not kill him with far-shooting, savage arrows like an
        Amazon,
    but in a manner which I shall tell you, Pallas,
    and you who sit to judge this matter by your votes.   630

    He had come from the war; his judgement had been good
    in most of what he did, she welcomed him with kindly words;
    she ran warm water in a silver bath, and then
    as he was stepping from it, at the edge
    she threw a robe right over him and struck him down –
    her husband, shackled by the close and endless meshes of the
        robe.
    There: that is how he met his end,
    a man revered by everyone, commander of the fleet.
    I've told you in this way, so all those people may be stung
    to wrath, who have been chosen to give judgement in this case.

1. F   According to your speech, Zeus gives the greater weighting
      to a father's death,   640
  but he put his own aged father, Kronos, into chains;
  how can you reconcile these points?
  Jurors, I call on you to witness this.

AP   You utterly revolting beasts, hated by all the gods,
    fetters can be removed – there is that cure,
    and many ways in which release is possible;
    but once a man has died, and thirsty dust
    has sucked up his black blood, he cannot be restored to life.
    For this my father has produced no countersong,
    although he turns and orders all things else   650
    at his desire with undiminished energy.

1. F   Beware: do not regard this as a valid plea for his release.
    Your client spilt his mother's kindred blood upon the earth;
    will he then live in Argos, in his father's halls?
    Will he officiate before the altars of the city?
    What brotherhood will let him share their sacred rites?

AP   I'll answer that as well; mark how I tell the truth.
    The person called the mother is no real parent
    of a child; she simply nurses foetuses once they've been sown.
    The parent is the man, who mounts; the woman is a hostess 660
    who preserves a stranger's offspring – if they are not harmed by
       any god.
    Now I will show you living proof of what I say.
    A father can beget a child without a mother; see, right here
    as witness stands the child of Zeus himself:
    she was not nurtured in the dark depths of a womb,
    yet she is such an offspring as no goddess ever bore.

    Pallas, I promise now as best I can
    to make your city and its army great in many ways.
    That's why I sent this man to take his refuge at your hearth,
    so that he might be pledged to you for all the rest of time.   670
    You would gain this man, goddess, as your ally,
    and his heirs – and it would be so evermore;
    all his descendants would be faithful to the pledge made here.

ATH   Have you both said enough? Shall I request
    the jurors to consider and return their votes?

AP   For our part, every arrow that I have has been unleashed,
      and now I wait to hear the judgement of the court.

ATH   Well, then, how shall I act and not be criticized by you?

1. F   You've heard what you have heard; and as you cast your
           votes,
       good citizens, revere within your hearts the oath you took.   680

ATH   Now hear the law I set for you, Athenians,
      as you cast the first judgement in a case of bloodshed.
      People of Aigeus, you will have this court
      of judges for the rest of time.
      Here they shall sit upon this rock, where Amazons
      once pitched their tents. They marched against us, built
      a high-walled rival to our citadel, and sacrificed
      to Ares, god of war. That's why it bears his name,
      this rock, the Areopagos, a place where reverence   690
      for all our fellow-citizens will soon become inborn, and so
      restrain injustice day and night alike,
      provided that the people don't destroy their ancient customs;
      if you allow polluted flows of muddy water in,
      you'll ruin your clear streams and never find a place to drink.
      Athenians, I beg you reverence and maintain
      a life neither anarchic nor beneath a tyrant's rule –
      and do not cast all elements of fear outside your walls;
      what man stays just if he has naught to fear?
      So if you reverence and fear a court like this   700
      then you will have a fortress for your land, a saving grace
      upon your city like no other men,
      unequalled by barbarians or other Greeks.
      This place of counsel, free from bribes,
      inspiring awe, sharp in its anger, wakeful guardian
      while others are asleep – I found it now.

      That speech was my advice, extended
      to our future citizens; now you must rise
      and take your votes and judge this case,
      in reverence to the oath you took. I have said all.   710

*The eleven human jurors step up, one during each speech, and cast
their votes into the first, active urn. They discard the other pebble
into the second urn.*

1. F   We are a heavy burden on the land;
          I counsel you, whatever else you do, do not offend us.

AP   And I advise you hold in awe my oracles
          (they come from Zeus) and do not make them fruitless.

1. F   You've interfered before in bloody murders which aren't
              your concern;
          now you'll give oracles from a polluted shrine.

AP   My father's judgement was in error, then,
          when he protected Ixion, the first suppliant murderer?

1. F   You've said it! And if I don't get fair treatment here,
          I'll settle, as a heavy burden, on this earth.   720

AP   You have no credit with the older gods
          nor with the younger; I shall win.

1. F   It's just the kind of trick you played at Pheres' house:
          you got the powers of Destiny to make a mortal live for all
              eternity.

AP   Is it not right to help a worshipper of mine,
          especially when he stands in need of help?

1. F   You plied the aged Fates with drink
          and then broke down the fundamental order of the world.

AP   You will not win this case; soon you'll be shooting arrows—
          harmless to everyone, even your enemies.   730

1. F   You, though a younger god, are riding roughshod over me;
          so now I wait to hear the outcome of this case,
          still in two minds whether to vent my fury on this city.

*Athena has approached the urns with her voting pebbles in her
hands.*

ATH   It is my task to cast the final judgement here;
          and I will give Orestes' cause this vote.
          There is no mother who gave birth to me;
          in everything I'm for the male with all my heart (except
          I would not marry one); I am the true child of my father Zeus.
          And so I will not give a greater status to a woman's death
          who killed the man, the guardian of the house.   740

Athena casts her vote.

Orestes conquers, even if the judgement comes to equal votes.
Now cast the lots out of the urns, quick as you can,
those of the judges who have been assigned this task.

The votes are counted.

OR   Phoibos Apollo, how will the contest end?

1. F Night, my black mother, do you look on this?

OR   Here I shall die by strangling, or shall live and see the light.

1. F And we shall wander outcast, or preserve our rightful role.

AP   Be careful, friends, in counting out the votes –
    and as you sort them, see injustice is not done.
    Without good care great damage might result,   750
    and just one vote can save a house.

ATH   *(after scrutinizing the ballots.)*
    This man escapes the penalty;
    the votes are equal on each side.

Exit Apollo, right.

OR   Oh Pallas, you have saved my house,
    and have returned me to the native land
    of which I was deprived. The Greeks will say:
    'He is an Argive once again, and now he lives
    on his ancestral property; all this is due
    to Pallas, Loxias, and Zeus the third, the Saviour and
    fulfiller of all things' – for he paid tribute to my father's
      death   760
    and saved me, though he had to face my mother's advocates.
    Now I shall go back home – but first
    I pledge my oath to Pallas and her people
    for the future, for the whole eternity of Time
    that never shall the man who rules my city dare
    to lead our splendid army out against this land.
    I will use all my power, out of my grave,
    and will wreak havoc if there should be anyone to break

these oaths which I swear now; I'll make their road
a hopeless journey, blasted by counter-omens   770
so they will regret their toil.
But if this oath is kept straight, and they aid
Athena's city by supporting you in war,
then I shall be more favourable to them.

So now farewell! Farewell to you, and to the people of this
    place;
may you possess a wrestling-stance no enemy can beat,
so you'll preserve your city and gain victory in war!

Exit Orestes, right.

FINALE

FURIES   You younger gods, you override
      the ancient laws, and snatch them from my hands.
      We are deprived of all we live for; in our misery   780
      our anger will be terrible, and we'll let
      the arrows fly out from our hearts
      to cause this country suffering in return—
      unbearable! The blight will drip
      to kill your plants and children.
      Justice! Justice!
      I will rush down to the plain, and pour into the earth
      the stain that will destroy all human life.
      I'll weep. What shall I do?
      They laugh at me. In Athens I have suffered
      terribly.   790
      We are the miserable, greatly suffering Daughters of the
        Night;
      no one respects us, so we grieve.

ATHENA   Let me persuade you not to take the trial so heavily;
    you were not beaten—no, the case came down
    to equal votes, and truly took no credit from you;
    for shining testimony was brought to us from Zeus,
    and he who gave the oracle stood as witness to the truth;
    Orestes had to do this and receive no punishment.
    So you should not cast down your heavy fury   800

on this land; do not be angry, do not wreck
our fruits with deadly, dripping poison from your breath,
a deadly froth that will devour the seed.
For I now promise you as fairly as I can
a place to live, here in a land
devoted to the cause of Justice; you shall rest
on gleaming thrones beside the hearth, and all
my citizens will pay you the respect that you deserve.

F   You younger gods, you override
    the ancient laws, and snatch them from my hands.
    We are deprived of all we live for; in our misery   810
    our anger will be terrible, and we'll let
    the arrows fly out from our hearts
    to cause this country suffering in return—
    unbearable! The blight will drip
    to kill your plants and children.
    Justice! Justice!
    I will rush down to the plain, and pour into the earth
    the stain that will destroy all human life.
    I'll weep. What shall I do?
    They laugh at me. In Athens I have suffered
    terribly.   820
    We are the miserable, greatly suffering Daughters of the
      Night;
    no one respects us, so we grieve.

ATH   You have not been discredited; you're goddesses, and
    should not be
  so furious with mortals, nor desire to wreck their land.
  Besides, I have my confidence in Zeus, and (need I mention
    this?)
  I am the only god or goddess who can open up
  the chamber where his thunderbolt is sealed.
  But we do not need that. Let me persuade you, and
  do not inflict your reckless threats upon this land,   830
  to make blight fall on all its plants.
  Please lay to rest the bitter force of that black wave of bile;
  for you are deeply honoured here, and may soon share my
    dwelling-place.
  Then you will praise my words, since for the rest of time
  you will receive the first-fruits of this splendid land

in offerings whenever there is childbirth or a marriage
   solemnized.

F   Me to suffer this!
    Ah! Me with my old-age wisdom
    to live underground
    buried like garbage!
    Ah!
    I hate you, I'll let loose my rage.   840
    Ah!
    The pain beneath my ribs.
    Oh mother Night!
    I have been cheated of
    my ancient privileges by the clever tricks
    of these deceitful gods.

ATH   I will tolerate your fury; you are older;
   then, in many ways, you are the wiser too,
   although I have a little bit of wisdom granted me by Zeus.   850
   But if you go off to another land with other leaves
   you will then long for Athens. I foresee – the flowing course
   of Time will bring greater renown
   to these my citizens, and if you have a place
   of honour near the palace of Erechtheus
   an endless line of men and women will present to you
   gifts you would never get from any other race.
   This is my country; do not cast upon it
   bloody strife that sharpens knives and causes wounds
   when young men rage in anger, maddened not by wine   860
   but by your venom; do not give them hearts that seethe
   like fighting-cocks by planting in my citizens a God
   who makes them fight each other, in the strife of civil war.
   Let War be with our enemies, it won't be hard to find –
   that war in which men can enjoy the fearful love of glory.
   Domestic, civil violence is no proper contest (so I say).

   This is the sort of gift that you may take from me;
   do well here, you will fare well here, and you will take your
     place
   with honour and reward; the gods all love this land.

F   Me to suffer this!   870
    Ah! Me with my age-old wisdom

to live underground
buried like garbage
Ah!
I hate you, I'll let loose my rage.
Ah!
The pain beneath my ribs.
O mother Night!
I have been cheated of
my ancient privileges by the clever tricks
of these deceitful gods.   880

ATH   I shall not rest from telling you these blessings;
      you will never say that I, a younger goddess,
      and my citizens evicted you and made an elder god
      wander away dishonoured and rejected from this land.
      So if the glorious goddess of Persuasion has some sanctity for
            you —
      she who will give my words a honeyed and a soothing charm —
      you'll stay; and if you still don't want to, then
      you could not fairly measure out your anger's weight
      against this city, injuring its men of war.
      For here you have a chance to be part-owner of this land   890
      forever, given all the privileges you deserve.

1. FURY   Lady Athena, what is this place you say I'll have?

ATH   One free from every kind of pain; please take it.

1. F   Well, suppose I do; what privileges will I have?

ATH   That no one's home may flourish unless you approve.

1. F   You'll really do this, grant me so much power?

ATH   Yes, you and I will give prosperity to those who reverence
      us.

1. F   And you will give your word on this for all the rest of time?

ATH   Of course; I would not speak of anything I will not do.

1. F   You seem to soften me; my rage abates.   900

ATH   So you will live here in our land and help us, as your
      friends?

1. F   How would you have me bless this place?

ATH   With songs that aim for glorious victory;
    blessings both from the earth and from the ocean's purity
    and from the heavens; pray for breaths of wind
    on sunny days to sweep over the land,
    and that the earth's fruit and abundant wealth of herds
    may never cease to flourish for my citizens,
    and human seed be fertile – so they will produce
    more and more children who revere the gods.   910
    I'm like a gardener, and I will cultivate the offspring of
    this noble seed; they must not grieve. All that is in
    your power; while I shall never cease, in any combat where
    men show distinction in the arts of war,
    to see that all respect this city's victories.

F (A1)   I will accept, I will live here;
    I will not hurt the city
    which is ruled by Zeus the conqueror
    and Ares, guardian of the gods –
    the glorious city which defends
    the gods of Greece.   920
    I wish it well; I pray
    the clear light of the Sun will make
    the blessings of good fortune
    flow in streams upon them.

ATH   This I have done because I love my citizens;
    I have inspired these goddesses both great and hard to please
    to settle here; for they have power   930
    in all affairs of men.
    If anyone encounters them
    he doesn't even realize they've struck him down.
    For all the errors of his ancestors
    drag him into their net, and silent death,
    for all his mighty noise,
    turns him to dust beneath their rage.

F (A2)   Diseases will not blight their trees
    (I tell you of the favours I shall bring);
    no fiery heat will trespass here
    to rob plants of their buds.   940
    No fearful sicknesses
    will creep upon them.

      May Pan ensure
      that their flocks thrive,
      and bring to birth twin lambs
      at the appointed time.
      This land is rich;
      its dwellers will repay
      with offerings the lucky finds
      the gods have given them.

ATH   Guardians of the city, do you hear this,
      what they are promising?
      A Fury can do much, and has great power   950
      both with the gods above and those below;
      and in the world of men, it's clear they always work their will
      right to the end; some they give cause to sing,
      to others a life dimmed by tears.

F (B1)   I say their men must not endure
      untimely death.
      Grant their lovely maidens
      men to live with – all you gods who have that power,   960
      especially the goddesses of Destiny,
      my mother's sisters,
      powers of Right;
      you have a share in every house's fate,
      and you are seldom gentle;
      but you never come without a cause,
      and so you are the most respected of the gods.

ATH   As they fulfil these pledges
      of such favour to my land
      I'm happy, and I thank Persuasion –   970
      she guided my speech
      when they were angrily refusing me.
      Zeus the persuader won the day;
      and now we are competing to do good
      we have the victory for evermore.

F (B2)   This is what I claim:
      that civil war, the most insatiable of miseries,
      will not rage here;
      so may the dust not drink   980
      the citizens' black blood

through lust to take revenge,
embracing Ruin for the city by
a mutual slaughter;
may they give each other joy,
may they share their thoughts in friendship,
may they hate as one!
That is the cure for many human sufferings.

ATH   Do you not see?
They are trying to find
words that will lead us on the road to good.
From these terrifying faces   990
I see great advantage for my citizens;
for if you always honour them
they will be happy, you will be happy,
everyone will see that Athens is a land
where Justice rules.

F (C1)   Hail, then, hail, Athenians!
You're destined to be rich –
you sit close by the throne
of Zeus' dearest daughter, her dear friends,
wise in good time.   1000
Zeus the father loves the people who
live under Pallas' wing.

*Enter Women and Girls of Athens left, some carrying crimson
robes for the Furies, others torches.*

ATH   Hail to you too; I must go first
to show you where your chambers lie
as this escort lifts
the sacred light.
Go now; and we will speed you there
with solemn sacrifice to keep
destruction down below, and send us everything
that will bring profit to the city
for its victory. Now you,
descendants of Kranaos, keepers of this city,   1010
you must lead these honoured immigrants;
the citizens must learn to understand
their riches.

F (C2)   Hail, hail, and now farewell;
         all of you – men, and the gods
         who steer the course of Pallas' city –
         as long as you revere your new-found immigrants
         you'll never have to blame what happens in your life.

ATH   I praise you for these words of invocation;
         I shall escort you now, while torches shine and light our way,
         to those deep places down below the earth,
         the finest place in all of Theseus' land,
         with these attendants who keep watch beside my image.
         These Furies I now name the Solemn Goddesses.
         Clothe them in garments rich in crimson dye
         and honour them; kindle the fire
         so they may make their friendly presence felt   1030
         by giving us good fortune ever more!

WOMEN AND GIRLS OF ATHENS (A1)   Go now to your
             home, oh great and honour-loving
         ageless daughters of the Night; we are your friends
         and we escort you.
         People of the country, keep silence.

   (A2)   In the ancient depths of the earth
         you will receive great honour,
         gifts and sacrifices.
         People of the city, keep silence.

   (B1)   Graceful to us, and strict in your goodwill,   1040
         Solemn Goddesses, rejoice as you go
         upon your way lit by our torches;
         raise a glad shout in echo to our song.

   (B2)   These torches mark your everlasting bond
         with the Athenians. Zeus, who sees all,
         and Destiny came down to aid our truce;
         raise a glad shout in echo to our song.

Exeunt Athena, Solemn Goddesses, citizens, Women and Girls,
left.

NOTES

Agamemnon

Dramatic Structure and Form

Agamemnon is formed around the king's return from the Trojan War.[1] During the first half of the drama Klytaimestra perverts all the normal customs which underlie a Greek homecoming. The hope of a successful return which the Watchman expresses in Scene 1 is progressively removed. We see the ever-increasing power of Klytaimestra, as her successive political and psychological engagements with the Elders and the Herald establish her possession and control of the playing space. At the same time we see the hope of a safe return for the Trojan expedition gradually diminished, until Agamemnon comes back alone, in just one ship, having lost Menelaos and all the rest of the fleet.

Aischylos uses the Elders' songs to blur the audience's sense of time, so the key stages can be presented consecutively, despite the fact that in real life the action of Scenes 2, 3 and 4 would have been separated over several days. Klytaimestra's actions create the Elders' complex blend of hope and increasing apprehension, as they respond in Choroses 1–3 to the events unfolding before them.

Her triumph over Agamemnon at the midpoint, in Scene 4, is so effective – and the setback, when Kassandra refuses to obey her in Scene 5 and forces her to delay the sacrifice, is so telling – precisely because these scenes are the culmination of her intrigue. The gathering momentum of Klytaimestra's perversions of ritual,

---

[1] The pattern of the *nostos* or homecoming story in *Ag* is discussed in Ewans (1982a). NB the parallel with Sophokles' *Women of Trachis*, in which, as in *Agamemnon*, the king sends an advance Herald on to the palace while he makes a first sacrifice to the gods of his homeland at the place where he has landed.

sacrifice and ceremony[2] gives a compelling feeling of tragic inevitability to the climax, the death of Agamemnon; by dramatizing all this, and adding on top of it the revelations of the Kassandra scene, Aischylos fulfils his fundamental aim of explaining why the death of the king took place.

In *Agamemnon*, Aischylos uses the recently developed wooden *skene* building to represent the house of Atreus, and exploits its resources: the flat roof (in Scene 1), the threshold and double doors (throughout), and the *ekkuklêma* (in Scenes 7 and 8).

The first half of the drama uses words, music and movement alone; the only props are the walking-staves on which the Elders lean. The absence of props symbolizes in theatre terms the emptiness of a kingdom without a king,[3] and so reinforces the expectation and apprehension as everyone in Argos waits for Agamemnon's return. Klytaimestra's ever-increasing power is indicated by the fact that she alone enters and exits through the doors of the house of Atreus, and does so at moments carefully chosen by herself for maximum effect.[4]

Then, at the mid-point of the drama, Aischylos deploys in rapid succession two remarkable visual images: Agamemnon's return, alone in a chariot with Kassandra beside him, and then the tapestries. These new properties give dramatic shape to the subsequent scenes.

Scene 4 is focussed around the chariot, the tapestries, and the doorway to which they mark the path. The most important and dominant focus in the *orchêstra* is normally the centre-point. Aischylos now exploits the fact that when they are in use, the double doors inevitably pull the focus away from it, and make the line from C to EBC the main axis for establishing presence in the *orchêstra*. (Actors are most powerful in the *orchêstra* when they advance down this line; they only start to lose power when they pass C and begin to advance towards FC, as from C forwards the percentage of the audience to whom the actor is presenting his back increases rapidly.)

Then the tapestries are removed, and Scene 5, in which

[2] Cf. Zeitlin 1965.

[3] Conversely, the use of props and extras can be used to communicate the presence and power of the king, as with the suppliant tableau in *Oidipous the King*, scene 1.

[4] See below. The importance of Klytaimestra's dominance of the threshold in *Agamemnon* was perceived by Taplin 1977a, 299–300.

Klytaimestra attempts to persuade Kassandra to leave the chariot, is focussed around the now vacant space between chariot and doorway. The chariot is removed for Scene 6, in which Kassandra (who up until now, as she has stayed silent and motionless in Agamemnon's chariot, could herself also be regarded as another, very striking property) dominates the action with the first solo actor lyrics in *Agamemnon*.[5] Although this scene uses the entire *orchêstra* and no props, it frequently focusses on her interaction with the *skene* doors, which have remained open (for the first time) since Klytaimestra's last departure; and on the route, formerly marked out by the tapestries, which Kassandra must follow, in Agamemnon's footsteps, to meet her fate.

After Kassandra has gone in, the Elders are helpless: for the first time since Agamemnon's arrival, they are left alone in the *orchêstra* without a prop or person to interact with. They are rapidly relieved of their confusion. Klytaimestra appears on the *ekkuklêma* in triumph over the bodies of Agamemnon and Kassandra, and the last third of the drama crystallizes around her defence of, and the Elders' attack on, her deed. The corpses remain visibly present, and centrally in the thoughts of the characters and the audience, from the moment they are first displayed until the end.

Roles

Late in the 460s one of the leading tragedians[6] successfully applied to the authorities to raise the number of solo actors from two to three. This trilogy is the first surviving work in which a third actor is used – and it is evident from the parts of Kassandra and Elektra that Aischylos had an actor available who could specialize in young female roles with a lyric dimension.

---

[5] In the first half, the absence of properties allows Aischylos to erect a complex interaction between the past events recalled in the three wide-ranging choral odes and the developing situation in the dramatic present. After Agamemnon's arrival, the only two choral odes are brief responses to the specific situation in which the Elders find themselves at the end of Scenes 4 and 6; the remainder of *Agamemnon* is focussed around the use of properties in the space and the power of the threshold. However, the pressure to which events have built up by this time permits Aischylos to compose two intense lyric scenes for choros and solo actor.

[6] Different sources name Aischylos and Sophokles.

Interaction between more than two solo actors is avoided throughout the *Oresteia*, and is rare even in much later tragedies, doubtless because[7] problems arise in distinguishing between the voices of more than two male solo actors in a complex interaction with a group of twelve choros members. Indeed, the normal mode in dialogue scenes throughout the *Oresteia* is interaction between one solo actor and the choros; careful blocking and greater use of gesture are needed during interplay with two or three masked, male actors.

In *Agamemnon*, the organization of parts makes a precise statement through doubling possible. The first actor (presumably Aischylos himself) played Klytaimestra throughout; the second actor played the sequence of inadequate males who encounter her, and the lover who is – like Claudius in *Hamlet* – a counterfeit, inferior replacement for the king he has just played; the third actor represented the one character who, though young, female and a slave, is able to check Klytaimestra's course.

In *Libation Bearers* the first actor again plays the central figure – now Orestes; the rest of the distribution is dictated by the fact that the third actor must play Elektra, who has an extensive singing part. In *Eumenides* the first actor again plays the person on whom a tragic dilemma devolves – Athena.[8]

The drama contrasts the heroic Greek virtues of the kingdom of Argos with the effete, barbarian culture of Priam's Troy, which Aischylos figures, by a deliberate anachronism, as if it were the Persian Empire which his own generation of Athenians had twice repelled from Greece. It is important to bring this out in the costumes and masks or make-up, sharply marking off both Klytaimestra's handmaidens and Kassandra herself as oriental in their features. The fact that the Libation Bearers are foreign should also be marked in the second drama.

Scene 1

This scene establishes the return of Agamemnon, and the reception which he will receive on his arrival, as the main action of the drama (cf. especially 34–5).

In Homer,[9] Aigisthos posted a Watchman to warn him of

---

[7] Gould (1985, 275); cf. Baldry 1971, 56.

[8] Like Klytaimestra in *Agamemnon*, Athena is required to chant anapaests but does not sing full lyrics.

[9] *Odyssey* 3.265f., 4.521f.

Agamemnon's arrival in Argive territory. Aischylos significantly changes the story. This Watchman has been set at his post by a Klytaimestra who transcends gender expectations, in a way which the original audience would have found sinister and dangerous. She exhibits 'masculine' planning ability (10–11), and shows at once that the initiative will lie with her, and not with Aigisthos. It is Klytaimestra's purpose to know as soon as Troy has fallen, not just when Agamemnon's actual return to Argos is imminent.

Scene 1 lays down the fundamental emotional pattern of the drama.[10] It proceeds from expectation to the joy of fulfilment, and then into apprehension. This pattern is replicated many times – most overtly in Choroses 1–3; and it does more to establish the feeling of blighted homecoming than any other single aspect of Aischylos' dramaturgy. Agamemnon's return is overshadowed, even before it has begun, by the Watchman's cautious but firm allusions to the 'masculine' strength of Klytaimestra's intellect (11), the Fear that will not leave him (14f.), and the troubles in the house (18–19). He waits for 'release [. . .] from these sufferings' (1; another recurrent verbal motif in the drama),[11] and he receives it; but the direction of his thoughts in 9–20 prefigures a reprise as soon as his first rejoicing is exhausted. In 36f. the Watchman returns to the deeper reality which underlies the news that Troy has fallen; and his sudden, sinister withdrawal into silence does more than any further words to consolidate the final tone of apprehension for the future.

In many modern productions the Watchman stays motionless throughout; but Aischylos must have been alive to the potential for movement from side to side on a flat roof. The monologue should begin with the Watchman lying down (cf. 2); but the text contains strong inducements for him to rise at 8, and walk up and down (to illustrate his restless anxiety to a vast audience) at 12. Then his hope is illuminated effectively by bringing him to rest again – perhaps slumped at one end of the *skene* roof – at 20–21.

It is unlikely that a real beacon was kindled behind the *theatron* at this moment in Aischylos' performance. After a pause, the Watchman simply has to mime attention to a distant spot, disbelief – and celebration. He runs to just above the central doors

[10] Cf. Ewans (1975, 18–19) and Stanford (1985, 122–3).
[11] And a sinister one: 'release from sufferings' was also a euphemism for death (cf. e.g., Soph. *Tr* 1171f.)

for the outcry at 25, and rapid, excited movements illuminate his summons to Klytaimestra and his ecstatic victory-dance. Then the retreat into ominous silence at 36f. becomes a retreat also into a depressed body posture, matching and exceeding the weariness expressed during the opening lines; the actor then turns away as abruptly as is needed to convey the bitterness and finality of 39, before descending the internal stairs back into the *skene*.

Choros 1

It was a normal feature of Greek life for the city council to assemble to discuss strange news; this became a convenient opening convention in dramas with male choroses.[12] The group played by the choros can meditate on recent events, and expand on the background, before the first individual characters appear.

With the first entry of the Elders many productions of the *Oresteia* lose the audience,[13] as twelve greybeards totter on, take up almost fixed positions and start declaiming what apparently is a long theological meditation on behalf of the author.[14] The use of staves, an essential prop to characterize the Elders (and very useful in the choreography), does not imply that they doddered around ineffectively throughout the drama, presenting an image of senile immobility. Athenian choros members were young men at the peak of their physical ability, who rehearsed the trilogy for many months in preparation for the competition, and trained as intensively as an Olympic athlete; the lyric images in *Agamemnon* demand for their illumination some of the most evocative dance of any surviving Greek tragedy.

There would have been nothing incongruous to Athenian eyes when Aischylos' team of young men, dressed and masked as old

[12] Cf. e.g. Aischylos' *Persians*, Sophokles' *Antigone* and *Oidipous the King*.

[13] And give them a permanently distorted view of Greek tragedy as dull and boring. The same effect (Peter Brook's 'deadly theatre') can also be achieved in the opening choros of Sophokles' *Oidipous*.

[14] Neuburg (1981, 163ff. and 210ff.) rightly stresses that the narrative is the Elders' response to the sacrifices which Klytaimestra has organized, their own in-character reliving of Aulis, not Aischylos' authorial account. Note also the traditional mistranslation of *pathei mathos* 178, (correctly: 'learn by experience'; i.e. human beings can only learn for certain through experience), as 'learn through suffering' with the full Christian (and Wagnerian) overtones of redemption through repentance. The recurrent impetus to make Greek tragedy didactic is well and rightly criticized by Vickers (1973, 64–66 + notes).

men, danced vigorously to match the verbal imagery: in classical Greek culture, men danced actively right into old age. Accordingly, the convention of this drama (and others where the choros play the parts of old men) was, I believe, that the choros members mimed the Elders' age and feebleness at the few moments when the audience needed to be reminded of them for the purposes of the plot.[15] Elsewhere they moved at least as vigorously as the Athenians would have expected their senior counsellors to move –with a lot more sprightliness than *we* would imagine!

This is the longest choral ode in the surviving Greek tragedies, and arguably also the most powerful. It is exceptionally challenging in performance: Aischylos took a calculated risk when he asked his choros to sing and dance their most extended song in the entire trilogy immediately, before they have warmed up.

Introduction (40–103). The Elders march into the *orchêstra* full of confidence, and the picture which must be evoked in the choreography is clear: for them, the expedition against Troy is to be seen as a legal act of justified vengeance, to exact recompense for a violation of *xenia*.

This perspective is one-sided and it is rapidly undermined, by the momentum of the chanted narrative itself, at 60f. Now there are both favourable and unfavourable aspects to the expedition:[16] the good was obvious at the outset, while the bad has stolen in as the Elders develop their theme. The pattern is identical with that of the Watchman's thoughts after the appearance of the beacon.

Then a remarkable conclusion (72f.). Ostensibly only introducing themselves, explaining why they were debarred from joining the expedition, the Elders refer to the weakness of the marrow in their limbs – no stronger than a child's. The unsung implication is strong: only between childhood and age, in the prime of life, is man able to act; but we have already heard of the questionable nature of action, the sufferings it involves, and the inexorable, but unforeseeable consequences. The opening dance thus descends from the mime of an heroic departure, of angry

[15] Perhaps when they are first introduced at 72f., at the opening of Scene 7, and in the confrontation with Aigisthos and his bodyguards in Scene 8.

[16] The war is being fought just for one promiscuous woman, and it is the cause of Greek suffering as well as Trojan. These are two major motifs which Aischylos will develop in the second and third choroses.

vultures and their justified revenge, through the evocation of wartime suffering to the pathetic, hobbled gestures of old men.

The Elders have gathered before the palace because they have seen sacrifices all around the city; they are apprehensive and worried. In the absence of the king, they have come to the queen, who is acting as regent, to seek accurate news. When Klytaimestra declines to emerge,[17] they attempt to understand the past. They brood on the departure of the Trojan expedition, and their attempt ends in a disastrous evocation of the sacrifice of Iphigeneia.[18] They thus immediately set before the audience a picture of Agamemnon so trenchant and memorable that it will underlie the first half of the drama.[19]

Aulis i (104–59). The Elders retrace their path, and embark upon a complex lyric narrative of the setting-out of the expedition; but much has changed since their opening presentation. The Atreidai are no longer sent out by the avenging hand of Zeus, but by the portent; and the complexity of the verse in these three stanzas matches the way in which both the men at Aulis then, and the Elders in the dramatic present now, have to feel around in the dark, trying to see into an obscure and ominous future – which later becomes revealed and tragic.

In stanza A2 Kalchas interprets the portent. The eagles, he says, stand for the sons of Atreus, who are about to go to conquer Troy.

---

[17] Performances both ways have shown that Taplin (1977a, 280–5) is right as against the psychologizing approach of e.g., Pool (1983). The people whose psyches are affected by the narrative of Aulis are the Elders and the audience, not Klytaimestra (who resolved long ago to murder Agamemnon; 1377–8). Goldhill's indifference to the first major staging question posed by the trilogy (1984, 16–17) is depressing. In our production, the Elders first turned in formation towards the *skene,* came to a despairing close as the chant drew to an end unanswered, and then turned forwards – after a pause – into a new dance formation, as the song begins at 104f. Neither the actress playing Klytaimestra, nor any of the Elders, felt a need, still less an enthusiasm, to have her come on at 83 and either pull focus by 'stage business' or watch the rest of Choros 1. On the contrary, her entrance after 257 became highly effective – with a moment of pointed silence when she is seen for the first time, as she stood just outside the doors of the *skene* and coldly confronted the Elders.

[18] Another example of expectation – fulfilment – apprehension. The patterns of this ode are discussed in Ewans 1975; cf. Lattimore 1964, 40–1.

[19] It is, significantly, thrown in his face by one of the Elders when he arrives, 799f.

We are left to conclude for ourselves that the pregnant hare stands for Troy, and its young for the city's inhabitants. Destiny will destroy Priam's city forcibly, with this expedition as its medium; but once again the reassuring note is qualified. Kalchas fears lest some divine anger may overshadow the army – for Artemis 'hates the eagles' feast' – and if we translate the symbolism of the portent,[20] she is angry as the protectress of all the young innocents who will be destroyed when the sack of Troy avenges Paris' crime. As his vision flows on, into the *epode* A3, Kalchas is able to see the future, to predict, and fear, the winds. More obscurely, he is also able to see, although dimly, the goddess's eagerness for monstrous sacrifice, and the consequences for the house of Atreus; an implacable hostility (which the audience will interpret as that of Klytaimestra) which will await Agamemnon on his return home.

As the Elders narrate these events, a refrain steals in (121), focussing on the moment of suffering, and the optimism of the hope that the outcome will be better. Repeated and transformed, as a disastrous outcome is more and more seen to be unavoidable, it becomes a recurring verbal motif to express the tragic cadence of the drama, the widening chasm between man's hopes and what actually happens in the real world. At first it simply appears, gently, as the Elders' own comment to round off A1; it is then repeated, as an outcry by Kalchas, at the end of A2 – adding emphasis and anxiety to his reading of the omen; and finally, when both the perils and the blessings of the expedition are complete in Kalchas' prophecy, the Elders join their voices 'in harmony' with those of all the men at Aulis; their own emotions now are fused with those of the others, ten years ago.

In the lyric verse of Greek tragedy *strophe* responds to *antistrophe*; the metrical pattern of matching stanzas was exactly the same in the original, and the meaning is greatly enhanced in performance if such stanzas are choreographed identically. In this group there is also an *epode*, A3, in the same metre, but different in detail from A1 and A2 and therefore requiring a different but related patterning in the choreography.

The parallels between matching stanzas cannot all be brought

---

[20] Note however – despite a wealth of modern speculation – that neither Kalchas nor Agamemnon pursues the question *why* Artemis demands human sacrifice in fulfilment of the portent of the dead hare; cf. Neuburg 1981, 139ff.

over into English, since no translator can locate every key word at exactly the same point in the line as in the original;[21] but if some of the main points of relationship are preserved, the choreographer can devise suggestive patterns which will bring out the aspects of the Greek playwright's meaning which this device expresses. In these two stanzas, for example, Aischylos places the Elders' narrative (A1) in parallel with Kalchas' (A2), setting their sense of their own authority to speak in parallel with his authority to interpret. After matching Kalchas' opening to theirs, Aischylos then enforces the parallel between the portent and the army whose fate it interprets, by matching all the details of the description in A2 to that in A1. Then he ends by bringing the act which symbolizes why Artemis is angry (the eating of the hare, 119–20) into alignment with Artemis' pity for that act (134–5), and reinforces the convergence of meaning at this point by repeating the refrain.[22]

Aulis ii (160–257). The full burden of the prophecy which they have just reported is obscure to the Elders, even in the dramatic present, for Klytaimestra's hatred of her husband is still concealed from them. Aischylos needs a pause between Kalchas' prophecy and the implementation of the first thing which he feared, to measure and reflect the time which elapsed at Aulis, before it became plain exactly what the demand of Artemis was.

It is appropriate that in the darkness of this moment the Elders turn to Zeus, for he, they believe, is the only source by whose agency vain burdens of reflection may be cast away. But a subtle irony undermines their attempt to find comfort. The praise of Zeus leads them on at 182–3 to confront an aspect of his powers which is highly, and unpleasantly, relevant to the situation which they are in the middle of describing. Zeus has given Agamemnon the great gift, or favour, of sacking Troy; but such favours are dangerous to mortal men: the gods may well demand a price. And because his gift from Zeus exacts so much from others who are

----

[21] Indeed, it is usually not even possible to translate matching stanzas with totally corresponding English verse patterns, and remain faithful to the sense of such complex lyrics.

[22] Close study of the text often reveals further detailed correspondences, which should be brought out by setting them to identical movements in the choreography.

under her protection, the goddess Artemis demanded such a recompense from Agamemnon at Aulis.

This sequence of thought explains how, with a seamless transition, without change of metre – indeed, in the middle of a strophic pair – the Elders shift their focus from their meditation on the powers of Zeus to the situation of Agamemnon at Aulis; and here again the matching responsion of the danced stanzas makes the point. The powerful connection at 183 'ranges the special case under the general law';[23] we see the sufferings of the Greeks, as they languished at Aulis, danced to the same steps in C2 as was the pain that accompanies the favours of the gods in C1.

Then the narrative flows seamlessly into its final phase. Once again strophic patterning is central to the meaning. In D1 the Elders sing first of indecision and suffering which the gale inflicted on the expedition, and then of the terrible remedy which Kalchas saw was Artemis' demand. This is matched in D2 by the way in which Agamemnon's agonized indecision is followed, in the second part of the stanza, by his movement to accepting that remedy. Aischylos then emphasizes the madness of the deed by setting the E2 account of it in parallel to E1, the Elders' fierce denunciation of Agamemnon's state of mind.

The account of Iphigeneia's last moments runs directly onward in mid-sentence into the F stanzas (a rare writing technique in Greek tragedy), and sets the choreographer the acute challenge of devising movements which will evoke both the appalling pathos of the picture evoked in F1, and the reckless abandon of the Elders in F2, as they attempt to retreat from that picture into unjustified optimism. The extended choral dance comes through to a highly ominous conclusion.

Scene 2

Klytaimestra's part in the first half of *Agamemnon* is conceived in theatrical terms, as a series of rehearsals for the return of Agamemnon – a commanding performance, which is finally frustrated and upstaged by Kassandra, when Klytaimestra attempts to create the climax of the drama after Scene 4. The power struggle between Klytaimestra and a succession of men

[23] Wecklein, quoted by Fraenkel 1950, 114.

begins in Scene 2; as Agamemnon begins his return home, his wife tests her ability to think and act as strongly as a man against the chief citizens of Argos – and she succeeds. The Elders are left at the end with nothing but their scepticism, which will be undermined at the start of Scene 3.[24]

The Greek theatre shape is most effective in illuminating the ebb and flow of a confrontation. This is evident in Scene 2 from the moment the doors open, framing Klytaimestra as she steps into the playing area. She comes out for the first time to confront the Elders – in their conference space, but on her terms – and they retreat. Wherever she goes during 264f. (ERC or ELC work best), the Elders have to advance towards Klytaimestra one by one during the *stichomythia*, only to be swept away as she breaks out from the locked-in confrontation and drives them back towards the perimeter with the opening words of the beacon speech.

There are many possibilities for performing the rest of the scene. One promising approach is to take advantage of the fact that in the Greek theatre the line from EBC to C is the most commanding: points on this axis can be used as Klytaimestra's resting-places for those moments in the two long speeches when she is at her most emphatic. Then, by contrast, she can range around the *orchêstra* during those passages where the speech flows more freely, annihilating the Elders' attempt to maintain their own physical solidarity in the space. This movement visually complements the command of geography in her rhetoric.

Klytaimestra's second speech, her response to the studied insult to her intelligence in 318–9, is an enigmatic performance. In terms of movement it is perhaps best seen as an appeal to the Elders to become emotionally involved in a situation whose exact parameters and relevance are initially opaque to them. The spatial metaphor then remains similar to that in the first speech; once again EBC/BC is the most effective position for the key points of rest (especially the crucial warning at 338f.). Her sallies before that point are, however, quite different from the triumphant circlings appropriate to the beacon speech: here, by contrast, she must quit

---

[24] Aischylos pours into the confrontation the bitter fruit of ten years of growing mutual suspicion and political conflict. Lines 258f. make it plain that the Elders tolerate Klytaimestra's political position only because they are obliged to; 270 can be played as expressing the totally feigned public emotion of the politically subservient in the face of an official statement which, inwardly, they totally disbelieve.

Once again, in preparation for the arrival of Agamemnon himself, a character first arrives to take possession of the *orchêstra*, and is then driven by Klytaimestra from that possession to the perimeter. In our production the Herald entered at a run and then collapsed, exhausted, at FC as he delivered his opening line. He rose gradually, first to his knees and then to his feet, during the ensuing greetings to the earth, the gods and the heroes of Argos. Then he began to assert possession of the space, moving up the centreline (obviously) towards the *skene* before and during 518f., and turning (BC) to face forward as he addresses the Elders from 522. Whether he moves again during 527f. or not, the last section of the speech must be played as an attempt to persuade the Elders from a static, commanding position, culminating in a triumphal declaration at 532f. The Herald's confident mood can then be systematically undermined. After retreating from their initial curiosity in the face of his aggressive, rhetorical address to them, a few of the Elders draw closer for 538f., one by one. (This *stichomythia* plays well with one or at most two interlocutors.) The Herald naturally moves forward too, reaching out to them in a dialogue in which both partners truly attempt to communicate with each other. However a chasm grows between them: in his political naivety the Herald – after finally, at 549, getting the point at which they are driving – then misses it totally, when he misunderstands 550 and uses it as the springboard for a second optimistic speech. In our production the Elders at this point broke up their increasingly close concentration around the Herald – the first contact by the people of Argos with the returned expedition –and retreated in disgust to positions around the front perimeter.

Their retreat forces the Herald to address the first of his appeals (555f.) to their turned backs. In what follows the Elders only gradually overcome their reluctance, turning to face him again one by one in response to the increasing pressure of his rhetoric, and of his movement around and between them. At 568f., as he tries desperately to recreate the joy of victory, his mood changes, and the Elders all turn to follow the flow of his rhetoric. Lines 572f. play well with the Herald just off-centre at the back (EBL), as he builds up to the climactic declaration at 577f., and then approaches the Elders to address to them the admonition of his last three lines.

Finally he turns back again and begins to advance towards the palace. This again accords with a familiar practice: it was customary for the bearer of good news to convey it in person, and receive a reward from the king or queen. But this Herald is interrupted. Klytaimestra appears, as if by magic, at the exact moment when she can subvert his move towards the house; she deprives him both of the fulfilment of his duty and of his reward.[28]

Her sudden entry disrupts the pattern of triumphant Herald and attentive Elders. She drives them all back to the perimeter of the *orchêstra* by the vehemence and speed of her entry and subsequent movements, as she delivers an astonishingly bold and challenging speech which she uses as a second, even more aggressive, rehearsal for the control of the *orchêstra* which she will exercise – and the grand hypocrisy she will raise on the basis of that control – when she greets Agamemnon himself. She then departs as swiftly as she came, before either the Herald or the Elders can muster a reply.

This dynamic, whirlwind speech is best played fast, and with violent contrasts between the sections in which Klytaimestra is still and those in which she is on the move. Most of it is an attack on the Elders, though two small parts (598–9, 604–7) are addressed to the Herald; one section (607–12) can be played as pure introversion, addressed over all their heads to air and sky.

Alone in the *orchêstra*, the Herald now has no choice but to suffer interrogation by the Elders on the one subject he was hoping to avoid. The sudden, aggressive new tack taken by the Elders (after their incisive comment at 615–6 on Klytaimestra's performance, which is lost on the Herald and is therefore best played as an internal comment from one Elder to the others) is met with evasion; accordingly the final *stichomythia* must be blocked to express the Herald's various attempts to escape, and the ways in which the Elders corner him. Lines 632–3 can then be played as a last, futile attempt to turn away from their interrogation before he settles down to the narrative, in which Aischylos makes fine creative re-use of Menelaos' story, in *Odyssey* 4, of what happened after the fall of Troy.

In the last speech, the Herald's syntax becomes increasingly complex in order to express his continuing reluctance to speak; the movement must also reflect this. The speech begins in a very

---

[28] This theatrical effect, which will be replicated at 851, justifies Taplin (1977a, 294–7 and 299–300) in firmly rejecting all attempts to have her present earlier in the scene.

elevated tone, with the Herald circling around in fragmentary patterns as he tries to convince the Elders (who have now retreated to the perimeter) that they do not really want to hear his story; but at 649, almost by accident, he blurts out the fact that there was a storm. After this the narrative settles down, and 650–66 can be delivered virtually from one spot (e.g. BC).

More movement is helpful in the closing section, after 667 – especially at 675f., when the Herald approaches the Elders (who should now have come in a little and re-formed, to express their involvement in the disaster he has told them). He attempts to impose his hopefulness upon them, but their silence (aided in production by motionlessness) speaks louder than his words, and he circles, turning to no avail inside their formation. The audience realizes that Agamemnon will now return alone, without an army to protect him from the conspirators. After 662, the Herald's optimism sounds far more hollow (674f.), and the echo of the play's main recurrent theme, 'yet may the good prevail', as he attempts for the second and last time to make a closure, is full of irony. He is finally obliged to exit[29] with no response to his ringing, optimistic assertion of truth.

Choros 3

The Elders pass, for the first time without prelude or introduction, into a depressed, introverted meditation on the sheer scale of the disaster caused by Helen; they arrive as Agamemnon is about to enter at their fullest illumination yet of the general truth that all actions have their inexorable consequences. The last example is the furthest, in both space and time, from the action of the drama – for the final image is of the avenging Fury settling in Troy on the arrival of Helen; but the last statement is the most detailed and the most universal, as well as being the one most applicable to the present situation in the house of Atreus (which is now seen to be parallel in many respects to the royal house of Troy).[30] The Elders'

[29] Which side? If he is to obey Klytaimestra's instruction (604f.), and take a message back to Agamemnon, then he should return the way he came, and exit right; but it seems better to have him leave by the left *parodos*, as if that command has been forgotten in the last part of the scene, and he goes on into the city to rest after his journey.

[30] Cf. Kitto 1956, 12–19.

final words are ominous in the extreme for a 'sacker of cities' whose house has the *miasma* of ancestral crime.

This third and final choros of recall is also the most direct; it takes the pattern of almost irresistible flow from subject to subject, already established in Choros 2, to its furthest extent. The argument again exploits the parallelism of *strophe* and *anti-strophe*; the A stanzas pair Helen, as the destroyer, with Troy, and the way that city incurred the wrath of Zeus by accepting her into a bigamous marriage. Then the B stanzas figure Paris' nature through the parable of a lion cub, and set its loveable behaviour when first born in a hideous contrast with the terrible destruction it wreaked when full-grown.

Finally the C stanzas break up this pattern. The Elders return in the *strophe* to the event which started all this destruction, the settling of the Fury in Troy when Helen first arrived; but the *antistrophe*, instead of pursuing this theme, launches into a generalization. On the basis of all they have seen and heard in the drama so far, the Elders dispute the old, fatalistic belief that prosperity in itself gives birth to violence and misery. Aischylos then allows them to hint in the D strophic pair at the past of the house of Atreus, the previous impieties which threaten the destiny of the surviving king – a part of the legend which will not be heard in *Agamemnon* until Scene 6.

The choreography has only one task; to match the ever-continuing flow of the argument, from the meditative opening to the lapidary conclusion, with images of ever-intensifying power and force. Paradoxically, we found that angular movements of almost military precision, set in deliberate opposition to the flowing movement of the words, achieved a better effect than attempting to match the style to the content.

Scene 4

This famous scene makes simple but powerful use of the *orchêstra*. At the mid-point of the drama, Agamemnon arrives back in front of his home and places his chariot in the central position appropriate to the power that he, and the Elders, believe is his due: Klytaimestra then converts that position to powerless-ness, as she first demonstrates that the remainder of the *orchêstra* is her territory, and then fills with the tapestries what has now become the most significant part of it: that which lies between Agamemnon's chariot and his threshold.

Aischylos uses his first props single-mindedly to illustrate the only theme which concerns him at this moment: the subversion of Agamemnon's homecoming, as Klytaimestra proves that she is the stronger, conquering the conqueror of Troy. When the gods' eyes are on him (cf. 461–2), she persuades this 'man who has killed many' to incur their jealousy (924, 947f.), trampling over crimson (to be exact, brownish or blood-red)[31] fabrics. He voluntarily wastes fine property, part of the substance of his *oikos*, just as he did at Aulis, and not now at a god's command but simply under the influence of Klytaimestra's Persuasion, enacting the pattern set out by the Elders in 369f. There are other overtones;[32] but the psychological combat of genders and wills between Klytaimestra and Agamemnon is the primary focus of Scene 4, and the movements implied by the text illuminate it continually. The two large properties enable a detailed reconstruction of the action to be made.

Agamemnon comes slowly into the view of the stage-left spectators during the final stanza of Choros 3 – ominous words for him – at the moment when the Elders finish singing (782), his chariot enters the *orchêstra*.[33] It was accompanied by at least one attendant, to hold the horse(s) still; perhaps also by one or two foot-soldiers, but no more.[34] The main visual image which needs to be established at his entry is that Agamemnon's triumph as conqueror of Troy is less than total, reinforcing the Herald's narrative of the loss of the fleet.[35]

[31] Goheen (1955, 115f.); rightly emphasized in Vickers (1973, 366f.).

[32] Cf. the fine discussions by Easterling (1973, 7ff.), Vickers (1973, 363ff.), Winnington-Ingram (1983, 88ff.), and Taplin (1977a, 310ff.).

[33] *Pace* Taplin (1977a, 303–4), written as if sudden entry down a *parodos* was possible.

[34] The practice of making Agamemnon's entry more spectacular, with Kassandra appearing on one of several extra wagons laden with the spoils of war, dates back at least to Hellenistic times (Anon. *Hypothesis to Agamemnon* 8–9). It is still prevalent (cf. e.g. the BBC's 1979 production of the *Oresteia* under the title of *The Serpent Son* and Hall's National Theatre production), but is rightly opposed by Taplin (1977a, 304f.). Kassandra must be in the same chariot as Agamemnon, to visually establish the intimacy between them which motivates Klytaimestra's determination to kill her; Rehm (1992, 84) rightly notes that the image of a man and woman standing together in a chariot evokes Athenian wedding custom.

[35] An effective contrast will then be made in Scene 8, if Aigisthos enters accompanied by an impressive number of armed retainers.

Agamemnon's opening speech shows that he is blind to the wider implications of the sack of Troy and deaf to the Elders' guarded warning. He is firmly confident in the gods' support and his own ability to resume power at Argos. The chariot therefore comes to rest with Agamemnon in the most commanding position in the *orchêstra* – at the centrepoint;[36] his arrival forces the Elders back into the front left quadrant of the *orchêstra*.

Klytaimestra's power is then shown by the ease with which, on her entry after 851[37] ('late' as in Scene 2, and exactly at the right moment to control a man's attempt to enter her palace, as in Scene 3), she converts his position of dominance into one of subservience. When she comes down to above FC and begins to speak, she has a captive audience, with Agamemnon to her left and the Elders ahead of her and to her right. Agamemnon is trapped between her rhetorical performance in front and the tapestries behind him, which now cover the dominant movement line in the *orchêstra*, from C to EBC.

Her speech breaks down into five parts:

(1) 855–75. Klytaimestra turns her back on Agamemnon, and establishes her total control over the front portion of the *orchêstra* in vigorous, sweeping movements. She dominates the Elders by hyperbole and brazen hypocrisy, and approaches Agamemnon only as if he was the illustration for a lecture to them, a specimen under examination, at 866f.

(2) 876–86. Klytaimestra addresses Agamemnon for the first time. This section needs to be played quietly, close to Agamemnon – perhaps even as a quasi-aside, with Klytaimestra

---

[36] Any position L or R of centre is unsatisfactory because it would necessitate an asymmetrical layout of the tapestries, as well as taking Agamemnon himself away from the centre of attention; he must be placed somewhere on the centre-line between EBC and EFC. A location behind C unacceptably truncates the space to be covered by the tapestries; but one in front of C constricts the action, since Agamemnon, in the chariot and facing forward, can only interact naturally with people to his front and right.

[37] Not 855 as Taplin (1977a, 306) and almost all translations; she needs to be within Agamemnon's field of vision as he completes 854, to stop him leaving the chariot, presumably by a gesture; a commanding appearance at the *skene* doors is not enough – *pace* Reinhardt (1949, 94). Keeping her present from 258 to 974, pulling focus from the choros, is highly undramatic, and the idea should not have been revived – after Taplin (1977a) – by Conacher (1987, 97ff.).

deliberately turning away from the Elders – to establish a contrast with the rhetoric which follows.

(3) 887–94, played to the Elders and including Agamemnon only by a half-turn at 890; the springboard for

(4) 895–901, the climax of the speech, directly addressed to Agamemnon from L of FC.

At 919 Agamemnon implies that Klytaimestra has prostrated herself full-length before him in the homage which the Persian monarchs required of their subjects, and the Greeks found deeply offensive. The best place in her speech for this to happen is at the culmination of the rhetoric, which then reaches its climax in a contrived swoon into total self-abasement after 901.

(5) 902–13. Klytaimestra recovers from the outrageous climax of her homage, and calmly prays for the *daimôn* Jealousy to stand far away – after which she immediately proceeds to ensure that Jealousy will be present here and now, and hostile to Agamemnon, by making him walk across the tapestries. Crossing to close by the rear of the chariot, so she can be seen by the maidservant to the right of the *skene* doors, she finally gives her permission for Agamemnon to approach his own halls, but only over the finely woven robes.

The Elders are ignored after 904; the scene is now set for a total confrontation – the first interchange between two solo actors in *Agamemnon*. Given the king's position in the chariot at C, this can only be achieved by placing Klytaimestra between EFL and FL by 930. This shows that she has the confidence to begin the argument with her back to the Elders; Agamemnon's vulnerability is acutely symbolized by his position, trapped with the tapestries behind him and Klytaimestra directly facing him on his opposite side.

The text seems to suggest that Agamemnon should leave the chariot at 957, when he verbally accepts her command (904f.). But this creates two practical difficulties: firstly, 951f. play very awkwardly if Agamemnon is right beside Kassandra in the chariot; the introduction of Kassandra is a counter-attack against Klytaimestra, and Agamemnon needs some playing space to make it effective. Secondly, Agamemnon cannot step at the end of his speech out of a central chariot directly onto the tapestries, and then walk towards the *skene* doors. A crucial moment in the action would then be obscured from the view of a large portion of the audience, since the horse and chariot would debar everyone in the front half of the *theatron*, except the very highest spectators, from seeing the moment at which Agamemnon first places his foot on the tapestries.

Both difficulties are removed if Agamemnon has his own small moment of rebellion, and steps from the chariot to the ground at the end of 949. It should then be moved immediately towards the left *parodos*, to free the focal point of the *orchêstra* as a usable position for the actors.

Agamemnon must have entered the *skene* by 972. Just before that, Klytaimestra delivers fifteen lines of superbly focussed rhetoric. Most commentators imagine or assume that he begins to walk at 957, and completes the walk by entering the *skene* at 972: but her speech is far too long for this purpose, unless Agamemnon creeps over the ten metres of his direct path to the door at a comically inappropriate pace, or Klytaimestra rushes through some of her finest lines.

There are no lines in the middle of the speech which could be played as suddenly overpowering Agamemnon's hesitation and motivating him to walk over the tapestries. So one possibility is for Agamemnon to be seen as firmly committed – walking without hesitation as soon as he has expressed his intention to obey Klytaimestra (956) – and submissive enough to pause at the threshold and listen passively to her final, climactic celebration of his return (perhaps from 966) before making his exit into the house.

Another blocking makes more exciting and effective theatre. Agamemnon advances at 957 to the brink of the tapestries, but then hesitates at C, and does not move until after 972. Klytaimestra is then obliged to create the speech, with its outrageous comparison of their *oikos*'s wealth to that of the sea, as desperate rhetoric to persuade a still reluctant Agamemnon. To do this she must move on the first lines, crossing F of Agamemnon by the beginning of 962 to a position (BR/EBR) from which she can confront him directly.

Lines 973–4 are of course delivered after Agamemnon has gone into the *skene*. The whole first half of the drama has led up to this moment, at which Klytaimestra, having made Agamemnon enter the household on her own terms, attains her supreme triumph, aligning herself (correctly) with the will of Zeus as she is on the point of fulfilling her design. The moment demands a position commanding the whole theatre. For this reason, and to avoid obliging Klytaimestra herself to walk on the tapestries, the maidservants must remove them, and disappear inside, as soon as Agamemnon has completed his walk and passed into the house.

Klytaimestra advances to C while they do this. She is then able to deliver the last two lines from the position of maximum strength before she departs, asserting her own total domination by striding at will from C to EBC – over the same line, now free of tapestries, which Agamemnon has just walked under her control.

Choros 4

After what they have just seen and heard, the Elders are no longer capable of offering a lengthy choros of narrative and argument. The homecoming which they have desired throughout the first half of the drama has happened, but still they cannot suppress their fears. Here is the final development of the pattern which the Watchman began; the fulfilment of their expectations has plunged the Elders into an extreme apprehension (note 1019–21, the sinister thought, generated by the image of the blood-red tapestries, which dominates the close of this drama and the start of *Libation Bearers*; the possible solution offered in the B stanzas provides no release.)

After Scene 4, Agamemnon's death is almost inevitable. But the Elders do not express any premonition; they simply brood on their fears. If he were to die now, the implications for the future would be unclear. The events between Agamemnon's exit and his death-cry will generate the action of the next drama and so perpetuate the narrative of the trilogy.

Aischylos signals that Agamemnon's death will not happen immediately simply by leaving the Trojan prophetess on the chariot in the *orchêstra*, motionless, wordless, and still unidentified. In Aischylean drama nothing is introduced without a purpose, and the conventions of the Athenian theatre are broken only for good reasons.[38] Agamemnon's death therefore cannot take place until Kassandra has made a contribution.

The continuing presence of Kassandra and her chariot also

---

[38] The puzzlement created by Kassandra's silence, and the delay in identifying her, are well discussed by Taplin (1972, 77–8; cf. *idem* 1977a, 305–6).

constricts the choreography of Choros 4. For the first time the Elders are obliged to sing and dance in a physically restricted space; and the position of the chariot, together with the brevity of the ode, virtually confines them to stunted, introverted movements in the front half of the *orchêstra*, matching the mood of the text.

Scene 5

Kassandra knows exactly what Klytaimestra is inviting her to,[39] and her immediate reaction is a defiant silence, accompanied now by quivering spasms of terror, at the latest by 1062–3, in preparation for the sudden explosion of dance and song at 1077.

Visually, Aischylos opposes Kassandra's unrelenting refusal to respond, let alone leave the chariot, to the angular movements which illustrate Klytaimestra's consuming desire for revenge, and her frustration. This is Klytaimestra's first rebuff – an indication, even before the murders, that her power is not absolute and she too will be brought down. She can make a male, a great Greek king and the conqueror of Troy, cross from chariot to threshold and over the tapestries at her will; but after the men have gone she cannot make a foreign, female slave obey her command.

The first speech must be played as by a woman on edge, using all her strength to submerge her seething, devouring need beneath a veneer of gentle persuasion. Her impatience then becomes explicit, as Kassandra's refusal to respond exasperates Klytaimestra beyond endurance, and increasingly agitated movements illuminate her feelings. At 1055 Klytaimestra breaks away suddenly, moving back slightly to face Kassandra at 1059, but then wheeling around at the start of 1064, to turn in fury on the Elder who spoke 1062–3. Then perhaps (as one effective way of ending) a lunge down towards ERC as 1064 is completed, a vigorous cross towards the back during the next three lines, the exit line 1068 hurled back at the Elders from between BC and EBC – and Klytaimestra, temporarily defeated, is gone as swiftly as she came.

---

[39] With the chariot now in an angled position, between C and BL, Kassandra is staring directly past Klytaimestra at the *skene* doors.

Scene 6

Kassandra's terror and agony are those of a seer – the only character in the trilogy who possesses true insight into the past, the hidden present and the future. Aischylos interweaves the three elements closely. In the past lies the 'first-beginning crime', the adultery of Thyestes – and the consequent murder of his children by Atreus. Kassandra's vision of this introduces for the first time in the trilogy a past crime in the house, explaining Aigisthos' part in the conspiracy and adding another direction from which Agamemnon's life is threatened, since Kassandra sees in the hidden present the children's avenging Furies summoning Aigisthos. In the immediate future lie the deaths of Agamemnon and Kassandra; but as the scene unfolds Kassandra sees further and realizes that they, too, like the children of Thyestes, will be avenged; so the consequences of Klytaimestra's deed are brought before us before she has even done it.

Kassandra's prophecies cannot be believed (1202f.); and so we watch the Elders groping towards a truth which they do not want to hear. They cannot overcome the barrier imposed by Apollo's punishment, even when in desperation she prophesies the death of Agamemnon directly (1246). But by the end, as they watch Kassandra accept her fate, they have come as close as Apollo's curse permits to believing her. The doors remain open after Klytaimestra's exit; so from the start of this scene, Kassandra's outcries as she peers into the darkness inside the *skene* begin to establish the threshold as a metaphor for passing into Hades.

Part one (1072–1177). Kassandra leaps from the chariot (it must then be withdrawn, by the left *parodos*),[40] and her long silence erupts into lyrics. This unexpected large-scale scene unfolds almost as if the introduction of lyrics suspends time between Klytaimestra's furious exit and Kassandra's final departure to meet her fate.[41]

In this part of the scene (to 1177) Kassandra sings – initially with extreme emotion, as her visions show her that Apollo has brought her here to die;[42] this is reflected in the short-lined,

[40] This lyric scene requires the whole of the *orchêstra*; and when staging Aischylos any property should be removed as soon as its purpose is fulfilled.

[41] Cf. Taplin 1977a, 322.

[42] In Greek, Aischylos puns at the outset on the similarity of sound between 'Oh Apollo' and *apôlesas me* ('you have destroyed me').

repetitive lyrics. Gradually she calms down, and the stanzas become longer and more lucid. The Elders attempt to contain their anxiety by defensive, pedestrian (and twice downright comic) responses to her agony; but at 1121 her reminders of the bloody past of the house of Atreus and her vision of Klytaimestra's preparation for the murders provokes them from individual spoken responses into unison lyrics.[43] The dance must reflect the initial violence (the metre in Greek of Kassandra's lyrics is the extremely agitated dochmiac), the increasingly expansive thrust of Kassandra's visions, and the sudden passionate involvement, against their will, of the Elders. Kassandra's last stanzas are relatively meditative and gentle, but 1172 is well illuminated if, after the line, she collapses for a few moments as the Elders bring the dance pattern to an end.

Part two (1178–1330). Now Kassandra tries to explain in spoken words what she can see. Each of three speeches is followed by a four-line response from one of the Elders, and then by a *stichomythia* interchange with several of them. An onset of prophetic pain, imposed by Apollo to prevent her from communicating closely with them, twice suddenly regenerates the sequence; but during the third pattern Kassandra frees herself from the constraints of the god, and the final section, after her last outcry at 1307, is written in a loose combination of dialogue and speech, to express the freedom she has achieved.

Until 1264f., when she throws away her emblems as his prophetess, Kassandra is struggling to communicate with the Elders through the barrier of Apollo's curse; only after that does she fully regain her human dignity, as she gathers from her prophecy at 1279f. the courage to face her fate. She knows that neither she nor Agamemnon will die unavenged, and even her death has a place in the long sequence which will only end after Orestes' deed. The closing mood is triumphant, as we see the mortal young woman emerge from under the terrible possession of the god, which has made her at once superhuman in her clarity of vision and subhuman in the bestial subjection of her prophetic agonies. Then she recreates, conscious of her fate and therefore hesitant, the last walk towards the doors of the house of Atreus which Agamemnon made freely and blindly.[44]

[43] Rehm 1985, 240–1, cf. Taplin 1978, 190.
[44] Reinhardt (1949, 101–4, cf. Taplin (1977a, 321). Rehm (1985, 89) notes parallels in the language used of Kassandra in her last moments and of Iphigeneia at Aulis.

Aischylos establishes a strong contrast between the possessed movements of the first two speeches, in which Kassandra ranges over most of the *orchêstra* – coming far forward to escape from the horrors which she sees inside the *oikos*, and driving the Elders back to the perimeter with the intensity of her conviction – and the brief points of rest during the four-line interventions and dialogue. This leads forward to the contrast within the third speech between the initial activity, in Kassandra's final moments of possession, and Kassandra motionless in the visionary closing section 1279f.

Kassandra needs to begin her final walk after 1290 at C, to replicate Agamemnon's movements. The opening section of the third speech must therefore be enacted in the front half of the *orchêstra*. Lines 1279f. play well if addressed not directly to the Elders but forward, facing from FC into the centre of the audience – like the corresponding moment (*Eu* 681f.) at which Athena sees into the future.

For the last section the Elders must withdraw, to flank her journey on both sides. It has now become a theatrical metaphor for the gradual acceptance of death, as Kassandra moves slowly towards the *skene* door, twice recoiling and twice hesitating. The script implies these movements:

1286 At FC, turns back to address the Elders
1290 Moves slowly towards C
1291 Kneels at C facing the *skene*
      1295–1301, rises, advances to BC
1305 and 1307 Recoils, e.g., towards L
1313 Resumes the centre-line, and again walks up past BC
1315 Above BC, turns forward and addresses the Elders
1320 Resumes her movement towards the doors
1322 At EBC, turns forward to address her last words to the sun
1330 After the last word, exits swiftly. Doors close.

Kassandra reaches, in her last words, a mood which is almost unique in Aischylean tragedy. Poised just before the climactic moment in *Agamemnon* (the death of the king), both playwright and character stand back as she accepts her fate, inviting us at 1327f. to seek a bitter, momentary comfort in the transitory condition of humanity as a whole.[45]

[45] Cf. Stanford (1983, 152).

Choros 5

The Elders now have virtually no doubt that Agamemnon will die. They sum up the issues which have dominated the drama in twelve pivotal lines; a fast, trenchant summary, chanted in anapaests in the original, of the hazardous implications for all mankind *if* (the keyword; 1338) that happens. The Elders surge forward as they march and chant, perhaps tossing the lines from speaker to speaker (they divide easily 4,3,5), to create as much distance as possible from the door by the end of the stanza, to prepare for the immediate, abrupt opening of Scene 7.

Scene 7

The Elders alone. The death-cry is heard at once. The tragedy dissolves into farce as the Elders are first paralysed into immobility,[46] and then scurry comically around the *orchêstra*, talking about the importance of not talking in the aftermath of Agamemnon's death.[47]

Aischylos' company have just performed one of the greatest scenes in surviving Greek tragedy – and are about to plunge into another. He therefore separates the Kassandra scene clearly from the confrontation between Klytaimestra and the Elders, by inflicting two drastic changes of tone in as many minutes: from the high pathos of Kassandra's exit and Choros 5 into the increasingly absurd dithering of the Elders, and then into Klytaimestra's speech of exultant triumph.

The contrast at 1371 is acute between the Elders, who as the

---

[46] Lines 1343–7 are in trochaic tetrameters in the original Greek. This metre expresses greater agitation than regular iambic dialogue (cf. 1649f.). There is also something slightly comic, at least to my ear (and A. E. Housman's, cf. *Fragment of a Greek Tragedy*, 1989, 238) in Agamemnon's ability to utter two perfectly formed four–*metron* verses as he is being ruthlessly murdered. (Contrast the inarticulate cries normally uttered by victims in tragedy, e.g. Aigisthos at *LB* 869.)

[47] It was, by convention, a very rare effect for the choros to enter the *skene* during the course of the play (in surviving tragedy, only in Euripides *Helen* [330f.], and by a subsidiary choros in the fragments of *Phaethon* [245f.]) The dramatist could however generate suspense by threatening to do this and then escaping from the situation by other means – as here; cf. Euripides *Medeia* (1275), *Hippolytos* (782) and *Hekabe* (1042).

chief men of Argos should be in a position at least to determine what to do, and Klytaimestra, who has already acted and, as the rest of the scene makes plain, is totally aware of what she needs to do next. It is so great, and so striking, that the *ekkuklêma* must have been employed to provide the requisite sudden transition from empty space to tableau,[48] thrusting the dark events from the interior into the full public light of day.

The agon *with Klytaimestra.* This is the climax of *Agamemnon.* Here, and in the deliberately anti-climactic final scene, Aischylos discharges all the energies which he has built steadily since Scene 1. The macabre tableau of the bodies of Agamemnon and Kassandra remains in sight to the end, to remind both the Elders and the audience of the utter finality of Klytaimestra's act. Now the focus turns inexorably from the deed itself to its consequences, and Klytaimestra's position becomes completely undermined. Though she begins in absolute triumph over the bodies, she is soon obliged to retreat from her stance. The Elders are armed, after her death has proved her veracity, with all that Kassandra has said; they add that knowledge to the wisdom they have gained from their own earlier meditations on the pattern implied by the sack of Troy. They find the power to counter much of Klytaimestra's self-justification, and make her see that her deed is merely one link in what now threatens to become an unending chain of vengeance and counter-vengeance.

The conflict also brings deeper knowledge to the Elders. At first they denounce the deed as monstrous and insane; Klytaimestra must have been high on drugs to dare such an act (1407f.). But this is not an adequate viewpoint, any more than her initial conviction that she is wholly justified. In two powerful speeches Klytaimestra puts before them the depth of the affront to her womanhood when Agamemnon slaughtered Iphigeneia, the humiliation of her husband's many infidelities, and the crowning insult, Kassandra. Nor will she shirk conflict: with Aigisthos as her consort, she is prepared to meet any and all opposition.

This forces the Elders to reflect more deeply. Klytaimestra's command of language and of the situation is total, and she is clearly not insane. They must seek further if they are to find the

---

[48] This is the majority view; though strangely, in view of the points made on p. 324, Taplin is undecided (1977a, 325–7).

true causes and make an adequate response to the death of the
king. By the end of the scene, the Elders come to apprehend fully
the powers at work in the situation. Klytaimestra too has some
right on her side: the *daimôn* is indeed present, and the house is
falling, under the threat of retribution and incessant shedding of
kindred blood. Their summary at 1560ff. contains no hope;
violence has now become endemic in the house of Atreus, and
there is no prospect that it will leave.

Part one (1372–1447). Like Scene 6, this massive scene is
carefully structured to mark out the stages through which the
confrontation between Klytaimestra and the Elders passes.
Klytaimestra begins her speech of orgasmic triumph (NB 1391–2,
and cf. 1447), whose impact must be total, over the bodies on the
ekkuklêma (see 1379); but clearly she does not remain there. EBC
is not the strongest position in the Greek theatre, even when the
focus of attention is pulled there by a striking tableau; and
Klytaimestra's verbal challenge to the Elders contains some of the
most powerful imagery in the entire drama.

She therefore quits the tableau after a short time, like other
users of the *ekkuklêma* in later dramas, and advances to interact
with the Elders, who will have retreated to the front perimeters of
the *orchêstra* under the impact of the tableau. Klytaimestra then
comes forward down the centre-line soon after 1379 – perhaps to
BC on 1382. She must complete the advance to the most
dominant position, C, during 1391–2 so as to command the
orchêstra from there (or from even further forward on the centre-
line) for the final, totally defiant challenge to the Elders in 1393f.

The aggressive elaboration of her position in 1401f. goads them
out of their shock; after a relatively muted, spoken first response
they attack her vigorously at 1407, in the heightened intensity of
song.[49] Their initial reaction provokes a further series of com-
manding movements from Klytaimestra during her second speech
– back up to near the corpse, so she can exhibit it like a specimen
in 1404–5 before returning to the centre-line to accompany the
absolute finality of 1406. The movements for both characters are
intensely powerful and confrontational from 1399 right through

---

[49] They open in the dochmiac, the most violent of Greek lyric metres. For details
of the metrical forms used in the Greek see Fraenkel (1950, 660ff.) and Scott (1984,
73ff.).

to 1438f., where Klytaimestra concludes her final speech back by the bodies. Her absolute control of language in the four speeches of part one must be matched by a complementary control of space, to establish the commanding nature of her triumph, before it is undermined in the second part of the scene.

Part two (1448–1576). Klytaimestra's power is now so great that the Elders do not attempt to counter her, but ease at 1448 into a meditative, despairing mood. Agamemnon's more questionable actions are forgotten, expiated by his death, and he now begins to be rehabilitated, in preparation for the unequivocally favourable view which his surviving children and the Libation Bearers will take in the second drama.[50]

The B1 stanza is followed by an *ephymnion*, a lyric pendant in which the Elders brood on the destructive power of Helen; but this spurs Klytaimestra to the greater emotional intensity of anapaests;[51] the rest of the scene is a chanted/lyric interchange between solo actor and chorus.[52]

Slowly, as they begin the new dance after 1448, the Elders repossess the bulk of the *orchêstra*, isolating Klytaimestra and provoking her into argument. In 1462f. she challenges first what was sung in the first stanza and then the *ephymnion*; if the quiet opening has been sung by two soloists (as is appropriate to its mood), Klytaimestra is forced in turn to answer first one of the dancing Elders and then another – and then a third, after the singer of the B2 stanza rounds on her (preferably from a distance, e.g. from EFC, to make the most of 1471).

Through all this Klytaimestra remains fixed to one spot, near the tableau (cf. 1472–3); part two reverses the roles played by the characters in part one. Klytaimestra, although she comments – as if from a position of authority – on the truth or falsehood of the Elders' diagnoses, is now on the defensive, while they move increasingly freely.

---

[50] Cf. Vickers (1973, 382).

[51] Unlike Kassandra, Klytaimestra never expresses herself through the uninhibited emotionalism of full lyrics.

[52] The Elders counter the vividness and power of Klytaimestra's chanted, anapaestic rejoinders by thrice adding to their sung stanza another *ephymnion*: after each of the C stanzas a short, identically repeated refrain of mourning for the dead king, and then finally after D1 a lament that they should have lived to see her murder her own husband.

After 1489 the Elders begin an *ephymnion* of mourning for Agamemnon, and the text implies that they are to establish a close physical relationship with the body; they have therefore by now extended their possession of the *orchêstra* back into the extreme rear segment, passing around and beside Klytaimestra.

This motivates her vehement (and outrageous) counter-attack at 1497f., which animates the Elders' reflection in the next stanzas and so precipitates the closing movement. When they repeat the C *ephymnion*, she counters by reminding them once more of the sacrifice of Iphigeneia, so powerfully that by 1530f. (D1) the Elders feel totally helpless. The dance winds down into an exhausted half-truce; the Elders no longer attack her for her outrageous boldness, though in 1551f. her bitterness against Agamemnon reaches new heights of sarcasm, preparing us for the revelation in *Libation Bearers* that she mutilated his corpse before she buried it, spurring the Elders in 1560f. (D2) to a fierce, final summary. Klytaimestra's proud exultance, her firm self-justification, and even her bitterness against Agamemnon, have all disappeared. It is the measure of her weariness now that she agrees (1567f.) with what the Elders have said, and voices a modest wish to make a pact with the *daimôn*. Even this is utterly futile. Scene 7 has made it clear that the act of violence in which she has gloried will itself be avenged. But as yet there is no vision of how the cycle of ever-continuing violence may be averted. The drama has run down to an unresolved conclusion, which Aigisthos does nothing to change.

This closing section could be realized by having the Elders increasingly drawn apart from her, suggesting that their meditations on the scene become more inward as they consider the future, while Klytaimestra remains isolated by the bodies to emphasize how her vision remains backward-facing almost to the end of the scene.

It is however better to devise a bold image which will embody the psychological and dramatic situation just before Aigisthos' arrival. In our production Klytaimestra advanced towards the centre of the *orchêstra* during 1551f., to match the vehemence of her irony in that speech. She was then gradually surrounded by the Elders during 1560f.; at the end of the stanza they raised their staves to a horizontal position, with the ends all touching; Klytaimestra delivered her final stanza kneeling, as if imprisoned. An image like this embodies Aischylos' meaning more effectively than the alternative, and also explains how Aigisthos, with his guards, can enter down a *parodos*[53] and begin to speak without being noticed by either Klytaimestra or the Elders.

Scene 8

Aigisthos is expected, for his belated appearance both confirms the accuracy of Kassandra's prophecies and fulfils (albeit ironically) Klytaimestra's claim that he will be her protector. Scene 8 also answers the political question which the murder created, as Aigisthos dismisses the king's Elders, usurps Orestes' throne and establishes a tyranny in Argos.[54]

On a deeper level Aigisthos is superfluous. His glorious claim to Justice is undermined by cowardice. His tearful but banal account of the Thyestean banquet is fatally coloured, both for the Elders and for the spectators, since Kassandra has already told this appalling story, in appropriately intense language and without omitting the first crime, the adultery of Aigisthos' father, Thyestes. Aigisthos' brash self-righteousness contrasts so completely with Klytaimestra's justified passion in her defence that Scene 8 becomes a parody of Scene 7. Both begin with an avenger entering in triumph, to be challenged by the Elders; both end with a weary truce and the issues unresolved. Only this time the descent is deeper, and *Agamemnon* ends in a snarling, bitter conclusion without parallel in any other surviving tragedy.

Aigisthos' absurdity is patent in the linguistic inadequacy of his opening speech. The justice of his hereditary feud against the house of Atreus is fatally compromised by his bombast, self-righteousness, and frequent descents into cliché (beginning with 1577!). He also increasingly loses control over his syntax, unlike any other *agathos* in the *Oresteia*.[55] The speech invites extravagant movements and gestures, to reflect his over-developed self-image, and the low opinion which Elders and audience soon form.[56]

[53] I.e. in full view of an increasing number of spectators. Like Agamemnon's, this *cannot* be a 'surprise entry'; *pace* Taplin (1977a, 327).

[54] Aischylos dramatizes in Scene 8 a political *putsch* and suspension of constitutional rule: events which were all too familiar to fifth-century Greeks.

[55] Cf. only the Herald and the Nurse.

[56] Rosenmeyer (1982, 73) wrongly supposing Taplin to be in agreement with him, has Klytaimestra exit at the end of Scene 7, and re-enter before 1654.

The Elders must fall back to the far right side of the *orchêstra* before the military strength of the bodyguards, as they follow Aigisthos in and deploy themselves in the left section;[57] this permits him to use virtually all of the playing area to match the expansive thrust of his rhetoric. In the course of his narrative Aigisthos needs to face in several directions – addressing the opening apostrophe to the heavens at large, but then inspecting the body of Agamemnon (1580–3), and telling the story of the Thyestean banquet (1584f.). This narrative plays much better if parts of it are delivered rhetorically out from the front of the *orchêstra* towards the audience, rather than to the Elders (whose disdain remains total throughout the speech); he then turns finally in self-justification directly to the Elders at 1603.

The Elders counter-attack at 1612f., moving as far against him as they dare (given the presence of Aigisthos' bodyguards) during the cut-and-thrust of the following exchanges. They gradually advance from R until Aigisthos, Klytaimestra and the guards only possess the left half of the playing space. This move forces Aigisthos from the centre, and cuts him off from the house of Atreus, which he has come here to occupy. Aigisthos' increasing paranoia, as the argument develops, is then explained in visual terms, as well as his sudden threat at 1649.[58] Here Aischylos increased the intensity of the scene, in Greek, by changing the metre from iambic trimeters to trochaic tetrameters; modern productions must find some visual or musical means to mark the heightened level for the rest of the drama.

However, 1576 does not provide a cue for an exit; 1654f. are far more natural if Klytaimestra has been visibly present, watching the development of the quarrel before her anxious intervention; and the omniscience which she showed in appearing 'on cue' from inside to prevent the entry of both the Herald and Agamemnon into the house is part of the 'masculine' powers which she has lost as a result of the events of Scenes 5 and 7. Finally, an effective point can be made if she is present from the outset of the scene as an alternative focus, but is ignored by Aigisthos as he attempts to take all the credit for the death of Agamemnon away from her. (To reflect this we had her cross angrily around 1584 from C to the position [EBL] where she remains until just before her intervention at 1654.)

[57] The entry in Peter Hall's production of a full hoplite phalanx – with helmets, shields, spears and full body armour – made exactly the right effect.

[58] Lines 1617–8 have sometimes been pressed into service as evidence for a raised stage. However, the dramatic point is precisely that Aigisthos does not have the commanding physical position which his nautical metaphor implies.

There is a case for making Klytaimestra cross a substantial space (e.g. from EBL to between FC and FL) before she can intervene in the ensuing conflict, so she begins to move around 1650-1, and arrives by Aigisthos only just before she tries to soothe him.[59] Clearly she must then also be between the contending parties, so she can turn easily first from him to the Elders at 1657, then for the deeper reflection of 1659-60 away from both groups, before turning back to face them all as she delivers 1661 –a line which reflects her full, rueful, awareness that now, after Scene 7, she has been far reduced from her earlier ability to combine the strengths of both genders, and is ('just') a woman.[60]

Nothing is resolved at the end of *Agamemnon*. The choral exit is unparalleled in any other surviving drama; in opposition to the principal characters and without any comforting words sung in conclusion. The Elders' last words are a series of angry taunts, verbal protests against the physical brutality of the new régime, which are effectively underscored if they depart in successive small groups during each individual Elder's speech after 1665, so that Aigisthos has to shout his defiant counter-threats at their departing backs.

To gain access to the interior of the palace, Klytaimestra and Aigisthos have to step past the bloody tableau on the *ekkuklêma*.[61] This indignity undermines both the victorious defiance which Klytaimestra attempts to impose by her closing couplet, and the triumphal procession in which she leads Aigisthos, for the first time, to cross the threshold of the house which she has now made his.

When the actors are all gone, the tableau stands for a moment before it is withdrawn, as a silent, implacable statement of the shed blood which cannot be recalled, which demands and will inevitably receive revenge.[62]

---

[59] Audiences will not miss the irony of 1656 if it is spoken, as in our production, by a Klytaimestra whose clothes are covered in blood.

[60] Cf. Vickers (1973, 387). She will remain in this diminished role on her two appearances in *LB*: meanwhile the Elders have stigmatized Aigisthos' cowardice by reducing him also to female status (1625; cf. Orestes at *L B* 304-5).

[61] So too will the guards, unless they remained outside until after the drama is over and the *ekkuklêma* withdrawn.

[62] Cf. Reinhardt 1949, 110.

Libation Bearers

Introduction

The murder of Agamemnon has locked the action into the house of Atreus. The death of the king and the godless rule of the usurpers are wounds so serious that the outside world recedes, not to return to our sight until *Eumenides*. This short, intensely powerful drama is the dark night, the winter at the centre of the trilogy, in and through which the quest for a new light must be pursued.[1]

This atmosphere is established almost at once, in Choros 1. The Libation Bearers return insistently to the motif which dominated the last scenes of *Agamemnon*: 'How can the house be purified, once blood's been shed?' (48). The shed blood of Agamemnon has confined the action to this house because only there can a cure be found for its self-inflicted wound (cf. 471f.).

Only children can save a man's glory, after he is dead. His descendants are duty-bound to pay honour to his grave. A male heir must avenge his murdered father, or his father's Furies will turn their anger onto him; and legitimate power descends, with spiritually cogent force, from father to son. *Libation Bearers* reflects completely these basic features of Greek belief. Only Agamemnon's heirs can lift the veils of *miasma* under which this house now lies; only when Agamemnon's son removes the tyrant Aigisthos and takes his rightful place on his father's throne will its greatness be restored.

This is a drama of sharp contrasts, developed from the acrimonious division between the Elders and Aigisthos in Scene 8 of *Agamemnon*. Here people and their actions are judged by only one criterion: do they remain true to the natural order, or do they

---

[1] Peradotto (1964) rightly notes the centrality of the progression from light, both literal and metaphorical, in the imagery surrounding Agamemnon's return through images of darkness in *Libation Bearers* through to the new, secure light of the torchlit procession at the end of *Eumenides*.

not? Are they the real *philoi* of Agamemnon, or have they become the instruments of Aigisthos and Klytaimestra, and so his enemies? Even physical objects, such as the locks of hair which Elektra finds on Agamemnon's grave, are subjected to this test.

Orestes declares at the outset his resolve to avenge Agamemnon (18–19, cf. 297–8); this is no drama of Hamlet-like indecision. Gradually there gather round him the powers, human and divine, that will aid him; like Klytaimestra in *Agamemnon* he slowly obtains the strength that will make his success inevitable. The difficulties of his task are firmly stressed: the Libation Bearers are only slave women, his sister is treated like one, and he has only one male companion. They are all exiles or outcasts, attempting to overthrow a régime which has abolished political processes and governs by force.

But we sense at once that Orestes' approach is very different from his mother's. Here is a man whose determination is calm and measured, and whose stance towards the gods is far from reckless. And this is why the relative weakness of Orestes' human allies is steadily counter-balanced, as the first half unfolds, by the ever-increasing aid which he is able to summon, as he comes to deserve it more, from the gods, both above and below. In Aischylos' world 'the gods help those who help themselves'.

The choros members now play characters on the side of the protagonist; the Libation Bearers take a central role in developing the audience's expectations. As Orestes nears his deed, they increasingly sing of the light that he will bring (809f., 863f., cf. 131); and after he has killed the usurpers they break out into unrestrained rejoicing.

To avenge Agamemnon is inevitably, after Aischylos' treatment of the story in *Agamemnon*, to take the life of Klytaimestra. The threat that Orestes' vengeance for Agamemnon – and his restoration to the throne of Argos – will involve matricide is present even in Kassandra's first vision of his return (*Ag* 1279f.); but Aischylos deliberately underplays it in the early stages of *Libation Bearers*, then makes it resurface powerfully just before the half-way point and overshadow the remainder. We are not allowed to know the nature of Klytaimestra's terrifying dream until it is right for Orestes to read it (523f.).

The climax is not simply a justified retribution. Mother confronts son before our eyes,[2] and Orestes finds himself in a

---

[2] The scene is unparalleled in subsequent Western drama; the confrontation

position as monstrous as that of Agamemnon at Aulis. Klytaimestra's femininity and her motherhood are placed fully before him; against them lie his duty to avenge his father, and the command of the gods. Once again, a real choice that is also no real choice, for the Furies will attack him – a father's or a mother's – whatever Orestes may do (924–5). By that point in the drama we expect that he will take his vengeance; when Orestes decides that Pylades' advice is right, he satisfies the deepest expectations of the audience. But once again, just as in *Agamemnon*, his deed is overshadowed – and far more terribly, because Klytaimestra's Furies rise almost immediately from her shed blood.

Dramatic structure

To point up the similarities and differences between Orestes and Klytaimestra, Aischylos dramatizes the story of Orestes' return through a structure parallel to that of *Agamemnon*. As in the first drama, the action reaches its climax in the murders, which take place approximately two-thirds of the way through; and once again the last scenes present the avenger appearing triumphantly on the *ekkuklêma* over the bodies of two victims, a man and woman who have been lovers, only to be reduced, by the end, from triumph to apprehension as the murderer is overwhelmed by the prospect of vengeance.

Also as in *Agamemnon*, there is a structural division at the mid-point. But in *Libation Bearers* this is far more marked. The drama is divided into two fundamentally opposed halves, around the scene-change which lies at the centre of the drama and the trilogy. First a slow section, framed around the grave of Agamemnon at the centre of the *orchêstra*,[3] with a steady and

---

between mother and son takes place inside the palace in Sophokles' and Euripides' *Elektra* dramas, and in all later plays based on this myth. In [Tourneur], *The Revengers' Tragedy* (4.4) the audience is aware in advance that Vindice and Hippolyto are only threatening Gratiana, and do not actually intend to kill her.

[3] Reinhardt (1949, 110–1). No other position is natural, or indeed practical; *pace* Arnott (1962, 59–61), Walton (1984, 115), and Garvie (1986, xliii).

The grave should not be represented by an elaborate funeral *stele*, as in some vase paintings of the myth; Aischylos makes plain that his Agamemnon was buried without honour. A low mound of earth and/or stones, set at the centre of the *orchêstra* and with its long side parallel to the *skene* façade, is most suited to the drama's production requirements.

unified development, during which Orestes and Elektra are reunited, and gain the support from Agamemnon and the gods which they need for their attempt at vengeance; then a rapid, suspense-filled second part set before the palace, in which Orestes deceives to gain access, and eventually succeeds in overcoming the usurpers.

The difference between them is marked in several different ways. In the first half, the *orchêstra* alone is used, the grave pulls the focus forward, and the *skene* is ignored. There are only two scenes and one full choral ode. Scene 2 is the longest scene in the surviving tragedies of Aischylos, and is given monumental shape by the massive *kommos*, the invocation to the spirit of Agamemnon), which is the most substantial lyric actor–choros interplay in the *Oresteia*. There are also only two speaking solo parts, two entrances, and no exits until the end.

In the second half, this steady build-up is replaced by constant surprises. The *skene* represents the house of Atreus, and its door is in frequent use; the focus is pulled towards the back of the *orchêstra*. This allows for many sudden entrances and exits,[4] and there are five short scenes, divided off from each other by equally short choral odes. Their brevity maintains the pace, as the unity created in part one by interweaving sung and spoken parts is replaced by a marked alternation between the two modes. There are no actor lyrics, and while Elektra is reduced to a silent part, five new speaking characters join Orestes.

The reunion of Orestes and Elektra at Agamemnon's grave, the invocation to gain his support and the plotting to subdue the tyrants are all conducted in an atmosphere of ever-increasing confidence; this is symbolized in the theatre by the Libation Bearers' confident possession of the playing area, especially when they envelop the heirs and the grave in the *kommos*.

In the second part, the Libation Bearers no longer participate in the action on equal terms; their involvement in the conspiracy is used to generate an air of suspense, and they are now at the mercy of events. There are violent contrasts, as the Libation Bearers begin each ode from a position of retreat, dispersed to the perimeter of the *orchêstra* in a feigned conformity to their proper social role. Four times they suddenly resume control of the

---

[4] Rehm (1992, 98) notes the disruption of the control of the threshold which Klytaimestra had imposed in *Agamemnon*.

playing space for a brief and intense choral lyric. This oscillation culminates in the sequence after Choros 7, a triumphant and hopefully a final repossession of the entire *orchêstra*, followed immediately by the horror of the tableau on the *ekkuklêma*, which drives the Libation Bearers back to the perimeter. Orestes himself then loses his command of the *orchêstra* to the Furies, and after he has been possessed and driven from the scene the closing chant is brief, hesitant and anxious.

Scene 1

Kassandra prophesied that Orestes would return from exile to avenge his father's death (*Ag* 1279f.). *Libation Bearers* opens at the moment when her prophecy is fulfilled. The sole descendants of Agamemnon are about to be united at the one place where they can enlist the support of their dead father's spirit, and of the gods who protect his interests.[5]

Scene 1 shows Orestes return and establish a relationship with his father's grave. Agamemnon was buried in the absence of his son and heir (8–9); we learn later that Klytaimestra mutilated his corpse, to hobble the dead man's spirit in the hope that his anger against her would be less potent (440f.); the burial was performed by Klytaimestra alone, as she threatened at the end of *Agamemnon* (1551f.); and the dead king was denied lament either by the citizens of Argos (429f.) or by his only daughter (444f.). In this scene Orestes begins to compensate Agamemnon for all those acts; he also begins to gather round himself the powers that will make possible his own restoration to his rightful place.

Orestes must first establish his possession of the *orchêstra*, which represents the soil of Argos, and then focus more on building a close relationship with the grave itself, at which he must claim his inheritance.[6] He should therefore stand motionless at EBR/BR, facing towards the grave, for a few moments after his entry. This action offsets the initial image of desolation presented by the isolated mound; his return gives some prospect of a solution to the problems of the house.

[5] Cf. Adkins 1970, 66ff.
[6] Cf. Vickers 1973, 389.

To complete the interaction, Orestes must move to ERC before he delivers the opening lines, perhaps then advancing to and around the front side of the grave during them, and arriving at C by the end of 3. This strategy allows him to circle the grave and kneel facing forward in the most dominant position possible (immediately BC of the mound) when he offers the locks at 6f.

Traditional commentaries neglect the role of Pylades, because he says nothing until his crucial lines in Scene 6. But Pylades is present in every scene, except the brief Scenes 4 and 5, and his role goes far beyond the three spoken lines. Pylades is Orestes' silent guardian or protector. At the climax he can credibly speak almost with the voice of Apollo because he has earlier witnessed, and given his silent support to, everything done by Agamemnon's heirs. His positioning in Scene 1 must establish this role from the outset. One way to do this is to have him follow into the playing area only after Orestes has moved up to ERC for the opening line. Pylades then moves almost immediately to between ERC and FR, observing and overseeing Orestes' interaction with the grave.

The approaching women become visible to Orestes and the spectators in the right-hand side of the *theatron* just before line 10. Orestes springs back to join Pylades, and both men then look across the grave towards the left *parodos*. Orestes needs to move back towards R, as he looks more closely at the women during 12–13; Pylades meanwhile crosses up ERC and then, after Orestes' final invocation to Zeus, joins him BR during 20–21 in preparation for their exit after 21 to conceal themselves.[7] The most obvious and effective place for this is the mouth of the right *parodos*; they shelter just outside the playing area, under the lee of the rising slope of the *theatron*.[8]

The manuscript in which *Libation Bearers* was transmitted

[7] This device intensifies the power of the recognition-scene between brother and sister; by the time they recognize each other, two important developments have taken place. (It was imitated by Euripides, *Elektra* 107f., and echoed by Sophokles, *O.K.* 113f.).

[8] Taplin's argument for the doorway of the *skene* (1977a, 335–6) should be rejected: the *skene* doors and the space in front of them are part of the acting area, and actors standing there would pull focus from Elektra and the Libation Bearers during Choros 1 and the start of Scene 2. Garvie's suggestion (1986, xlv) that Orestes and Pylades conceal themselves behind the grave is totally impractical, in view of the use which Elektra and the Libation Bearers make of it in the opening section of Scene 2.

through the Dark Ages begins at what is now line 10 of our texts; by great good fortune, eight and a half lines from the missing opening have been preserved in quotation by other ancient authors. Lines 1–5 are cited in Aristophanes' *Frogs* (1126–8, 1172–3; although the quotations are separated by dialogue, there is no good reason to doubt that the lines are consecutive). Lines 6–7 and 8–9 are presented consecutively in this script only for the actor's convenience; they are preserved to us in separate, later sources, and the fact that 8–9 follow on neatly from 6–7 is no guarantee that they did originally follow without a break, or indeed that the two couplets are presented in the right order.

Though the surviving lines play well, there is one important element missing from the scene as we have it. In Scene 2, Elektra is rewarded with the sight of the locks of hair that speak of Orestes' return only when she has affirmed her loyalty to Agamemnon and prayed for an avenger to return. Similarly, Orestes should use the lament in 8–9 as the springboard for a firm declaration of his readiness and resolve to avenge his father; he would then be rewarded at once with the arrival of Elektra and her companions. If lines to this effect originally preceded 10, 18–19 would become a closing, recapitulative invocation to Zeus, which could have been delivered almost as an aside.

Choros 1

Klytaimestra has buried Agamemnon far from the palace (22) to blunt and avert the anger of the king she has murdered. But during the very night that Orestes returned to Argos, the gods have sent Klytaimestra an ominous dream which shows that they are opposed to her. Agamemnon's anger from the grave has power – indeed, it has brought Orestes back, and the crucial moment is at hand. This terrifying dream, together with Orestes' return, generates the plot of the first half of the drama. The success of the vengeance is due to Klytaimestra's fear (42f.), and her lack of *philoi* apart from Aigisthos (revealed by the lie at 717). She must send the libations she needs, to appease Agamemnon's spirit, by the hands of slaves who are her enemies and a daughter who is easily convinced, at the start of Scene 2, to follow her true loyalties. Coming together at his grave on the outskirts of Argos, Orestes and Elektra are joined by both gods and slave women (the highest and the lowest strands of the Greek social order);

together, these provide the heirs with the strength needed to overthrow the tyranny.

Elektra and the Libation Bearers enter by the left *parodos*.[9] They begin to move before line 10; Orestes and Pylades withdraw into the opposite entrance after 21, and the Libation Bearers begin to sing at 22 as they step into the *orchêstra*. Elektra enters before the choros members, carrying garlands for the grave of Agamemnon, and takes up a neutral position (e.g. BL) for the duration of Choros 1.

The choreography must reflect the structure of the lyric: a strophic pair as introduction, violently contrasting the women's torment with Orestes' calm;[10] then two pairs of stanzas which present the central theme of the drama, and a brief concluding epode. It must also show the tentative but firm relationship which the Libation Bearers establish with the *orchêstra* and the grave. A way of securing both these aims is for the choros members to take up a position between EBC and BC during the A1 stanza, splitting up and moving around the grave as individuals to reach a matching position between FC and EFC by the end of A2.[11] Agitated, divided formations are needed during the B and C strophic pairs, to convey the extent of the *miasma* and the Libation Bearers' certainty that there will be continued vengeance.

Since the epode is non-strophic, it allows the Libation Bearers to move towards a final tableau in counterpoint to Elektra, in a form not symmetrical with any previous choreography. Since she is BL, this is achieved if they adopt a posture of grief on the FR side of the grave, and freeze in that position on the last line. The transition to Scene 2 is then easy, if they open out into a semicircle facing the grave, BR–EBC–BL, ready to respond to Elektra.

[9] Scott (1984, 82 and 201) does nothing to refute Taplin (1977a, 336). Choros entry through the *skene* door, like all special effects in Greek tragedy, would not be made unless there is some point (as at *Eu* Choros 1). If the Libation Bearers entered through the *skene* then the *skene* would represent the house of Atreus and the grave of Agamemnon would be in sight of the house; neither is the case.

[10] Cf. Bowen 1986, 35.

[11] The pots and mixing bowl for the libations must be placed by the grave early in the dance movements of these stanzas.

Scene 2

Part one: Elektra's offering (85–164).

> '[The Libation Bearers] encourage her [Elektra] to turn the
> weapons against the inventor by offering the libations as if from
> herself, with a prayer conceived in a directly opposite sense to that
> which Klytaimestra intended [. . .] The attempt was monstrous,
> and it has failed; the libations have been restored to their proper
> office; and Agamemnon's wrath, instead of being propitiated, has
> been aggravated by his child's prayer [. . .] That which Klytai-
> mestra, in insult or fear, has denied to Agamemnon for years is
> conceded at last, and being entrusted to the hands of others is
> turned to the very purpose she would most have deprecated.'[12]

Elektra's offering is the next stage in the queen's down-
fall. It matches Orestes' lock of hair; the spirit and manner of the
address which Elektra makes are parallel to his;[13] and she speaks
124f. in the same place, behind the grave at C, to stress her affinity
with Orestes.

The staging of this section is straightforward. Elektra must first
establish her relationship with the grave: given the importance of
her first speech, she should move to it as early as possible (perhaps
to the L end of the grave during the opening lines, then around to
C directly behind it on the strong lines 89–90). Next (100f.), she
must engage more closely with the Libation Bearers, preparing for
the *stichomythia*; Elektra moves to and beyond BC, turning
towards the various members of the choros as she delivers the
appeal.

The *stichomythia* is best played between Elektra and one
member of the choros, since the text implies an increasingly close
involvement between them.[14] Elektra is between BC and C, so if
the speaker is near the L end of the semicircle, her movements
towards Elektra (106, 117, 119) are also movements towards the
grave, establishing in spatial terms its importance to the Libation
Bearers.

Elektra's speech 124f. is beautifully modulated, providing a
fine opportunity for an actor to control his or her audience

---

[12] Conington 1857, xv–xvi.
[13] Cf. Garvie 1986, 67–8.
[14] Adverse *stichomythia*, as at the opening of *Ag* Scene 2, or between the Furies
and Orestes in *Eu* Scene 5, profits more from division.

through the power of pathos and rhetoric alone. The key to its delivery is to take a diminuendo from 130 and treat the central section from 135 as a close and intimate address to the corpse. This then allows a steady build from 142 to the climax at 148.

Choros 2 is a short lyric in one single, non-responding stanza. After the first four lines it was composed in dochmiacs, the most violent Greek lyric metre; it requires an agitated outpouring of grief, to discharge the rhetorical emotion built up in Elektra's speech into the other world of lyric. The choreography must both evoke the act of ritual lamentation and express the intensity of the Libation Bearers' desire for the avenger; but it must not obscure the audience's view of Elektra as she pours the libations, and then sees the lock of hair; most of the dancing is therefore in the rear half of the *orchêstra*.

Part two: the reunion (165–305). Euripides' brilliant critique (*Elektra* 508–46) comes from the very different and more cynical Athens of 413 BC. The main role of the lock and footprints in *Libation Bearers* is to establish the oneness of Orestes and Elektra (221) before they meet. The primary element is the divine guidance which leads Elektra to the lock,[15] later to the footprints and the premonition that they are Orestes', and to mental anguish based on the fear that they may, despite this, not be his; then to the reunion at his grave of Agamemnon's heirs.

If Elektra has poured the offerings at the L end of the grave, the lock of hair will naturally be discovered by her attention moving R, and she should go close to it during the last lines of Choros 2. The Libation Bearers then come forward during 169–70, to cluster round Elektra just behind the grave. She picks up the lock of hair during 170 (she will use this prop throughout 183–204),[16] and should immediately break forward, for example, to between R and ERC, to get enough distance from the Libation Bearers to play the rest of the *stichomythia* and the monologue effectively.

Lines 183f. play best if Elektra moves in a semicircle round

[15] Orestes left two locks, but Elektra always uses the singular. Does she ignore one, or bunch the two up into one?

[16] Elektra still holds the lock at 230. We solved the problem of disposal by having her drop it to the ground as she advances towards Orestes after 234 – a marvellous moment; she no longer needs his token after she has finally recognized the man himself.

from FR via FC to between ELC and L. The main implied moves are: a short move on 183; a substantial movement (to FC) during 187; a pause from 193–196, and a stop at the end of 200.

The discovery of Orestes' footprints takes Elektra from L to C in 205f., tracing them in front of the grave while the Libation Bearers, still grouped (e.g., in a semicircle) behind it, follow her moves.[17] Line 211 can then be delivered FC facing F; this allows Orestes to surprise her as he enters rapidly, advancing to just R of the front of the grave. When they see him, Elektra starts back a little towards FL, and the Libation Bearers retreat much further, back to EBR/C/L.

The recognition *stichomythia* can now become a slow re-possession by Elektra of the area in front of the grave, which she has just abandoned to Orestes. Line 220 implies a move away from him; but from 224 onwards she gradually comes nearer and nearer to him, so that they are almost touching at 234, when he has shown her the piece of weaving.[18] After the recognition, they are close together, just F of the grave, for Orestes' prayers at 247f.

Pylades should be kept out of focus up to this point (ERC?). At 269, however, he can come into his own, countering the Libation Bearer's fear in 264f. by coming forward to give Orestes strength and provide him with a springboard for his speech of confidence in Apollo.[19]

Lines 269f. are another major speech, setting out at length the powerful forces which demand that Orestes accomplish the revenge of his father. In retrospect, these words also preview what his mother's Furies will threaten to do to him, even before we have been squarely confronted with the reality of his coming act of matricide. Its rhetorical variations cry out to be complemented by movement.[20]

---

[17] No transposition or deletion of lines is desirable here; Taplin (1977a, 337) and Bowen (1986, 177f.) add nothing to the weak arguments in Fraenkel (1950, 815f.) Lloyd-Jones presents a sound defence of the transmitted text (1961, 171–84).

[18] It must be something which can be produced speedily (in our production, an elaborate belt which has hitherto been concealed under his cloak).

[19] In our production this was symbolized by Pylades passing to Orestes the spear he has been holding. Orestes then advanced to EFC, holding the spear vertical for 269f.; and returned it decisively to Pylades on 305f.

[20] e.g., advance to EFC on 269; 275 kneel; 283f. rise, circle round EFR/ERC/EBR (in front of the Libation Bearers, who remain in a semicircle EBR round to ELC, but rise and retreat individually to the perimeter as Orestes involves them by

Part three: the invocation (306–509). For the Greeks, the spirits of the dead inhabited a shadowy, ill-defined underworld. They are within the power of the gods below, perhaps in 'Hades'. But they are also in their graves. The dead are present when a dirge is sung for them, and are aware of what is done beside their tombs. This murdered man would have had the power to haunt his murderess, had she dared to come near; and he has the power to help his children, now they are assembled at this grave. He can both profit from the *time* paid by those who owe it to him, and suffer, losing respect among the other dead if he does not receive his dues. But the senses are dulled by death, and strenuous effort is needed to ensure that a prayer or offering truly reaches the dead.

Out of these basic conditions of belief Aischylos created the lyric invocation, or *kommos*, in which Agamemnon's reunited heirs attempt to gain his attention and seek his aid and that of the gods. It is – or should be – one of the most powerful scenes in Greek tragedy. It should not be cut, as it all too frequently is in modern production.

The heirs and the Libation Bearers pass through an intense psychological drama. Orestes begins with little hope, despairing of ever communicating with Agamemnon. The opening mood is slow and solemn, as both he and his sister dwell on the miseries of the past; their first prayers are hopeless, impossible wishes that Agamemnon had met a better fate, or had not been killed at all. But the *kommos* must become faster and more impassioned for Elektra's outcry at 363f.; and then suddenly, under the prompting of the Libation Bearers' optimism, hopes for the future start to overcome despair (372f.). After a slight rallentando at 405f. there is a moment of equipoise at 410–17; and then there are no more doubts. The tempo picks up gradually to 428. Elektra's anguish is there in 418f.; but so is her savage determination; and so, as the second section begins (423f.), the Libation Bearers increase their emotional intensity, from chant to full song.

The murder of Agamemnon can now be recalled in all its horror (rall. again 429f., but with ever-increasing intensity to the climax at 456f.). Orestes states his resolve directly to his father (434f.),

the pressure of his rhetoric); 288–90 pause at EBR, addressing the Libation Bearers; arrive L before 297, and deliver the rest of the speech directly to, first, the Libation Bearer who intervened at 264 (she remains between C and FL), then Elektra (who has retreated to C in front of the grave) and finally to Pylades (BC?).

and brother and sister confront all that their mother did –
including even (440f.) the mutilation of Agamemnon's corpse in
an attempt to deprive his shade of the power to take vengeance.

She was too late. The *kommos* itself transcends her attempt,
and as it reaches its fierce, elliptical climax (456f.) we hear no
more of hopes and fears. The past has been consumed in the
intensity of the scene, and Agamemnon's heirs now confront the
present and immediate future firmly, and with disciplined and
solemn emotion. After the *kommos*, Orestes has lost his
dependence on others, and he takes total command of the
vengeance.

For the Greeks, a fated thing will inevitably occur – but the
precise time at which it will come to fulfilment is not fixed. The
right appeal, at the right time, may make it come. So too with this
act of vengeance; the *kommos* has made the right time, now – and
for a few moments the power of their achievement fills the
Libation Bearers with awe (463–5).

This lyric invocation, cast in the form of a highly complex
pattern of responding stanzas,[21] requires a use of space which will
reflect both its ritual solemnity and its ever-increasing dramatic
intensity. Here the relationship and interaction between the
Libation Bearers, – Orestes and Elektra, – and the grave is vital. A
regrouping is needed to mark the beginning of the *kommos*, either
before or during the opening stanza. Orestes and Elektra must
take up their basic positions for the scene, which are clearly at the
head (LC) and foot (RC) of the grave respectively. Pylades, since
he takes no active part in this section, should move to a position
where his role as overseer may be communicated to the whole
audience (e.g. EBL).

The placing for the Libation Bearers is more conjectural. The
concept finally adopted in our production was for them to begin
the invocation equally spaced around the perimeter of the
orchêstra, facing inward, and to make their way successively, in
the choreography of the choral stanzas, towards the centre,
ending the scene in a close ellipse around the grave (incorporating
Elektra and Orestes in this pattern), and kneeling facing the grave
for part or all of the final section (463f.). This has three main
advantages: (1) two magical, ritually complete formations are

[21] On the structure see Garvie (1986, 124–5); and for the metres used in the
original Greek, cf. Scott (1984, 85–9).

placed at the start and end of the *kommos* – the opening one spread out and tentative in its approach to the grave, and the last one in a close relationship with it, with an incomplete, transitional pattern in between to symbolize the struggle and anguish during the intervening lyrics; (2) the Libation Bearers can easily address both the grave and one or other of the heirs; (3) it leaves plenty of room for the heirs to make their own movements and gestures.[22]

Emotionally, 479–509 form a cooling-off period, a calmer representation in spoken verse of that which was earlier conveyed to Agamemnon in the passionate intensity of song. Scott[23] imagines the choros as withdrawing from the grave, leaving the heirs close beside it. This fits in with his view that this section is the climax of the invocation scene (though the pause while the twelve choros members withdraw is messy). Some repositioning after the lyric *kommos* is clearly called for, but the better alternative is to reposition the heirs, leaving the Libation Bearers in their position close around the grave. The *stichomythia*, and the speeches at 497f., both gain power if Orestes and Elektra are now together facing the grave in unity, rather than separated. Accordingly we moved them during the choral epilogue to stand between BR and BC: the oblique angle to the grave, with Orestes and Elektra now together and facing the bulk of the audience, gave the required variation from the *kommos* positions, while still making possible an effective interaction with the grave.

Part four (510–84). Orestes needs to be brought forward, away from Elektra for the reading of the dream. This is achieved by selecting the speaker of 510f. from between C and L. (Her intervention goes well if it is spoken over the grave to disrupt the unity of the heirs.) Orestes has to come round, perhaps via BL to ELC during his response, and the Libation Bearer who speaks in

---

[22] These obviously include: 363f. – Elektra, in sudden rebellion or dissent against the picture the others have built up in the two previous stanzas, breaks away from the mound (e.g. in the direction of EFR), returning to her place by 394; 380f. – Orestes addresses the mound more closely; 429f. – Elektra turns outward again, this time further, e.g. towards ERC; (she goes back to her place during 444f.); 434f. – Orestes rises, apostrophizes Klytaimestra, then closes in; 461f. – Orestes and Elektra turn and face F, to show that they have now completed their address to the spirit of Agamemnon and can confront directly what will now happen.

[23] 1984, 94–5, cf. 74–5.

523–53 crosses to between FL and L to engage with him. Orestes
is then near the grave at 540f., and Pylades should come down
from EBL to join him at the end of this speech, in view of his
increased importance from 561.

Orestes' plan requires an interaction with both Elektra and the
Libation Bearers. It plays well with the bulk of the action in the
front half of the *orchêstra*, and the Libation Bearers – with the one
exception, who is now FL – still in their ellipse around the grave,
but now turned to face Orestes.[24] As Orestes quits his interaction
with the one Libation Bearer, he moves – e.g., via FC – towards
FR during 554f. Meanwhile Elektra comes down to ERC to be
given her instructions. Lines 560f. are then animated by small
movements of Orestes in the FC/EFR area, with Pylades coming
down to join Elektra and Orestes during 560–3.[25]

Line 579 is addressed to Elektra, close to her between R and
FR; from this position Orestes has an easy turn to address the
remainder of the speech to the Libation Bearers and Agamemnon.

The directions after 584. In the first half of *Libation Bearers*
the *skene* and its doors are not used, and therefore by conversation it
does not represent anything; the grave of Agamemnon is imagined,
for obvious political, psychological and religious reasons, as not
being anywhere near the palace.[26] At 653 Orestes knocks on the
doors, establishing that they now represent the entrance to the house
of Atreus. A change of scene therefore takes place before 653;[27] in
fact before 585, since the last two stanzas of Choros 3 accompany
Orestes' entry to begin the revenge attempt.

A scene-change in Greek tragedy requires that everyone –
especially the choros – leaves the first location before anyone
enters in the second location; so the Libation Bearers must exit
after 584 along with Orestes, Pylades and Elektra.

[24] The rear of the *orchêstra* is of course a possible position for them; but they
would all have to move during 510f., and these are not appropriate lines for a
retreat.

[25] Orestes might well use his sword as a prop to give vigour to the fantasy plan
of revenge: drawing it at 575, miming the death-thrust at 576, and saluting the
Fury at 577–8. (He could then salute Agamemnon in a similar fashion before his
exit at the end of the scene.)

[26] Lines 722f. do *not* imply that it must be present in the second half of the
drama!

[27] *Pace* Taplin (1977a, 338–9) and many other scholars. I discuss the issues at
greater length in a forthcoming article, 'Scene-change in Greek Tragedy'.

It also requires a change of props, to refocus the playing area. Accordingly attendants must strike the grave of Agamemnon after all the actors have left. While this is being done the actors have to move round behind the *skene*, on the lower level out of sight of the audience, from the left *parodos*, by which they have made their exit to show they are going from the grave towards the city, to the right *parodos*, from which they must re-enter to show that they are coming to the palace from the country.

My last direction raises the whole issue of realism in Greek tragedy. Orestes has ordered Elektra (554, 579) to go home and play a part, inside the house, in the action of the vengeance attempt. Most translators and commentators assume that she vanishes from the drama after Scene 2 (primarily, I believe, because she never speaks again). But her presence as a silent face in Scenes 3 and 7 is very effective, and if Elektra comes out of the palace for either or both of these scenes, then logically she should have been seen to return to it from the grave. If she returns and enters the *skene*, this establishes, before the re-entry of the Libation Bearers for Choros 3, that it is now in use. This also prepares the audience for Orestes' entry, and makes a nice contrast between Elektra's ease and his difficulty in gaining access to the house.

Choros 3

An inner dialogue between the Libation Bearers, placing Klytaimestra's crime in the full focus of other unnatural crimes which have been caused by the total readiness of a woman seized by passion to take risks (A2). This widens the focus of the drama, bringing in mythical examples in a way which is appropriate both for the mid-point of the trilogy, and for the central ode of a drama which is otherwise focussed relentlessly on the fortunes of this house alone. They also begin here their attempt (which develops through the next two songs to a climax in Choros 6) to impose the view that Orestes is completely justified, and may commit even matricide in the cause of avenging Agamemnon without deserving any consequences. This prepares by contrast for the sensational undermining of Orestes' defence in Scene 7.

The initial mood is philosophical and reflective; in our production, mindful of the approach of nightfall (NB 660–1) the Libation Bearers entered individually, and collapsed exhausted around the perimeter of the *orchêstra*. Then the choreography began with one of them rising slowly to dance and sing the first stanza. The song gains intensity and momentum through the B and C stanzas, until (settling in the original Greek firmly into the iambic metre) it achieves directness and power in the final strophic pair, by which time the Libation Bearers have summoned all the strength they need to welcome Orestes and Pylades.[28]

Scene 3

After the choros ends, in two stanzas whose choreography should be a triumphal hailing of the returning hero, there is a complete contrast. As Orestes and Pylades approach the doors, the Libation Bearers retreat to the EF perimeter,[29] feigning non-involvement for the first – but by no means the last – time.

The scene begins with a remarkable shift in tone, a sequence which has surviving parallels only in comedy.[30] The house at first completely ignores its rightful master – fulfilling Orestes' prediction of the maimed state of the *oikos* (566f.). He has to knock three times before a Servant emerges,[31] grumbling the first half of his line from inside the *skene*, and delivers the rest of it reluctantly through partly open doors. The régime has withdrawn into the palace; the *agora* of Argos (represented now by the *orchêstra*) is dangerous territory, viewed with suspicion by Klytaimestra and her followers.

Orestes' speech begins as a direct response to the Servant, but he soon opens out first into the expansive rhetoric of 660–2 and then (663f.) into speculations which are better addressed to Pylades, as a confidential aside. This allows two further comic effects: first, the Servant can retreat in disdain before Orestes' affected, ornamental imagery (closing the door precisely so as to

[28] Orestes and Pylades therefore enter just before 639, not 653; *pace* Kranz (1933, 165) and Taplin (1977a, 338).

[29] *Not* up by the *skene* (Melchinger 1979, 100); far from being 'almost invisible in their black robes', they would pull focus from the action in one of the rare sequences in Aischylos where the choros character is deliberately withdrawn from interaction with the individual actors.

[30] Bain (1981, 46) rightly notes the comic technique; cf. e.g. Aristophanes *Frogs* 37.

[31] *Pace* Taplin (1977a, 341) and Bowen (1986, 116), who suggest that the Servant does not appear at all.

undermine 662); and then, Klytaimestra can enter early at 665 (not 668), to overhear the last three lines of Orestes' speech – directed, as a man-to-man confidence, to Pylades – and then score a rich ironic point with her opening line.

This scene is a re-creation and inversion of the arrival of Agamemnon.[32] Klytaimestra's entry disrupts Orestes' expectations, perhaps even more strikingly than Agamemnon's. It is not simply that Orestes expected Aigisthos (554f., 656): the vehemence of the language of the murder fantasy at 571f., when taken now together with the evasive, sexist phrasing of 664f., indicates that he actively wanted to meet Aigisthos first. Instead he is forced to confront his mother at once.

This is the first scene after the *skene* doors come into use, and is therefore played largely towards the back of the *orchêstra*. Orestes begins his interaction with the Servant up by the doorway, but leaves him and comes forward in a leisurely way during the rhetorical amplification at 658f. However, as Orestes' tale unfolds, Klytaimestra will inevitably be drawn forward around 686f., in preparation for the great outburst at 691f., in which she temporarily breaks out of the web of Orestes' schemes. The substantial move here, clear into the front sector of the *orchêstra*, is Klytaimestra's only sally into a public arena which is increasingly controlled by her enemies.

Klytaimestra is clearly attended (cf. 712f.) – but by whom? Some scholars[33] have assigned to Elektra Klytaimestra's central speech at 691f. I am sure this is wrong: it is *Klytaimestra's* reaction to the news of 'Orestes' death' that we want to hear at this point. The idea has unfortunately led almost everyone[34] to discount the possibility of Elektra's re-entering now, played by a silent face.[35] If Elektra does re-enter, it shows up the grand lie with which Klytaimestra ends the scene, even in advance of Scene 4, where the only person she can find to take her message to Aigisthos is an old Nurse totally loyal to Orestes. To receive Agamemnon, Klytaimestra came out in total command, symbolized in the theatre by the anonymous maidservants ready to do her bidding, as well as by her free use of the whole *orchêstra*. Now

---

[32] Cf. Taplin 1977a, 343.

[33] First in the Aldine edition. The case is made by Thomson (1966, 161–5), Winnington-Ingram (1983, 216–8) and Seaford (1989).

[34] Except Fagles 1977, 206.

[35] Cf. Tekmessa in the later stages of *Aias*, and Ismene in *Oidipous at Kolonos*.

she does not control the playing space, and to receive Orestes she can call as attendant upon no one but the daughter who hates her.[36] Klytaimestra's every move is undermined by Elektra's presence at EBC, metaphorically 'upstaging' her and performing exactly the role which Orestes asked of her at 579.[37]

The meeting between Orestes and Klytaimestra is portrayed with great psychological subtlety. Klytaimestra is not now the monster whom the Libation Bearers portrayed to us in Choros 3. Even if there is macabre irony when she offers 'warm baths' to Agamemnon's son, Klytaimestra is hospitable. She remains, as in the last scene of *Agamemnon*, firmly within the traditional limits of a proper woman's role.

Orestes therefore has to deceive a Klytaimestra who is receiving strangers correctly and properly. So his speech at 674f. begins hesitantly, with head averted, and only takes flight – once again, in clichéd rhetoric – at 685f. Then Orestes gathers the strength for a sudden, vicious attack (690), and receives in reply not the hypocritical reaction which both he and we might have expected, but a sincere meditation on the troubles of the *oikos*. Though she fears her son's return, Klytaimestra, when she first hears of his fictive death, sees it as yet another undermining of the household. (We will only be told later, by the hostile Nurse, that her second, secret reaction was rejoicing.)

Orestes overrides the pathos of 699 with the direct thrust of 700 – unfair even if he only refers to material goods, and outrageously insensitive when delivered by a man purporting to bring the news that an only son is lost. In what follows he continues to play the travelling Daulian – note for example the facile rhetoric of 702–3. But his hypocritical speech allows Klytaimestra time to recover, and with a sudden new energy (710f.) she welcomes her murderers into the house.[38] She does this

[36] Line 715 is very imperious if addressed to an anonymous maidservant, but plays well if designed to keep a rebellious Elektra under control. (Orestes and Pylades are not attended; Taplin 1977a, 341–2).

[37] Elektra perhaps carries a torch, to reinforce in visual terms the fact that night is drawing on during this scene (660f., 710f.). Torches could then become an important motif: one can be carried from the palace by the Nurse, and brought back by Aigisthos in the following scene, to remind the audience of the increasingly dark psychological atmosphere (in opposition to the literal broad daylight of the original performance) as Orestes' vengeance attempt comes nearer to its crisis.

[38] Taplin (1977a, 343–4) would have Klytaimestra leave last, controlling the man's entry as in *Agamemnon* Scene 4. But the last place now, without the

with sincerity; and she tells only one lie – in the final line, as she attempts to conceal the total isolation of the usurpers, which in the next scene will undo them.

Choros 4

The secret prayer referred to in 82f. now becomes an active desire to help in the deception. The Libation Bearers call on Hermes to help Orestes,[39] and they call on Persuasion to come and help themselves, correctly sensing that the crucial moments of the action, which are happening now, may give them an opportunity. They are praying for 581–2 to be fulfilled; in the next scene their prayer is answered, and they save Orestes.

In this ode the Libation Bearers express their increasing anxiety, their suspense as they hope that they can guide or direct the action, and through that the fact that the drama is now nearing its climax. Given their starting position on the front perimeter, the structure of the words implies a rapid flow towards the centre during the first three lines, vivid invocatory gestures from a position surrounding the centre during the four-line prayer, and then a rapid movement away from the centre, which must be completed during the last three lines. Then they must freeze quickly in position the moment the doors begin to open.

Scene 4

The gods answer the Libation Bearers' prayer immediately, and from a totally unexpected direction.[40]

triumphal exit lines which indicated her control then, is weak – the usher's position. Better to have Klytaimestra disengage from Orestes at 710f., turn commandingly back towards Elektra, and then sweep out as she speaks 718, leaving the men to follow. It is her last, false victory; and the dramatic point at 930, where obviously she goes first, is to create a parallel not with this scene, but with Agamemnon's controlled, defeated final exit. Then Elektra will be the last to leave. Escorting Orestes and Pylades into the house, she is doing exactly what her brother asked of her.

[39] Kitto 1956, 51–2.

[40] Aigisthos is away from the palace, and needs to be sent for (672–3 and 718). It is probable that this will be done next; so the course of the action is not so entirely up in the air at this point as Taplin implies (1977a, 345). The Nurse is at the periphery of the action, but gives reality to the central issue of the drama, the mother–son relationship: 'both Orestes and Clytaimestra have been slightly distant figures, functionaries of fate . . . ; the Nurse makes them flesh and blood again, and just when Orestes least wants them to be' (Bowen 1986, 133).

This scene begins with one of the Libation Bearers interrupting the Nurse, to prevent her from leaving the *orchêstra* directly via the left *parodos*. The contrast between the section up to 742 and what follows is easily established if the Nurse delivers the opening of the speech from one position (e.g. just F of BC), and then comes forward to engage the Libation Bearers at 743–6. The movements must exhibit throughout the contrast in tempo between the Nurse's almost comic garrulity and the Libation Bearers' increasing impatience, with the Nurse circling around individual Libation Bearers to give visual form to her rambling discourse. She then disengages partially from them as she concludes.

By 763 the Nurse should have reached the centre, in view of the importance of what is to follow. The Libation Bearers intervene to change the message[41] – an action unparalleled in surviving Greek tragedy; even the Furies themselves, for all their power in *Eumenides*, do not have the ability to change the course of the plot. The Libation Bearer who speaks to the Nurse can be initially at some distance; a substantial cross during 763f. brings the audience's full attention onto her intervention. The dialogue requires to be played with urgent intensity until 775, and then eases back until 778–9, in which the speaker feigns detachment; the Libation Bearers close in a little towards the Nurse from 763, and then finally yield outwards again. This allows the Nurse to make directly for her exit BL, watched by them all. Choros 5 begins as soon as she steps out of the *orchêstra*.

Choros 5[42]

As the action nears its climax, Aischylos varies the pattern of short, intense, astrophic odes between the scenes with this longer lyric. He reinforced the impression of stillness and spaciousness by opting for an unusual Greek metrical scheme, with the strophically responding stanzas interspersed by *mesodes* in a contrasting metre, which do not respond to each other (A1a, B1a, C1a). Each *mesode* intrudes, with disturbingly stronger content, on the normal choreographic sequence of pattern and matched

[41] The excitement makes the speaker break out of the regular *stichomythia* pattern for four lines at 770f.

[42] The text of this ode is deeply corrupt in the one surviving manuscript of *Libation Bearers*. Though much scholarly labour has been devoted to attempts at restoration, any translation rests on several speculative conjectures.

counterpattern. Though the argument of the text continues through them, each *mesode* is an intensifying, heightening element in relation to the two matching stanzas which frame it. There is a complication, which qualifies what is otherwise a steady, serene development through the ode, reflecting the constant emphasis on the absolute rightness of what Orestes will do (overt in every stanza except A1a). The choreography must flow – perhaps beginning in a stately manner, but with a gradual rise in intensity and speed through the prayer to Zeus in the A stanzas; then with an overall calm, on a new level of emotion, during the address to other gods in the B stanzas; finally with a firm pattern for C1 acting as the foundation for an increasing level of emphasis through to the end.

Circular patterns, with much use of interweaving of choros members and of gesture, are appropriate for the first six stanzas with their sequence of supplications and their overall feeling of completeness. The C stanzas call for a much more direct, angular treatment to complement the combination of confidence and anxiety with which the Libation Bearers turn from the gods to address Orestes directly (presumably facing towards the *skene* during much of the last three stanzas).

Scene 5

Aigisthos enters 'summoned by a messenger' (838); and we know how the Libation Bearers reshaped that message. Deception and teacherous persuasion are clearly working, and once again the Libation Bearers take extraordinary action. Just as there is no surviving parallel for their intervention in Scene 4, so too there is no parallel for a character played by the choros luring someone to his death.

Aigisthos makes his approach while the Libation Bearers conclude their lyrics with an appeal for Orestes to kill him without hesitation. His step from the *parados* into the playing area is the cue for a violent transition – from expression of their inner emotions to feigned subservience – which is the most important aspect of the Libation Bearers' part in Scenes 3 to 6. In our production the Libation Bearers moved at this moment from an erect posture, with arms extended in salutation of Orestes' imminent triumph, to the total submissiveness of an oriental salaam, in an echo of Klytaimestra's homage to Agamemnon in the tapestry scene.

This short scene[43] allows the director to consolidate the atmosphere of political menace under the tyranny of the usurpers. In the speech the actor can establish not merely the hypocrisy of Aigisthos' condolences on the 'death of Orestes' but also the sinister, decadent character into whom power has corrupted the self-justified poseur seen in *Ag* Scene 8. There is also the dynamic tension between the Libation Bearers, apparently weak and cowering before the tyrant – but in fact strong – and Aigisthos, who is the exact reverse. We tried to express all this by having the Libation Bearers kneel and prostrate themselves in a supposedly reverent – but in fact menacing – ellipse in the rear part of the *orchêstra*; Aigisthos delivered his speech circling nervously around the centre of this ellipse, pausing only to ruminate (841–3) on the implications of the 'death of Orestes'.

Aischylos crystallizes the contrast between Aigisthos and his deceivers around a central issue of the trilogy: gender conflict. Aigisthos pours scorn on Klytaimestra's message in 845f., and these lines remind the audience both of Orestes' confidential aside to Pylades at 665f. and – more directly, though over a larger span of time – of the Elders' sudden distrust of Klytaimestra's beacons at *Ag* 475f. Those parallel essays in male sexism, though subjected to almost immediate deflation, were at least addressed at the time to men alone: here however, with supreme irony, Aigisthos is made to voice his distrust of women's words to a woman, who then with consummate hypocrisy agrees with him and applies his teaching to herself. Aischylos then takes the irony of the scene even further: going to his death more blindly than Agamemnon, Aigisthos tells the woman who has duped him that 'My mind has eyes; it cannot be deceived'.

The movements and gestures here must establish the contrast between Aigisthos' false assumption that he has power and the true power of the slave woman who answers him and lures him to his death. For example, in our production Aigisthos suddenly grasped one of the Libation Bearers by the chin at 847, jerking her half erect to make her answer his question; but she rose fully to her feet on 'We've heard', and delivered the rest of her speech

---

[43] The shortest in Greek tragedy. Scene 4 is the second shortest; Taplin (1977a, 346–8, 351–3) rightly emphasizes the unrelenting pace of the events in Scenes 5–7.

standing uncowed, after backing away slightly to assert her control over her own space. Aigisthos' transition from sadism to bemused acceptance was conveyed simply by his steady, oblique move towards the doors during the next three lines.[44] It was then almost irresistible to play the last line as a parting address; Aigisthos turns back towards her at the doorway before a purposeful, unsuspecting exit.

Choros 6

Now the parallel with *Agamemnon* reaches its closest. As the lesser victim, Aigisthos is technically parallel to Kassandra – though their difference in moral stature is shown by his being assigned the shortest scene in Greek tragedy, while she received one of the longest and greatest. The pattern of *Agamemnon* Choroses 4 and 5 is therefore replicated in the contrast between the two odes (5 and 6) which frame the Aigisthos scene. Here again the excitement is whipped up after the victim's exit by a very short chanted sequence, which builds up steadily to a climax.

If the Libation Bearers are with one exception kneeling as Aigisthos exits, as was the case in our production, the only possible choreography – given the brevity of the ode – is for them to come successively to their feet, surging nearer to the palace and into a more and more excited stance as the words verge towards their final outcry.[45]

Scene 6

Just as in *Agamemnon*, the second of the two victims has now passed into the house; the choros has summed up, in a brief lyric outpouring, all the issues which are at stake; the death-cry is heard from within; and the action breaks down into turbulent chaos in the immediate moments after the deed. But this chaos is not now stilled by the triumphant emergence of the murderer: here the male is the easier victim.

[44] He should not be allowed to replicate the dignified direct path from C to EBC walked by Agamemnon and Kassandra – and by Klytaimestra in Scene 6 of this drama.

[45] This ode profits, even more than most, from division among individuals. Both the arch shape and the gathering momentum are reflected if the lines are divided 2/3/6/2/1, with the entire Choros chanting the last line in unison.

The impact of the climax is achieved by a startling change of pace. First comes the hectic, almost comic confusion created by the Servant in the moments after Aigisthos' death, followed instantly by Klytaimestra's brief reversion to male valour in the attempt to make a counter-attack. But she is too late, and the restless action is stilled when Orestes appears and corners her. The texture of the verse changes completely at 892, and the issues are then exposed more slowly, in a confrontational *stichomythia* of remorseless power and economy.

Aigisthos rates only an inarticulate death-cry; as it rings out, the Libation Bearers respond with extreme excitement (870–1 are still in lyric metres). But their reaction turns rapidly from exultation to confusion, and then to circumspection. This should be reflected both in the gradual falling-away of the excitement from their words, and also by dividing the speeches.[46]

The Libation Bearers need to be moved by 874 into a neutral position, so as not to pull focus from the climactic confrontation. This is the last and most important of their retreats from the action in the second half of this drama.[47] The most neutral place for the Libation Bearers is in two groups, FR–EFR and EFL–FL.

This leaves the Servant with the whole *orchêstra* to scurry around, articulating the frenzied energy of his panic in the face of the totally unresponsive, disdainful Libation Bearers. Until 880 his speech is directed to them;[48] then at 'Hey . . .' he turns away towards the back of the *orchêstra*, arriving BC in time for Klytaimestra to intercept him as she comes out.

The frenzied, almost surrealistic tempo continues with Klytaimestra's entry. She immediately engages the Servant in dialogue around BC, turns briefly away from him for the recognition and meditation 887–8, and then back to send him off.

He cannot leave before 889, since this line motivates his exit.[49] Scholars have made strenuous efforts to preserve the 'three-actor rule' for Athenian tragedy, by making him leave earlier, and

[46] Perhaps there is even a case for splitting 870 and 871. The pause for a double-take would then come after 871.

[47] Not of course into the mouth of a *parodos* (Taplin 1977a, 348): first because that movement would suggest that a scene change is imminent; second because they would still be very visible to over half the audience; and finally because the Servant needs someone in the playing area to address in the next section.

[48] *Pace* the ingenious theories in Bain (1981, 56–61).

[49] Taplin (1977a, 353–4); *pace* e.g. Bain 1981, 62.

postponing the entry of Pylades to give the actor time to change. However, performance experience shows that Pylades cannot enter at any other moment except with (to be precise, just after) Orestes.[50] This leaves only two lines between the Servant's exit and Pylades' entry – far too little time for a change; a fourth actor must therefore have been used.

This was a remarkable breach of convention.[51] The extreme surprise, when Pylades spoke the three crucial lines which seal Klytaimestra's fate, was caused not merely by his total silence until this point, but also by the fact that all three actors were apparently employed elsewhere, when a voice spoke from behind his mask. The audience would have had every reason, after the successive entries of the Servant and Klytaimestra, to suppose that the mask and costume of Pylades are still worn by a mute extra or 'silent face'.

Lines 892f. must be played BR/BC/BL, in a dominant, but not the most predominant, part of the *orchêstra*. Orestes sees Pylades' intervention, when he himself hesitates, as one of two advocated pleas – the one which he accepts; Pylades' three lines match, answer and defeat Klytaimestra's 896–98. He should not, however, be between Pylades and Klytaimestra. Pylades himself must be in the central position of the triangle, judging between Klytaimestra and Orestes, to indicate how 'in his one utterance we sense an awful authority, as if the god had possessed the seeming-mute and spoken through him'.[52] He then retreats instantly after 903, out of the way for the ensuing dialogue.

Aischylos now presents another major actor–actor *stichomythia*, comparable to that by which Klytaimestra lured Agamemnon to his death in the parallel tapestry-scene. This scene equals that dialogue in intensity and doubles it in length; only here she fails to persuade. As in *Agamemnon*, a relatively static blocking is desirable: only a few, slight movements are required during 908–29.

Success in performance depends on a strong change of pace and tone at 922. Up until that point, the exchanges are cumulatively faster and more intense as Orestes' rebuttals are implacable and ruthless. But then, after Klytaimestra's realization that she is doomed, she once again threatens him with a mother's Furies; and

[50] cf. Taplin *loc. cit.*; *pace* e.g. Garvie 1986, l.

[51] So rightly Bowen (1986, 147). Note however that at no time are all four speaking actors on together.

[52] Jones 1962, 102.

now he does not simply brush that aside, as he did at 913, with a superficial tit-for-tat, but gives the fullest possible answer, revealing in 925 all the tragedy of his position. Here Aischylos undermines the hope (805–6) that there may be no more bloodshed, and prefigures the consequences of his impending act: the combat for Orestes' life between Apollo and the Furies, which dominates the final drama.

Accordingly, solemnity is needed from here to the end. With his father's Furies set in the balance against his mother's, Orestes has placed against Klytaimestra all the forces which bound him to do this deed (cf. 272f.); and this final recognition, that of the two evils he must inevitably choose his mother's death, is matched by Klytaimestra: as she reads the dream, she accepts its meaning and recognizes that she is doomed.

The parallel with the *stichomythia* in *Agamemnon* must be enforced by creating an echo of the end of the tapestry scene – and therefore also of Kassandra's exit – since once again, as in *Agamemnon* Scene 6, the open *skene* doors have become a metaphor for the mouth of Hades. This can be done without replicating the *Agamemnon* blocking in every way. Orestes shows his mastery at this point by understatement, concluding the 1–1 *stichomythia* simply by speaking two lines; unlike Klytaimestra, he does not need a pyrotechnic display of rhetoric to conquer his victim. Thus she advances up the centre-line from C to the *skene* doorway, controlled by Orestes with his drawn, bloodstained sword.

Choros 7

As if to lay to rest the fear explicit in their sober, muted closing comment on Scene 6, the Libation Bearers embark on an ode of rejoicing, composed in the original Greek in dochmiacs, the most frenzied metre. In Greek, the lyrics of this drama have so far been metrically unified. The unity is now violently broken, to show their extreme emotion. Paradoxically, the ode works particularly well when choreographed with regular patterns of movement – in rectangular blocks and straight lines – with the exultation left to the gestures as the Libation Bearers take over the *orchêstra*, totally confident now for the first time in the second half of the drama that the space is truly theirs.

Clearly this is in retrospect premature rejoicing, expressing an almost desperate desire to see Orestes' act at the end of a chain of violence. But the traumatic effect of the final scene does not completely undermine what they sing; on the contrary, Choros 7 reminds us of truths which could otherwise easily be forgotten in Scene 7. Orestes has come back as the instrument of Justice; Apollo has given victory to Justice; and the house of Atreus has been purified. Only 969–72 express a premature hope.

Scene 7

Now a total reversal, as the Libation Bearers retreat towards the front extremity of the *orchêstra*, abandoning the final, triumphant posture of Choros 7 in a horrified response to the tableau.

This is the most remarkable 'mirror-scene' in surviving Greek tragedy.[53] As Kassandra virtually prophesied (*Ag* 1316f.), here again is a triumphant avenger posed over two bodies – one of each gender – and speaking in self-justification before horrified witnesses; and once again their response forces the murderer onto the defensive.

Orestes maintains a reticent stance, not merely abstaining from such glorying in the deed as Klytaimestra indulged, but actively rejecting it (1014–7, cf. 930). In return, where Klytaimestra was unequivocally overshadowed by the prospect of vengeance at the end of Agamemnon, Orestes receives Apollo's protection as his reward. At the end, the mother's Furies have their victory, as they drive Orestes from the *orchêstra*; but now there is something to set in the balance against them.

Once again the scene seems designed to exploit the theatrical power of the *ekkuklêma*. The continuity required, to achieve the effect of shocking contrast and suddenly undermine the Libation Bearers' rejoicing, cannot be obtained if Orestes' attendants have to bring the bodies on slowly, and Orestes has to take up his position, before the first speech.

On the platform are extras, wearing the clothes and masks of Klytaimestra and Aigisthos and placed under the net-like robe in which Klytaimestra entangled Agamemnon, the first actor playing Orestes, with bloodstained hands and sword[54] (1056–7),

[53] I am not persuaded by Arnott's suggestion that Orestes simply exhibited the severed heads of Aigisthos and Klytaimestra (1989, 168).

[54] Like Klytaimestra in *Ag* Scene 7 (*pace* Reinhardt 1947, 137). He carries this prop with him, since *Eu* 42 makes plain that he still has it when he arrives at Delphi.

and at least two attendants to display the net at 983.[55] Orestes cannot make the violent gestures required to realize the later part of his first speech if he is encumbered not only by his sword but also by the wreath-crowned olive branch, symbol of his future hope, which he needs to take to Delphi (1034f.). There is great advantage in bringing on Pylades:[56] if Apollo's representative carries them and hands them to Orestes during the third speech, the tokens of supplication take on a greater significance.

The other attendant should be Elektra. Lines 991f. work superbly if Orestes turns to his sister and visibly allies himself with her; and the whole tableau is enhanced if Orestes is supported by two *philoi*.[57] This makes yet another strong contrast with Klytaimestra in *Agamemnon*: her only *philos* was a lover so cowardly that she had to kill, and defend her act of murder, alone.[58] By contrast, even the support of the two people closest to him is not enough to save Orestes now.

The through-line is Orestes' gradual loss of self-control under the onslaught of the Furies. This is first openly admitted at 1021f., but the dementia has already set in at 995f.[59]

The first speech begins with Orestes in a dominant position on the *ekkuklêma*, behind the bodies; and as it proceeds he establishes an even closer relationship with them (e.g. by crouching at around 977, to deliver the sick irony of 979 directly). He then rises, picking up part of the death-robe, as he begins 980; Pylades and Elektra must stretch it out at 983 – perhaps with the Libation Bearers refusing and shrinking back, in preparation for their muted, horrified response at the end of the speech.

The intensity increases after 990: Orestes must advance to the

[55] It is theatrically weak to use any of the Libation Bearers; separating them from the tableau makes their chant of distress (1007f.) and Orestes' need to come forward to defend himself, far more effective.

[56] Cf. Fagles 1977, 221.

[57] Again, one of each gender; Aischylos knew, though he does not use, the version of the legend in which Elektra subsequently married Pylades.

[58] Elektra, Pylades and the Libation Bearers are the only people whom Orestes can correctly refer to as his *philoi* (1026); Taplin (1977a, 357–8) rightly rejects the idea of a crowd of Argive extras.

[59] Many scholars have argued for transposition or emendation in 997–1004; but in performance, using as props first the net itself – and then the corpse of Klytaimestra for 991f. (cf. *Ag* 1114f.) – the text works superbly for an actor, without any need for adjustment.

front corner of the *ekkuklêma*, on the side where Klytaimestra's body is placed, at 991; he seizes some part of her body – perhaps an arm – at 997; and continues to build to an extreme, almost demented climax at 1003–4 before easing off, to deliver the last two lines detached, at a short distance – off the *ekkuklêma*, but still EBC.

The anguish, and the strength of the prophecy in the chant at 1007f., arraign him at an imaginary bar (cf. 987f.) – as if he were already debating with the Furies: Orestes is forced on the defensive, and suddenly seizes the bloodstained death-robe again. He drops this, however, after the first four lines; 1016–7 need a visual image of his vulnerability best achieved by moving Orestes forward, away from his supporters.

Once again the Libation Bearers, as they face towards him and the gory tableau behind him, concentrate remorselessly on the suffering which they foresee; and now Orestes cannot offer a counter. Lines 1021f. are best played motionless, to prepare by contrast for the intense movement when the actual madness sets in.

Pylades advances towards Orestes at 1030, hands him the wreathed olive branch ritualistically during 1034–5, and returns by 1038 to his original place. This leaves Orestes free to advance a little down the centre-line, past BC, during the closing phases of the speech.

As in *Agamemnon*, *stichomythia* is used to raise the intensity in the last moments. The Libation Bearers now gain authority as Orestes loses it under the pressure of the consequences of kindred murder;[60] given that Orestes must leave by the right *parodos*, the Libation Bearer who intervenes should be drawn from FL, and advance at least half-way to him during her first four lines. Orestes then sees the Furies over her shoulder. He jumps back from BC towards BR; she follows him, perhaps taking his arm in 1051f. But her ideal is impossible: the Furies are more real to him now than Argos. They hurl Orestes first around, and then out of the *orchêstra* and his city.

Choros 8

A brief, grim choral chant sums up the balance which the action of

[60] Cf. Aischylos, *Seven against Thebes* 712f.

the trilogy has now reached. On the one hand, the hope of Apollo's protection in the future; on the other, the prospect of death at the hands of his mother's Furies. Just as Zeus – the third great god – is the saviour (cf. *Ag* 160f.), so Orestes – also the third – can be seen as a saviour; or will the curse never end? In the even balance between these two prospects, the final lines pose the question which will dominate *Eumenides*.

During this choros, the dance takes the Libation Bearers from the front of the playing area back towards the *skene*. This final repossession of the *orchêstra* is muted as well as brief. The *ekkuklêma* withdraws with the tableau, Pylades and Elektra taking with them 'the sad abandoned relics of this awful deed'.[61] Then the Libation Bearers leave, going away from the palace[62] with their heads hung; all that they have supported throughout the drama is now, for the moment, defeated.

[61] Bowen 1986, 164.
[62] Logically, as servants of this *oikos*, they should exit into the *skene*. There is no good point, however, in seeing them incommoded by having to step around the *ekkuklêma* (as there was with Klytaimestra and Aigisthos at the end of *Ag*). As with the Herald in *Ag* Scene 3, the 'downtown' *parodos*, though not the strictly consistent exit, is the best one (so too Melchinger 1979, 108).

Eumenides

Introduction

No other playwright ever dramatized the sequence of events which led eventually to Orestes' deliverance from pursuit by his mother's Furies. This phase of the legend was of special importance to Aischylos, who wanted to explore the implications and consequences of Orestes' deed in depth.

The plot of *Eumenides* is dominated by the question whether Orestes deserves to be saved or destroyed. And the drama crystallizes around that question the two main issues which have emerged in *Libation Bearers*: to which parent does the son owe more, his father or his mother; is there any remedy for blood spilt on the ground – can a house find release from the seed of violence, once it is sown?

In many previous versions of the story,[1] Orestes turned after the murder of his mother to the shrine of Apollo at Delphi, and received there both purification, and deliverance from the Furies. But there was a local legend that he made his way to Athens, and was tried on the Areopagos. For Aischylos, matricide is so extreme that taking refuge at Delphi is not enough to purify Orestes: he must also supplicate Athena and her city before he finds complete release. The problem of determining Orestes' fate devolves upon the people of Athens.

This creates the last tragic dilemma of the trilogy. The Athenians are faced with an 'impossible' choice between equally undesirable alternatives – just like Agamemnon at Aulis. A suppliant's claim to refuge was a fundamental right in Greece, guaranteed by Zeus himself. Yet on the other hand the Furies have their rights too, and will make Athens feel their full destructive powers if they are not satisfied (470f.). The way in which the Athenians make their decision, and the reasons why they deserve

[1] Details in Sommerstein 1989, 1–6.

to evade all retribution for the choice which they make, are the main subject of the second and third parts of the drama.

It was not customary to represent the gods in Greek tragedy.[2] The Furies in this drama are the only ancient chthonic deities, ill-omened powers from the realm of Hades, ever to appear (though Death, personified, speaks the first scene in Euripides' *Alkestis*); and the impact of their first entrance became a theatrical legend.[3] It was also a bold experiment, building on the success of the Danaid tetralogy in 463, to make the character played by the choros the central figure.

Aischylos normally avoided striking visual effects, unless they contribute directly to the drama's meaning. The decision to make the Furies materialize has a precise dramatic purpose. *Libation Bearers* closed with the Furies very much in the ascendant. This is natural: at that moment, in the immediate aftermath of matricide, our revulsion is so strong that we expect them to pursue Orestes and undermine his initial claim to full justification. But from the opening of *Eumenides* the movement is steadily in the opposite direction. The case in favour of Orestes' deed slowly makes up the lost ground, until he obtains his release by a hairsbreadth.

The subject-matter would in our terms be the evolving percep-tion of Orestes' deserts inside his mind and those of the Athenian jurors – material which the modern theatre can handle only with difficulty, using symbolism and expressionism. But the Greek vision, in which the boundaries of the human psyche are narrow, and the gods and *daimônes* intervene under the pressure of a moral crisis of this severity, meant that Aischylos had available more immediate means than ours – the means to make the gods themselves become characters in the drama, and fight out the issues. As we watch the contest, we must not hesitate to take a moral stance – just as we did with Agamemnon, Klytaimestra and

[2] There are some later dramas in which a god appears at the start, partly foreshadows what will happen and then departs, never to reappear (e.g. Sophokles' *Aias*, Euripides' *Trojan Women*); several others in which a god intervenes at the end 'from the machine' to resolve human conflicts; two in which different gods appear at the start and end (*Hippolytos, Ion*); and Euripides' *Bakchai* in which one god, disguised as a mortal, takes a major part in the action. The Prometheus trilogy is the only known work exclusively devoted to conflict between gods.

[3] 'Some say that when in the performance of *Eumenides* he brought on the choros individually, the audience was so startled that children fainted and women gave birth', Anon., *Life of Aischylos*, 9.

Orestes in the previous dramas. We are intended to estimate the changing relative strength of their cases as the drama unfolds; the meaning of the drama is embodied in this process of moral flux.

The opening image is a simple one: Apollo – radiant young male god of Light and Delphic certainty, is pitted against the Furies – hideous, old female daughters of the Night, loathsome creatures from the underworld. It would not have been difficult for the Athenian audience to take sides at the outset, and favour the defenders of Orestes. They were not cheated. Apollo's side gains ever greater successes, until finally it seems that Orestes just deserves to go free. Appearances are fundamentally not deceptive, and Aischylos satisfies our hope that Orestes should gradually come to evade the Furies' binding power.

It would have been extraordinary if this expectation had not been fulfilled. In the surviving dramas, Aischylos does not inflict drastic reversals on his audience. But the pattern of expectation and fulfilment in *Eumenides* is distinctly different from that of *Agamemnon* and *Libation Bearers*, in which as the plot unfolded everything came more and more to point our expectations in one direction. They are Iliadic dramas, in which the deaths of Agamemnon and Klytaimestra represent a tragic outcome which is as deeply expected, when it happens, as the moment in Book 22 when Homer's Achilleus, killing Hektor in implacable revenge, embraces as he does so the certainty of his own swift, inglorious death.

Eumenides by contrast is Odyssean. Here, just as in the battle in the hall on Ithaka, there is so much power deployed against the hero's quest for his deserts that his fate remains uncertain for the audience almost to the last – even after Athena has intervened and given her support.

As *Eumenides* unfolds, Orestes' side achieves an ever-growing prospect of success; but the Furies' case gains cogency as well. For Apollo is not simply the great god of prophecy, long and legally established on his ancient throne at Delphi – though this is how his Priestess would have us see him at the outset. In *Agamemnon*, he punished the girl who broke her pledge by a hideous death; in *Libation Bearers* he is ruthless once again, commanding matricide, warning of terrible penalties should Orestes try to evade it, and ordaining that Orestes must sink to treachery in order to achieve that end. Nor was his oracle, in real life, always above the charge of deviousness and trickery.[4]

4 Neither Aischylos nor the older members of his audience would have forgotten the expediency and cowardice of Delphi during the Persian invasion.

Eumenides seizes on these facts. Apollo breaks the initial deadlock by trickery, and argues against the Furies with more vehemence than logic. Then, at the trial, he cloaks the clinching arguments of Orestes' defence in sophistry and specious rhetoric. The 'right' case – or at any rate the one which will prevail – is increasingly undercut. And so our certainty that his prophecies will be fulfilled is less than absolute.

Conversely, simple pictures of the Furies also lose their force. Apollo's abuse at 71f. is corroborated by their physical appearance and by the terrifying verbal and dance images presented in Choroses 1–3. However in Scene 2, even under a torrent of abuse and threats, they respond with courtesy to Apollo and claim no more than their rights. Then in Choroses 3 and 4 we come to see that there is substance to their claims: simple black-and-white moral pictures lose their force, and we become aware of complexity. Apollo is both a deceitful thief, as the Furies rightly sing in Choros 1, and also the guardian of the view of Orestes' deed which will eventually prevail; so too the Furies are loathsome (as Apollo sees them) but also the incarnations of a profound moral law, and a great benefit to any city which can acquire them. After the masculist thrust of *Libation Bearers*, a re-evaluation of the true strength and value of female powers takes place as the trilogy reaches its conclusion.

This aspect of Aischylos' meaning is primarily communicated by music and dance. The initial images of Apollo and the Furies are conveyed by the costumes and faces; then this picture is gradually qualified. From their hideous opening song through to the radiant salutation of Athens in the Finale, the Furies change their aspect from *daimônes* of destruction and terror to goddesses of fertility and benediction, but without abandoning (indeed, by building upon) the powers that make them so menacing to human beings (cf. 990–1). The unchanging costumes and faces enforce the continuity, reminding us of their underlying nature; the music and dance must show us the development.

When the two sides come to trial, they both have equal force. The trilogy returns at its end to a moral crux as severe as that in which it was begun at Aulis. As the jurors cast their ballots, Aischylos brings us once more to a paradox: Orestes both ought and ought not to be acquitted. This time a resolution will be possible.

Dramatic Structure

The climax is still placed two-thirds of the way through the drama, but the pattern of parallel structures is now broken, to mark off the special subject-matter and new dramatic mode of *Eumenides*. This drama divides into three parts, with relatively short first and third parts, in symmetry and contrast with each other, surrounding an extended central section.

In the opening section, set at Delphi, Aischylos invents a unique structure for Scene 1 and deploys a number of special effects, to establish at the outset the disturbance created by Orestes' matricide, and the extraordinary new level of the action in this drama. The location then changes to Athens for the main action, which follows first the story-pattern of supplication, and then the format of an *agôn* in the trial-scene.

From Orestes' arrival at Athens through to the end of the trial, the action proceeds by a regular alternation of dialogue scenes and choral odes, disrupted only by the brief song interjected into Scene 3. Then the drama concludes with a Finale for actor and choros, in which a lyric harmony between them is established. This final section of the drama is as unusual in its structure as the first part; but here the extraordinary images created in the interplay between Athena and the Furies are images of unity, to counterbalance the ever-increasing disunity between Apollo and the Furies over the span of the opening scenes at Delphi.

After the hostility and turbulence of Scenes 1–4 (which is only partly calmed by the addition of Athena's image – the central prop around which the Athenian scenes are focussed), the half-circle of jurors around the front perimeter provides a point of rest in Scene 5. The trilogy then reaches its culmination in the Finale when two full circles are formed – jurors and female attendants surrounding the Furies, who themselves surround Athena. This is the final image before the processional departure.

Scene 1

The scene is divided into three parts, postponing the entry of the choros by a sequence of disjunct solo entries. There are also several remarkable effects: the unparalleled re-entry of the Priestess on all fours; the hideous sounds from inside the *skene*; and the entry of the Choros individually, in ones and twos, not from a *parodos* but from the *skene* building.[5]

5 There are only two extant parallels: Euripides' *Trojan Women* and the fragments of his *Phaethon*.

Aischylos wrote this highly unusual opening sequence, as
Taplin rightly observes, to create a continuous build-up of
'gradually mounting, threatening terror and horror'[6] until the
entry of the Furies after 142. In the previous drama they were
visible only to Orestes; now they have materialized, in the sacred
temple at the centre of the earth. They are first described, by the
terrified Priestess; then spoken about with contempt by Apollo;
then supplicated by the dream-image of Klytaimestra. At this
point they manifest themselves to the spectators for the first time
—but only as sounds from inside the *skene*; the audience does not
finally see the Furies until after the dream-image has departed –
apparently without success.

In 1–29 the Priestess establishes that Apollo owns the space
now represented by the *orchêstra* – the forecourt of his temple.
The playing space is energized after 33 by the interaction between
the *orchêstra*, which in Scene 1 is still 'safe' for the forces of light,
and the interior of the *skene*, possessed by the Furies. Apollo can
look, and move, back in confidence towards the *skene* doorway;
the human characters turn that way only in horror, and prefer to
stay in the front half of the *orchêstra*.

Klytaimestra's dream-image, by contrast, plays 1(c) in close
interaction with the doorway. When the Furies enter they transfer
their possession from the inner shrine to the forecourt itself; all
Apollo's energies are then required, in Scene 2, before they depart
from his territory. By this sequence Aischylos sets out in spatial
terms the opposition between Apollo and the Furies, and
establishes a visual image of how the Furies were treated at Delphi
against which to contrast their more courteous reception in
Athens.

---

[6] Taplin 1977a, 371. There is no good reason for spoiling this vital effect by
bringing the Furies on before 140. None the less, many scholars have imagined an
earlier entry: either a 'cancelled entry' to form a tableau before the drama starts
(e.g. Rosenmeyer 1982, 67f.; Scott 1984, 207; Rehm 1988, 290–301), or an entry
on the *ekkuklêma* at 64 by some (Arnott 1962, 82–3; Walton 1984, 98; Podlecki
1989, 12–13) or even, impractically, all of the sleeping Furies (Brown 1982, 28 –
together with Orestes, Apollo, twelve chairs and a terracotta replica of the
omphalos!). Actors playing Klytaimestra are naturally at first reluctant to attempt
1 (c) with nobody in the playing area to whom to address her pleas. However, we
soon discovered in rehearsal that the scene plays far more effectively with
Klytaimestra alone visible, than if she is attempting to arouse a tableau of visible
Furies.

1(a). Since she has to establish the role of the *skene* as well as the *orchêstra*, the Priestess should not advance directly to C, but should proceed on the opening lines first to EBC, and then forwards (perhaps during 3) towards BC. Then the remainder of the first beat invites performance as one continuous sweep in which the Priestess wheels right around the *orchêstra* until line 19, where she needs to end up in a central position, with arms upraised.

The prayers to other gods in 21f. are more animated, and once again this is a sweeping sequence, written for maximum use of the performing space. The Priestess needs to end at 28 as far as possible from the doors (e.g. EFL), so that 29 can be used for a long and dignified cross up via C towards EBC. The last section of this can continue into 31–3 (these lines require a gesture to imaginary potential clients). Then 33 is played facing forwards, standing in front of the doors.

In 34f. the Priestess must get as far as possible away from the doors, and clearly the first four lines are designed to be delivered as she scuttles out (e.g. towards LC). Then 38 provides a pause for breath, after which she rises slowly to her feet in 39f. – the narrative which lays the foundation for the drama.[7] It gives us a picture of the deadlock which – as the Priestess herself makes plain in her parting remarks – Apollo will now have to transcend.

She moves to the *parodos* on a slightly oblique route at first, heading up towards the *skene* on 60–1 to keep the temple in focus, ready for the last two lines. (Not of course right to it: she is very wary of what might come out of the open doors!) Then she should head directly for the exit, delivering 62–3 from a position by the *parodos* at BL, facing forwards towards FR to reach as much of the audience as possible – but including a side-glance and gesture towards the *skene* doors, before she turns abruptly and escapes from the scene.

1(b). The opening lines seem to imply that Apollo and Orestes entered in mid-conversation. There are no parallels for this in surviving Greek tragedy, so some scholars have argued that Orestes' last lines should be transposed up to here, to supply

[7] Brief, agitated movements are appropriate for most of the section. However directors should not miss the touch of pedantry which overcomes the Priestess's terror in 48f., as she becomes engrossed in her narrative; it provides a moment of contrast before the build to the climax at 56.

something for Apollo to respond to. But 85f. are needed where they appear in the manuscripts. Lines 64f. play well if Orestes makes a terrified, fugitive entry, and Apollo follows calmly to reassure him. Orestes gradually gains the courage to draw closer (64–73), and perhaps even take a tentative glance back inside the *skene*, to satisfy himself that Apollo has indeed subdued his pursuers.

Lines 85f. show that Orestes is not wholly impressed with Apollo's hearty assurances – this is the key to the movement and gesture after 74. He can refuse to set on his way when urged, then disengage from the god and move away – forcing Apollo to play the rest of the speech almost trailing after Orestes, as an attempt to overcome reluctance and scepticism.[8]

An extra playing Hermes is undesirable, as his presence would pull focus from the slightly barbed interplay between Apollo and Orestes.[9] Lines 89f. play well if addressed to an invisible god: the confident circling movements needed to conjure him out of the air, and direct him towards Athens, give Apollo a chance to assert his possession of the space in front of his temple. This foreshadows his energetic response to the Furies in Scene 2.

1(c). Aischylos now completes a contrast between Apollo – Orestes' loyal, active and mobile defender – and the sluggish, at first immobile Furies whom the dream-image can arouse only slowly, for all the plangency of her pathos-laden movements and appeals.

This sub-scene demands an extensive use of the *orchêstra*. The dream-image must first establish her relationship with the *skene* doorway soon after her entrance, perhaps circling round via FR to C to EBC during the build-up to the first climax at 104. But she can and should play 105–9 'out', facing towards the audience, detached from a literal relationship with the place where the Furies are.

After the Furies have begun to respond,[10] the dream-image

---

[8] A degree of tension between Orestes and his divine advocate can also be used in the trial scene, to make theatre sense of 609f.

[9] Hermes was normally invisible to human beings (cf. *LB* 818). It would also look strange if Orestes left Delphi escorted by a visible Hermes, and arrived at Athens without one.

[10] The directions for their moaning and groaning appear in the Greek text exactly as translated; they are among the very few stage-directions preserved in

increases the pressure of her rhetoric (with its remarkable combination of abuse and invocation). Here space is needed to establish by theatre metaphor the gulf between their inaction and her need. Accordingly in our production the dream-image came forward at 121, and once again addressed her reproaches to them from the front; she did not return to the rear half of the *orchêstra* until the climax at 129. Then she was close to the doors for the plangent apostrophe at 131f., and retreated from them only during 137–9.

Choros 1

Since the Choros entered individually, presumably they sung at least the first few stanzas as solos. The structure of the song reflects this. It is a powerful, straightforward choros which sets out in alternation in the first four stanzas both their anger against Apollo (A1, B1) and their justified complaint against him (A2, B2). Then the Furies settle down in the C stanzas, now that they are all in the *orchêstra*, to sing first exactly what, in their eyes, he has done wrong and then how committed they are to dealing with it.

In our production the choreography was a series of complex, hunting and circling patterns generated by each individual entry, with the choros gradually moving during the B stanzas towards formation into one unit, so that the C stanzas could be delivered in unison as a direct attacking address from the centre-line towards the *skene* building – almost as if challenging Apollo to dare to come out.

Scene 2

Apollo picks up the cue, and a powerful adversative scene follows, designed to set up in advance a contrast with Athena's reception of the Furies in Scene 4.

Simple images of the contending parties now start to be undermined. The god of reason deploys a highly emotive argument, while the goddesses who so far have seemed to be

our manuscripts. Though it is doubtful whether they go back to Aischylos himself, there is no reason to doubt the basic sequence and build-up of sound effects which these notations imply. Taplin 1977b, 122–3.

nothing but angry feeling give lucid, logical responses, which they present with courtesy and dignity. By the end the situation is deadlocked: Apollo has accused the Furies of inconsistency in the case of Orestes, and the Furies have accused him in return of exceeding his proper powers. Both are right.

This short but complex scene divides into five beats, requiring up to 45 separate moves to realize its ebb and flow effectively in performance.

First beat: 179–84. Apollo threatens the Furies, in an attempt to drive them from his temple. Here Apollo takes the lead, brandishing his bow vigorously, disrupting the pattern of the Furies, going close to several of them in turn and finally threatening one of them at close range with his bow.

Second beat: 185–97. Since the Furies have not been intimidated, Apollo tries to persuade them instead, but cannot maintain the calm which this requires, and returns to threats. Apollo's bluff has been called, and he resorts to aggressively vivid rhetoric (to 190). The rest of the speech demands a continuous sequence of movements, less violent in the quieter central section 190–5, but then suddenly bursting out in a new threat in 196–7.

Third beat: 198–212. The Furies begin a measured verbal response, gently advancing towards him and forcing him by 209 to retreat, to reinforce his irony by distance.

Fourth beat: 213–24. Apollo breaks out of the *stichomythia* with a new outburst of rhetoric – with wide, sweeping movements away from them, to give the speech room to flow – and ends by a disdainful turn on 224.

Fifth beat: 225–34. Apollo has proved to his own satisfaction that they are wrong, and confidently abandons the argument. The Furies make their own equally uncompromising position clear before they leave – forcing their attention on a reluctant Apollo in the *stichomythia*, and then suddenly breaking formation at 230, moving swiftly to the mouth of the *parodos*, facing Apollo from there for the last six words of 231, and then leaving rapidly in hunting posture. (To match this, Apollo too leaves suddenly after his own last words.)

Scene 3

The exit of the choros of Furies begins the scene change from Delphi to Athens. The *skene* doors are closed for the last time, and the change is completed by adding a prop which pulls the focus forward, away from the *skene*: the image of Athena. Since Orestes takes his refuge at this image, and the Furies then sing and dance their longest and most powerful ode (Choros 3) circling around him as he crouches there, the obvious and right place for it is at the centre of the *orchêstra*; like the grave of Agamemnon in *Libation Bearers*, this prop becomes the focal point for the action.[11]

Eumenides now overtly becomes a suppliant drama, a drama in which one character takes refuge at the image of a god in a foreign land, and begs the inhabitants for refuge and deliverance, while others come and demand that the suppliant be handed over to them at once. The dramatic issue then becomes whether the reluctant host country can resolve the dilemma without suffering harm.

The act of arriving as a suppliant, and the bond established between receiver and received, were fundamental institutions in Greek society. The right to protection was guaranteed by Zeus himself; to grant or withold it could literally make the difference between life and death.[12]

Orestes' first speech is a re-creation of *LB* Scene 1. It needs to be played as the fulfilment of an act of ritual, with Orestes standing reverently – or even kneeling – at the perimeter, as soon as he enters Athena's sanctuary, to deliver the first two lines; then gradually circling around the image (e.g. to BL) before finally moving in, on 241, to take up his refuge there.

The Furies are trying to follow the scent of Orestes' 'dripping

---

[11] Some commentators (e.g. Sommerstein 1989, 123–4) place it up-*orchêstra*, in front of the doors. This is of course theatrically weak (cf. Rehm 1992, 157). Unless the image is gigantic – as in Hall's production – there are no real difficulties in blocking the trial scene and finale with a central image. (It could even be removed, and replaced by the props for the voting, at the start of Scene 5; but this is unlikely, since 1024 probably implies that the Women and Girls of Athens take the image with them in procession at the end of the drama.)

[12] Several of the surviving tragedies are focussed around an act of supplication (Aischylos, *Suppliants, Eumenides*; Sophokles, *Oidipous at Kolonos*; Euripides, *Suppliants, Children of Herakles*), and many others make substantial use of it. Cf. Lattimore 1964, 46f.

blood' like tracking dogs. Their heads are lowered almost to the ground, and there is tragi-comic point (matching the bleak humour of 250–1) in the fact that they are now so exhausted that they do not see him until after they have all come into the *orchêstra*.

Aischylos clearly intended them to enter slowly, dividing into two groups led by the two speakers in 244f.; six Furies go in the direction Orestes actually went, via EBC towards BL.; the other group curves forward, so exhausted they have lost the track and can only smell that Orestes is somewhere near.

Choros 2 is a short, violent one-stanza lyric, inserted into the course of the scene, like *LB* Choros 2, to crystallize and give expression to a particular moment of extreme emotion. In performance it profits from being divided between many choros members. To match the development of the text, the choreography needs to be a sequence in which the Furies gradually close in on Orestes, and surround him more and more closely as they advance (from 261), becoming both more menacing and more solemn as they reach 269f.

Orestes' increasing confidence can be shown simply, by having him first stand up and answer them – and then break out forwards through them, away from literal reliance on the protection of the image, at 278f. This forces the Furies to turn and face him, as he now takes control of the events – following the plan which Loxias ordained.

After refuting their claim that he is still polluted, Orestes addresses a long-distance prayer to Athena herself. This sub-section can only be played properly if Orestes has now left the image – he must be at a distance from it to make the prayer. Since Athena is away from Athens, and will arrive for the next scene by the R *parodos*, it makes theatre sense if Orestes, after addressing the Furies at 280f., begins at 286f. from LC, facing towards the image, and beyond it towards that *parodos*. Then he needs, for 291f., to move a little in the direction of the rear section of the *orchêstra*,[13] to illuminate the broad sweep of his prayer. Finally the Furies rise up during 299f., threaten him, and drive him back to his original place beside the image.

---

[13] Not the front, since it is not possible to focus a speech on a *parodos* from there.

Choros 3

The Furies possess the playing space completely for the first time; they are assembled around Orestes as he crouches at the altar. And the ode is very different in tone from their first two short, violent choroses. Aischylos is preparing for the volte-face of 415f., where Athena, by making an issue of their claim to be fair (312), talks them out of an absolute stance (427, 429); and beyond that for the resolution in the Finale, where these Furies, who now seem to be so sinister and so threatening, turn out to be valuable, and needed by any society which seeks to be healthy.

Dance and song therefore need to establish a fine balance in this choros. The movement may be as menacing as the choreographer can devise and the actors execute; it can be used, together with the visual appearance of the Furies, to impress upon the audience the terrible powers which they possess; but there is a strong case for making their music a lyrical composition which brings out the solemn, proud and dignified aspects of the Furies – those which evoke awe rather than terror.

To establish the air of ritual solemnity which the 'binding song' requires, Aischylos supplied it with a substantial chanted introduction. Then there are four strophic pairs, of which the first three have a refrain, a mesode separating the strophe and antistrophe. The refrain of the first pair, the actual 'Song of the Furies', is repeated after the strophic pair for intensified effect.

The implications for the choreography are important. The fourteen-line introduction is 'cued' by 307 in a way rare in Greek tragedy: the Furies plainly use the introduction to form up into a circle around Orestes, and the text implies that during the stanza the circle closes inwards towards Orestes. Then the song proper begins. The singular forms in A1, A2, B1, B1a and C1a strongly suggest that to sing and dance some or all of these twelve stanzas individual Furies broke away, out and around the formation.

Scene 4

This is the crucial scene, in which the Furies alter their position. It also lays out the final tragic dilemma of this trilogy, the dilemma which now devolves upon the Athenians. So far the Furies have been uncompromising. Orestes has undeniably murdered his mother, and must therefore suffer at their hands (210f., 360f.). But when they meet Athena, they enter into a dialogue with her which closely resembles an Athenian magistrate's 'preliminary investigation'; and at 435 they turn the case over to her for decision.

Athena speaks for eight lines without noticing the Furies.[14] This implies that they withdrew into the left segment of the *orchêstra* in reverence and respect when they saw her arrive; also that Athena should be characterized at the outset as regally single-minded, intent only on one thing at a time. She begins to speak to Orestes the moment she enters the playing area, and does not stop to draw breath until after 404.

To make her failure to see the Furies plausible, and create good positions for the ensuing interaction with them, we found it best to have Athena wheel round from BR towards FC in a continuous sweep, nominally addressing Orestes but in reality, after the very first line or two, turning outward to play the rest of the section towards the audience. Then before 406 she makes her first pause, to take the measure of the newcomers. At 410f. she quietly comes closer to the Furies and inspects them; at the end of 412 she perhaps suppresses an instinct to draw back.

In rich but economical language Aischylos establishes an immediate reciprocity between the Furies and Athena. Unlike Apollo, she restrains herself from voicing her repugnance on seeing them, and treats them with the full courtesy due to *xenoi*. So they interact with her at once. But when she learns about their mission, it seems to her to be far too absolute. She rightly detects evasion and one-sidedness in their responses at 425f.; and she upsets the Furies with her reproach at 430.

Athena like them is wise, female and courteous. She is worthy of their respect and trust, and comes from a worthy lineage (435), so they have full confidence that she too will be fair. Nor does it yet occur to them that a just decision in the case of Orestes could possibly go against them. And so they yield the decision to her.

Lines 415f. precipitate a *stichomythia*, which must be blocked in visible contrast to that in Scene 2: the resolution of the drama's dilemmas depends on the contrast between Athena's courtesy,

[14] At the opening of the scene a line (405: 'yoking this chariot to powerful horses') appears in the manuscripts. It was clearly composed for a later production, as an addition to 404, so that Athena could make her entry by chariot. In Aischylos' production she entered on foot, perhaps miming the movement of the aigis; see Taplin (1977a, 388–90) against Hammond (1972, 440) and Podlecki (1989, 164).

and refusal to make hasty judgements, and Apollo's partisan hostility. The give and take can be shown if the Furies pass the role of spokesperson only between two or three individuals, and remain in one, non-adversative pattern (e.g. a loose ellipse), and Athena generally avoids violent movements and disruptions of that pattern.[15]

After 445, the blocking must show how Orestes' speech involves Athena gradually in a complex dilemma. Orestes begins the speech hesitantly, fixed to one point (e.g., just in front of the image at FC). But he turns suddenly at 454 to involve Athena closely in what he is saying, coming much closer to her and perhaps even – if the production concept permits it – drawing her aside into the R segment, away from the Furies, catching her up in his enthusiasm as he names his father; only to blight the picture, and place her in a dilemma, at 458f.

The open admission delights the Furies. It is also the cue for Athena to disengage increasingly from him – ready to pause, and go to the centre before 470f., to convey the gravity of the situation. Orestes will be to her right, and the Furies to her left, if she delivers this speech from just in front of the image, symbolizing directly and effectively how she is trapped in the middle between the two sides; this also prefigures the arrangement of the participants when the trial begins.

Athena should probably not move in this speech, after finally disengaging from Orestes during the first three lines, until she has completed the exposition of her dilemma at 482. After that, she moves decisively, to show that she has found a solution; 483f. is a long exit cue, perhaps best played with some of the lines (the last four, or just the last two?) delivered after turning back towards the contending parties, from just beside the mouth of the *parodos*, before she turns away again and leaves.

[15] From 426 to 430 the prospect of open antagonism threatens ever more strongly. One effective way of staging this crisis is for the Furies to almost break off the dialogue after 427, and turn away angrily, back to BL. One Fury then returns more aggressively towards Athena on 429; the goddess then manages to detain this one close to herself at FC, and negotiates the final settlement with her – after which the Fury withdraws again, to join the rest at FL.

Choros 4

The Furies now realize that in a court of law it is possible to lose a case. But they cannot seriously imagine this happening to them in the case of Orestes, so to show how far-fetched that would be they picture for the audience what would happen if they were defeated (A1–B1). Then (B2–C2) they proceed to supplement the account in Choros 3, telling us how useful they, and the values which they enforce, are to individuals and to society.[16] Finally they revert to the power they have to destroy the wicked, closing the ode in the D stanzas with a direct and terrifying attack on people like Orestes.

The second section of this ode is one of the most wide-ranging portions of the drama. It refers back to Ag Choroses 2 and 3: the goddesses of the underworld confirm all that the Elders feared about the dangers of impiety and violence, and they use the same imagery (NB especially 537f.). Even more importantly, the Furies' picture of their own role prepares for the final resolution of their conflict with the Athenians, through the parallel between their values and Athena's ideal for the Areopagos, which like the Furies will provide the essential element of fear in individual and *polis*.[17]

In choreography and music, this ode must begin to foreshadow the harmonious patterns which will dominate the concluding part of the Finale. The Furies' movements – in our production, sinister, complex but steady circling patterns which gradually became more stately to match the developing mood of the C stanzas – at first bypass Orestes almost completely. Abandoned to a degree of independence at EFR, he was then suddenly and almost imperceptibly drawn back in towards the image, to become the centre of the circular dances in the C stanzas. And even after his return to the centre he was ignored, as the patterns continued to flow away from him, out to the perimeter, to match the way the text is directed outwards as well.

Then, shockingly, the Furies revert in the D stanzas to savagery, perhaps even suddenly turning on Orestes, pursuing and surrounding him at the rear of the *orchêstra*, so absorbed in their

[16] The fact that the transition is made in the middle of a strophic pair shows how closely the first and second parts of the ode are connected.

[17] Lines 681f. For the 'silent guardian' (518) Aischylos used in Greek the technical term employed at Athens to describe the role of the Areopagos.

persecution that only Athena's re-entry into the playing space to begin the trial rescues him.

Scene 5

Preliminaries

The text does not support the suggestion that a Herald actually entered the playing area; but equally, there is no reason why the trumpeter should not have been visible to some, if not all, of the spectators. He probably came up to the mouth of the left *parodos* before 570, and sounded his fanfare to summon the jurors before 570 and/or immediately after 573.

Each juror[18] has two pebbles, one black and one white. Some of them must bring benches to sit on, and others must bring two urns, one 'active' urn for the actual votes cast and another, 'passive' urn, into which each juror discards his unused pebble to maintain the privacy of his vote. A table, onto which the votes are counted, is also useful in production. The acquittal of Orestes is the climactic moment in the drama, so the props for the voting must be placed in a central position, i.e. just in front of the image of Athena.

The jurors must plainly take up a neutral position from which they can follow the arguments of Apollo and the Furies, without being visually predominant until they actually come to cast their votes. This position, in an arena staging, must be a portion of the perimeter. But which portion? Hammond[19] would arrange them round the rear semicircle, so they face towards the audience; this was actually done in the London production by Sir Peter Hall.

In the Greek theatre, characters often turn their backs while speaking to some of the audience, but never for very long, and they always avoid facing away from the bulk of the audience. Apollo and the Furies must clearly direct their arguments against each other and forwards towards the audience. If the jurors are at

---

[18] There were no extra citizens present apart from the jurors themselves; cf. Taplin 1977a, 394–5 (*pace* e.g. Melchinger 1979, 134–5). The 20m diameter *orchêstra* has very little room for movement in this scene even with only the 26 essential characters present; twelve choros members, three solo actors and eleven jurors.

[19] 1972, 441.

the back of the *orchêstra*, the litigants (and Athena) face away from them for most of the trial. This seems unnecessarily antirealistic and stylized: the closeness with which the jurors are involved in the trial scene (especially towards the climax, where the prosecution and defence subject them to bribes and threats) makes it preferable for them to be seated just in front of the first row of audience seats EFR–EFC–EFL, facing back across the *orchêstra* towards the *skene*.[20] Then the arguments, and the 'foundation speech', can make their full impact simultaneously on the jurors and the audience.

Placing the jurors at the front for the trial also helps with the Finale. They are, so to speak, protected during the trial itself by the comforting presence of thousands of fellow-Athenians above and behind them. If they do not resume their seats after voting, but stand towards the back of the *orchêstra*, the blocking then captures their isolation when they and their goddess must face the anger of the Furies alone.

Apollo's Entry

Apollo's appearance is abrupt, unannounced, and disruptive. Entrances in the Greek theatre were invariably significant, conspicuous, and marked in the words. Apollo's sudden appearance here (like his even more sudden exit after the verdict) is unparalleled. It can be made to work today;[21] but it remains a breach of Greek dramatic convention. Taplin may even be right to suspect that some lines have been lost from the text before 574.[22]

The Prosecution

The positions at 582 are virtually dictated by the text.[23] Athena

[20] Cf. Pickard-Cambridge 1968, 46.

[21] For example with a reprise of his music, after the fanfare and some entry music for the jurors, to mark his entrance.

[22] 1977a, 395ff. He favours assigning 574–5 to Athena (so also Sommerstein 1989, 189–90). This would establish a curtness, verging on hostility, between the two Olympians much too early in the scene. Spoken by one of the Furies, the lines play perfectly as an angry challenge to Apollo.

[23] The democratic nature of the Athenian scenes can still be disregarded. Two productions, in Christchurch and Sydney, placed both Athena and Apollo on the

must be C, by or behind the urns and voting table, Orestes between FR and R, and the Furies in a group FL to L. Apollo first goes near to Orestes for 579, and then crosses to a position nearer Athena, at BR. The cross-examination of Orestes then becomes a perfect example of adversative *stichomythia*; he will step towards the Furies boldly on 588 (arriving near FC); but then they advance towards him one by one, attacking with ever-increasing vehemence and competence on each successive line. Eventually they surround him on three sides, so that finally at 609 Orestes beats a hasty retreat FR, turning to Apollo for assistance.

Apollo magisterially brushes Orestes aside, ignores the Furies, and steps in front of them to a point FC from which he can address the jury as co-defendant. From here Apollo attempts to dominate the trial, moving around freely in front of the jury, over most of the front half of the *orchêstra*, to add force to his arguments.

The Defence

The Furies will have retreated to L/BL, to hear the god do his best. With three perfectly phrased, deferential interventions they provoke Apollo into putting forward more and more flamboyant, increasingly less-convincing arguments. Each intervention should be played by an individual emerging from the group, coming forward behind Apollo's back, as he attempts to dominate the jury by commanding the sweep from EFL via EFC to EFR. This forces him to round on each of them, and now his possession of the front of the *orchêstra* is a hindrance rather than a help. He is trapped between the Furies and the jury, and has to swing right round from one to the other; this brings out the bluster which is very obviously one aspect of his text in this scene.

Equally clearly the issues in the trial are serious, and are intended to be taken seriously. These four speeches present the clinching arguments in Orestes' defence, and they will secure the freedom from pursuit which Apollo had promised Orestes before he did the deed. However, they are not decisive arguments for

---

roof of the *skene* for the rest of the drama, as if they as Olympians can talk down to the Furies and the human beings. This completely misunderstands the relationship between the four characters (especially in implying that Apollo has as much power and authority as Athena), as well as inflicting a static blocking which cannot do justice to the ebb and flow of the trial and the Finale.

matricide; *pace* Apollo, nothing could vindicate the son who had to take his loyalty to one parent to the extreme of murdering the other. Apollo's sophistry, evasiveness, specious rhetoric and final resort to bribery are designed to make us realize this. Since the verdict will show that the jurors appreciate this fact, no actor can succeed if he either plays Apollo's arguments totally straight or sends them up. Productions must reflect the double focus, showing how at the crux the key elements in the defence of Orestes are both significant and sophistic.

Apollo's opening moves are impressive; but as he plays 619f., the actor must bring out the fact that Zeus' commands are not a powerful point of *law* at all, but a barely concealed reminder that 'might is right' – followed in Apollo's second speech by a highly emotive appeal to the juror's male prejudices (631f.).

The Furies let that pass, but question Zeus' consistency. This evokes a furious, exasperated diatribe from Apollo (644f.), and their counter-argument shows that they have trapped him (652f.).

Apollo now (perhaps with difficulty?) recovers his cool tone. He is certain he can meet this new challenge head on, and he proceeds to his final demonstration (658f.), an argument which accords with some contemporary medical and philosophical speculations, and would therefore have possessed some credibility. But even for the Athenians, whose culture had a heavy bias towards the male, there is an air of sophistry about it;[24] and this feeling is violently reinforced when, to support his case, Apollo produces Athena – who is still in a dominant but relatively passive position, perhaps at BC – as evidence like a rabbit from a hat (in our production she made her disapproval very clear). He then proceeds, with hardly a pause for breath, to come in close to her and urge all the advantages which Athens stands to gain if Orestes is acquitted.[25]

No convincing argument can be made for claiming that one parent is more 'true' than the other. Feminism gives no more justification to Klytaimestra's claim on Orestes than Apollo's theory gives to Agamemnon's. It takes two people to make a baby,

[24] For a balanced discussion see Sommerstein 1989, 207–8. Cf. Rehm 1992, 104–5.

[25] During the last part of this speech he moves near to Orestes at 671f., to exhibit him too as part of the flow of the rhetoric, before finally retreating almost to BR again. The Furies will then move forward a little for 679–80, before they take up a position matching his, at BCL.

and circumstances, or social priorities, can only create a preference in one direction or the other. In the ultimate reckoning, even Zeus and Apollo have been obliged to show simple masculist bias, and no universal solution to the predicament which Orestes' deed has created is possible.

However, this does not mean that a fair and appropriate verdict cannot be reached. Orestes had to make an impossible choice. His was a special predicament, and it is matched by the specialness of his judges. He stands before a court composed of goddess and men combined, and Athena herself is unique in a way which is directly relevant to the case. She was the virgin daughter of Zeus, sprung from his head and not delivered from the womb of a goddess, let alone that of a woman. In a conflict, she may well feel even more favour for the father's side than for that of her own sex; Apollo was presumably well aware of this, when he dispatched his suppliant to her city.

The Foundation Speech

Just before the climactic deed, Athena displays the insight which will make us understand its consequences.[26] Kassandra's prophecy of the return of Orestes undermined Agamemnon's murderess, and Klytaimestra's twice-repeated threat that her Furies will hound him blighted Orestes' vengeance. The dramatic structure of *Eumenides* has now reached a position parallel to that when Kassandra's prophecy and Klytaimestra's threat were spoken, for the casting of the votes is the climactic moment of choice and action in this drama. However, in the third drama a hope for the future appears instead. Athena's speech shows that, although she is Apollo's sister and shares his preference for the male, she is in far deeper ways aligned with the values of the Furies

[26] Athena does not set down laws of procedure, as promised at 571f.; witnesses are not called and registered, and the jurors do not swear their oath of office. This led Taplin (1977a, 395ff.) to suspect corruption and omissions in the surviving text at the beginning of the scene; he revives as a partial remedy Kirchoff's idea of transposing 681f. to the opening of the trial. Most of these difficulties are more apparent in the study than the theatre. Since this is an image of a trial created in a drama, Aischylos was not obliged to show every formal procedure of real trials. The foundation-speech is in the right place: it creates a dramatic pause to separate the argument between the two sides from the voting and the climax.

(cf. esp. 517f.). This common ground extends to the audience the hope that their goddess may be able to placate the Furies, if they are defeated in the trial.

Athena also engages with the issues which had convulsed her city in 461, when Perikles' political mentor Ephialtes was assassinated during their campaign to reform the Areopagos, limiting its jurisdiction to cases of homicide and enlarging its membership. *Eumenides* reflects the extreme polarization between oligarchs and democrats in the year of performance; both here and in the Finale Aischylos warns all his fellow-citizens against the danger that excess may lead to civil war, and clearly advises that strengths like those of the Areopagos must be conserved.[27]

The speech plays best if delivered from FC. In a similar manner to the Furies in Choroses 2 and 3, Athena is pitching her remarks past the litigants and almost literally over the heads of the jurors to Aischylos' audience, in preparation for the second half of the Finale, which will bind the Athenians of the present into a deep relationship with these events from their past.

The Voting

Despite their element of sophistry, Apollo's arguments have seemed to make Orestes deserve victory, though the Furies' cross-examination has also been cogent. The dominant feeling is that Orestes will be acquitted; but by now the design of the scene has almost totally counterbalanced that feeling. In Athenian courts, the material consequences of acquittal or condemnation were almost always brought out openly; and in Orestes' case these, too, are evenly balanced. Apollo, with prophetic authority, has promised a permanent alliance with Argos; the Athenian audience would expect the jurors to weigh the benefits of this against the Furies' threat to blight their land.

An intense controversy has raged over the voting. Attempts

---

[27] Aischylos clearly approved of the more democratic alliance with Argos against the conservatives (see below); it is less likely (despite the powerful advocacy of Forrest 1966, 215) that Athena's words endorse the domestic reforms sought by the extreme democrats. Cf. Lloyd-Jones (1979, 75–7), Podlecki (1966, 80–100; 1989, 17–21) and Sommerstein (1989, 31–2).

have been made to suggest that there was an even number of human jurors, whose votes were evenly divided, and Athena's was a casting vote which breaks their deadlock.[28] This view creates difficulties on every level; language, performance and interpretation.

The Greek text of 734–5 cannot be distorted into having Athena say she will give either a non-voting decision or a casting vote; and Aischylos is careful never to say that she holds a position, such as court president, which might debar her from making an actual vote. The language clearly implies that Athena is a member of the jury.

In performance, the couplets 711f. begin as intimidatory remarks. Apollo steps forward a little from R towards the FC/C axis, and the Furies from L/BL, to deliver the opening couplets at the jurors as they file back one by one between the contending parties to C to vote. (They then rapidly turn to mutual recriminations, hurled over the jurors' heads.) Given the way in which actions are matched as far as possible to words in the Greek theatre, it is almost irresistible to conclude that one juror votes during each of the eleven couplets. A longer, three-line speech of the Furies then covers the additional time required when Athena returns from FC to her original position at BC, and shows that she too is going to vote. Either she places her white pebble in the urn at 735, or (better!) she exhibits it at 735, and casts it finally with a flourish on 740. After that she must step back, so the selected jurors can come forward to empty the urns.

At 742–3 she orders that the votes be taken out of the urns, and at 748f. the words of Apollo indicate that the votes are being counted. Athena has already announced at 741 that should the votes be equal, Orestes will be freed. The result of the counting is still unknown at 751, but then at 752–3 Athena announces that the votes are now found to be equal and (therefore) Orestes is free. The implication is clearly that Athena is the last to vote of twelve jurors. She has cast her vote by 740 at latest; the votes are counted out between 742 and 752, and at that point they are seen to have been equally divided, 6–6. During this section the issues are fully polarized in a short, tense four-line 1–1 *stichomythia* between

---

[28] Cf. especially Hester (1981) and Conacher (1987, 164–70). For additional arguments against the 'casting vote' see Kitto (1956, 65ff.), Vernant (1981, 10 n. 3, 23f.) and Sommerstein (1989, 222ff.).

Orestes and two of the Furies. The extreme suspense is intensified if the jurors who count the votes show black and white pebbles alternately, until finally, after Apollo (still BR) has begged for care, the last pebble appears, and is added to make the white pile equal with the black.

Line 741 has nothing to do with Athena's announcement of how she is to vote. This is the first time the court has ever sat, and it would clearly be dramatically absurd if, on arriving at the declaration of 753, the participants were convulsed by argument as to what verdict an equal vote was to be held to indicate. Athena here lays down in advance the required procedural rule, which is of course that later followed at Athens.[29] By that miraculous conjunction of prediction or expectation and succeeding event with which the trilogy has familiarized us ever since *Ag* Scene 1, the contingency envisaged by 741 in fact occurs at 752. Apollo, god of prophecy, was right when he pleaded for careful counting at 751. One vote *does* save the house.

The verdict therefore falls between the two alternatives rejected at the end of Scene 4 (471f.): for the case of Orestes to be judged by humans alone, which would be an unexplained human verdict; or for it to be decided by Athena alone, which would be an arbitrary divine decision. We are given a collective decision by Athens, in which Athena's vote is explained because it turns out to be decisive, since the human jurors have found 6–5 in favour of the Furies. Facing up to the fundamental issues of the drama, she aligns herself with, and accepts the arguments of, Apollo (739–40). Athena's vote has converted a verdict against Orestes into a technical acquittal, giving Orestes the benefit not of the doubt but of the deadlock.

The result precisely mirrors Orestes' position now. He deserves to be freed, but not vindicated.[30] Apollo wins no victory: a majority of the human jurors found in favour of the Furies' view that Orestes, since he murdered his mother Klytaimestra, deserves to be punished for it; the verdict of the court as a whole is therefore precisely equitable.

---

[29] Aristotle *Athenian Constitution* 69.1.
[30] If he was, Athena could not later placate the Furies in the terms which she uses at 794f.

After the Verdict

The anger of the Furies is so great that they say nothing.[31] Even more extraordinarily, Apollo (it would appear) leaves the playing area in silence at this point. Like his unannounced entry, his sudden exit, presumably at the end of 753, is totally unparalleled. A formal mime of curt, abrupt farewell will yield a smooth departure in the modern theatre; but if the text is sound it will show Aischylos' strikingly experimental way of conveying how Apollo's whole purpose and function in the trilogy vanish as soon as he has achieved his aim.[32]

These moves leave the main focus on Orestes, who must now be written out of the drama, to clear the *orchêstra* for the final confrontation. Orestes first thanks his saviours, and then inaugurates (762f.) an alliance with Argos (cf. 289f., 670f.). These words refer forward from the world of the drama to the thirty-year treaty with Argos which the Athenians had signed in 461 BC, signalling a major shift in foreign policy away from alignment with Sparta and its allies towards more liberal and democratic policies, which had led in 459 to the outbreak of the First Peloponnesian War.[33]

The playing style must match the mood of 'secure strength and confident elation.'[34] Clearly Orestes approaches Athena on the first two and a half lines; but the rhetoric then opens up, and he can face forward from 756–61, and range around the FR segment of the *orchêstra*. The second section from 762 needs to be played facing back towards Athena and the Athenians, who are now somewhere near the perimeter EBR to EBL. Then the last three lines will be delivered from EBR before a crisp, sudden departure.

[31] In our production they wheeled away and collapsed into a threatening, motionless heap at BL, gathering their powers ready for the onslaught which will begin the Finale.

[32] Taplin 1978, 39: 'His partial vision of the place of the Furies, his low abuse and tricky rhetoric at the trial – these might be taken to reduce [Apollo's] stature low enough for Aeschylus to push him from the stage without any attempt to justify him or to integrate him in the final scheme of things.' True (cf. also Neuburg 1981, 55); but is this enough to explain such a remarkable breach of convention?

[33] Thucydides 1.102. Cf. Sommerstein 1989, 26ff.; Podlecki 1989, 19–20.

[34] Taplin 1977a, 402.

Finale

The emotions unleashed by the judgement must be discharged. After the spoken arguments of the trial scene, the *orchêstra* is once again filled with vigorous dance and song. Aischylos contrasts the close of the whole trilogy in three ways with the bitter outcome of *Agamemnon*: a confrontation between lone protagonist and hostile choros (cf. *Ag* Scene 7) now ends not in exhausted bitterness but in ecstatic resolution; extras enter to bring not male violence but female gifts of honour; and crimson fabrics are used not recklessly to honour one man, but in proper moderation to honour gods.

In their resentment, the Furies revert temporarily to the imagery, and the vehemence, with which they complained at Delphi about Apollo. Once again their 'ancient laws' have been 'overriden' by the younger gods. They are the senior, and they have been 'dishonoured' (780, etc.).

Or so we say, since it is hard to give adequate English expression to the Greek concept of *timê*, which dominates the closing section of the trilogy.[35] 'Honour', 'dignity' and even oriental 'face' are abstract and intangible. *Timê* was not; and it was central to Greek values, since it was essential to self-respect and even to existence. The possessions and rights which give tangible, visible expression to status and prestige in modern society were for the Greeks themselves a part of *timê*. To be deprived of your appropriate degree of *timê* is to be without all that we commend by the separate ideas of respect, status, credibility, material possessions and a defined function and role in society.

Athena counters their feeling from two directions. First she turns to the past (793f.); then she turns to the future, offering them a positive *timê* at Athens to make up for their injuries, both real and imagined. At last, for the first time in the trilogy, here is a clash of perspectives which can be resolved. The Furies' felt injuries belong entirely to the past; for the future, Athena promises them a *timê* which will be self-increasing. If they come into residence at Athens, as their powers help the Athenians to become more prosperous, the Athenians will be able to pay them in return more *timê*.

[35] Ewans 1971, 202ff. Cf. Macleod (1982, 138ff.) and Ewans (1982b, 233ff.)

As she proceeds with her task, Athena unfolds aspects of her city and its action which make plain that they do not deserve any retribution; and in doing this she takes up once again the ideals of the foundation speech, and shows how greatly her city values the Furies' own most fundamental concerns. From negative to positive, from past to future, gradually Athena comes to establish a concord of mutual respect between herself and the Furies. This takes time, persistence, and the help of the goddess Persuasion.[36]

Subtly, Athena returns to full female power. Persuasion is used without deception; and when the Furies yield, the drama flows into a coda of unrivalled lyric reciprocity and concord — for these goddesses are able to bestow a wealth of blessing on the Athenians in return for the residence and the *timê* which the Athenians offer them.

Female fertility and creativity, balked at the outset in Klytaimestra by the sacrifice of Iphigeneia, now come into their own to end the cycle. At last the balance is restored: male intellect has, in the outcome, secured only a token 'victory' by the acquittal of Orestes; and so the values of femininity can at last achieve that full strength, both intellectual and emotional, which has been their due ever since Aischylos' cogent, deeply etched portraits of Klytaimestra, Kassandra and Elektra. The Furies, being goddesses of the earth, are powers of fecundity. In their concord with the Athenians a true harmony will be reached, in which the images of creation and generation, so often perverted into metaphors of violence in *Agamemnon* and *Libation Bearers*, at last regain their literal force. Crimson robes now become a symbol not of bloodshed but of integration and acceptance; and blazing light signals a victory which will bring no consequent destruction.

As the Finale opens, the Furies sing violent, multiply divided lyrics (in the dochmiac metre in the original) against Athena's calmly spoken persuasion; and Aischylos marks their unique position here with a unique device. They repeat both their first lyric outburst and their second *verbatim*; and this seems to symbolize the absolute sterility of their anger, in contrast with the consistency of Athena's patience and persistence as she first balances past with future, and then turns in the third and fourth speeches entirely away from the past. But here our loss of the original music and choreography are even more damaging than

---

[36] Cf. Buxton 1982, 105ff.

elsewhere, for perhaps in the interaction between his three media Aischylos was able to communicate both the static, backward- and inward-looking character of their anger, and the underlying aspects of their nature which will soon make the resolution of the trilogy's last conflict possible.

These lyrics are structured in the form of an arch. The Furies rise up into their attack over the first three lines, and the song reaches a pitch of expressionist intensity at 784f. But then, over the last five lines, the Furies turn from attack and rage to introspection; and the last three lines can be played as a quiet collapse back into despair. It is essential for the music and dance to capture this sequence, partly because the Furies must not be reduced to simple caricatures of monstrous demons, but also because below the Furies' anger lies a real grief. The basis for a settlement is contained in this alteration of attitude.[37]

The movement in this first part of the Finale must reflect the ebb and flow of the Furies' attack and Athena's counter-balancing attempts to persuade them. It is of course possible for the Athenian jurors to simply stand helpless as well as silent, rooted to their positions throughout; but here movement by the jurors, responding to the power of the Furies' attack and the gradual success of Athena's persuasion, is invaluable. Their involved presence gives reality to Athena's repeated references to her countrymen and to her people. So in our production the Furies rose up from BL and drove Athena and the Athenians (cowering behind their goddess for protection) back into EBR/ERC; the Furies only fell away again towards the end of the first stanza, as they moved during the last few lines of the song into postures of grief (some kneeling, some drooping), scattered around the *orchêstra*.

Athena comes to C or FC as her first speech opens (the jurors can then also advance a little forward from the perimeter); the difficulty of her task is immediately conveyed by the total reprise of the Furies' rising up, then closing in (perhaps even closer to Athena, surrounding her and threatening to overwhelm her) before they once more pull back (819f.) and collapse into a freeze in postures of grief.

[37] The choreography must also reflect the fact that the metrical patterns of the first four stanzas are violently irregular, in designed contrast to 916f.

So Athena can and must begin again. Heavy weather must not be made of the veiled threat in 826f.; a relatively quiet, light tone allows for the contrasts which are needed between this speech and what precedes and follows. For Athena's Persuasion does not persuade. Twice she has emphasized that the trial was no defeat for the Furies – and even if they have been slighted, she and her city can make it up to them; but now they explode once again, into another paranoid, irrational outburst. This second onslaught is even more emotional than the first; the Furies do almost nothing but express the intensity of their suffering, in fragmentary, explosive individual outcries. Once again Athena and her citizens are thrust back to the perimeter, though this time not so much by the conscious efforts of the Furies (who are now wholly self-involved), but by their sheer terror in the face of the power of this music and dance.

There is a hope of resolution. The last three lines, though powerful and angry, are a solid, lucid summary of how the Furies feel; and they give Athena a point on which she can build. Determinedly ignoring the past, Athena turns to the future: she is going to make them replace one emotion with another. She now begins the attempt to link up the Furies with the Athenians and their land, associating herself closely with the Athenians in 852f., and gesturing vehemently towards the earthen floor of the *orchêstra* at 858f., as she confronts the Furies from in front of her Athenians, in what can be best played as an angry, passionate appeal.

There is still a reprise of the second outburst. Athena perhaps even mimes near-despair, turning away for a few moments from the scene of a conflict which threatens to become endless. After that she returns, and advances determinedly at 881f. upon the Furies (who remain in control of the whole central section of the *orchêstra*) – accompanied, of course, by the citizens.

This speech must be played with the utmost intensity. It is her last and most powerful attempt to use 'the glorious goddess of Persuasion' to win the Furies over. And finally, after the burning-out of their emotion in the reprise of the second furious lyric, they are ready to listen.[38] One by one the Furies come closer to Athena,

---

[38] The offer is strong and arresting ('part-owner' is not adequate as a translation of *gamoros* (890), with its overtones of a share for all time in the ancestral, original division of Athenian land).

and each of them makes a movement as she speaks her line. With these movements and a slow but vital change in body posture (on 900 and 902) they are preparing for – but not signalling fully in advance – the sudden outburst of ecstasy as they accept Athena's offer. The second and last part of the Finale begins at 916.

This is one of those passages where the modern instinct is to cut; but it must be resisted. The sheer vehemence of the dance and song of attack and fury in the first part demands that it be counterbalanced now, by the contrasting vigour and energy of the dance and song of love and benediction. Only in this way can the trilogy be ended, with enough dramatic time and space devoted to celebrating the concord between Athena from Olympos above, the Furies from the Night below, and the Athenians who own and inhabit this part of the earth. The *Oresteia* closes only when the image of this reciprocal and mutually favourable interaction is firmly established; Aischylos extends to his fellow-citizens the hope that it will be valid for the rest of time. The more the Athenians pay *timê* to their new foreign residents, the more the Furies will increase the power and prosperity of Athens; and as the Furies increase the prosperity of Athens, the more *timê* the Athenians will be able to pay them.

The Furies do not change their powers or their nature.[39] Just as Athena, the goddess of wisdom, can also bestow its opposite on mortals who offend her, so too the Furies, goddesses of blight, can also be goddesses of fecundity. That is what Athena begs them to confer, and that is what they give in the lyric final part of the drama. Their conversion from opponents of Athens to its closest allies is shown, characteristically for Aischylos, as a conversion not from anger to passivity but from active anger to active blessing.

In the Greek theatre there is one powerful way to convey this transformation. Here at the end of *Eumenides* the (probably) circular shape of the *orchêstra* finally becomes a metaphor which can be fully shared by the participants. Circularity symbolizes completeness, and so the Furies must become placed, as the last of

[39] Directors must not reveal some underlying goodness by visual means, as e.g. in John Bell's Sydney production of 1980, where the players removed their horrific masks early in this final section, to reveal the human faces underneath. On the contrary, it is insisted throughout the Finale that Athens welcomes the Furies precisely because of their terrible, punitive powers; cf. 930f., 950f., and especially 990f.

them move slowly and hesitantly towards Athena during the *stichomythia*, in such a way that they can suddenly and effortlessly complete a circle at 916. The citizens fall back, to watch in wonder the spectacle of the hideous Furies turned from their rage to graceful dances of invocation and incantation. If the jurors fall back into a pattern which is itself a segment of another circle, then after Athena has drawn them back into the action at 948f., to witness the Furies' conversion, a complete large circle can be formed in which Athena, the Furies and the citizens all take a part. In our production this was achieved at 968 – to be echoed, of course, at 989, and then reinforced by adding the Women and Girls of Athens to the pattern after 1003.

After B1 the Furies turn outward more and more to involve the audience. So too, Athena at 928f. addresses the citizens present in the *orchêstra*, but continues from 968 once again – as in the foundation speech – in a way which also invites playing out to the whole audience.

At 996 the drama enters its closing phase. The transition to departure should be marked by an acceleration of the musical tempo and an intensification of the dance in these last two stanzas; but by a fascinating strategy Aischylos takes Athena (whose utterances have since 928 risen to the intensity of chant)[40] back to spoken words for 1021f., her final speech of acceptance and farewell.

Headlam argued convincingly[41] that the end of the trilogy echoes the procession to the statue of Athena in the Panathenaic Festival, in which the Athenians were joined by resident aliens cloaked in crimson. Did Aischylos embellish the final moments with a crowd of extras (attendants, women, bearers of sacrificial animals [cf. 1007] and torchbearers) and a large supplementary choros of Athenian citizens to sing the final four stanzas and bring the drama to a close; or did the jurors themselves form the escort which accompanies the Furies to their new homes? The assumption has so invariably been in favour of Hollywood-scale extravaganza that Taplin[42] rightly protested against crowds of extras and additional singing citizens (but even he felt that the

---

[40] Perhaps in deliberate echo of *Ag* Scene 7; cf. Taplin 1977a, 328, 410.

[41] 1906, 268–77.

[42] 1977a, 410f.; cf. 1978, 39.

'sacrificial victims, flaming torches, red robes and female attendants' of the cult must be present for the final procession).

I doubt whether any animals appeared in the *orchêstra*;[43] first because animal behaviour in performance is unpredictable and distracting, and second because they would hardly have time to establish their presence before they are taken off for the sacrifice. Athena's whole chant 1003f. is anticipatory and prophetic, and the animals she refers to are to be imagined as waiting out of sight.

If no other people enter, the jurors must themselves clothe the Furies in the cloaks which denote their new status as resident aliens (and also perfectly symbolize their new role; the robes – the first *timê* to the Solemn Goddesses[44] – overlay but do not fully conceal the revolting faces and garments of the terrible Furies); some jurors would have to exit to fetch them. This is awkward and unsatisfactory. It is therefore better to have a modest number of women and girls (cf. 1025) arrive in procession, during 1003f. They will carry the robes, which they place around the Furies' shoulders after 1031 – and also torches, to make real in the theatre this final appearance of the image of light out of darkness which has permeated the trilogy.[45] The *orchêstra* is now full with concentric circles of dance and song radiating out from Athena at the centre.

The final procession is symmetrical. Athena (first, cf. 1003f.) and the eleven human jurors escort the twelve Solemn Goddesses. They form up and begin to leave during the B stanzas, followed by the singing supplementary *choros* of females.[46] Those who brought the cloaks in probably now carry out the image of Athena (see 1025); the rest bear torches in their hands.

---

[43] Sommerstein (1989, 275ff.) holds out for one black cow.
[44] This point is rightly stressed by Macleod (1982, 139).
[45] Cf. *LB* Scene 3 and notes; on the imagery see Peradotto 1964, 392–3.
[46] Probably costumed as priestesses of Athena Polias. Cf. Sommerstein, *ibid.*

GLOSSARY

Proper Names

Where other surviving narratives conflict with the *Oresteia*, this glossary presents only the version used by Aischylos.

ACHAIANS   Aischylos follows Homer in using Achaians as a synonym for Greeks, reflecting the Achaian pre-eminence, especially throughout the Peloponnese, in the time at which the dramas are set.

ACHERON   A river in the underworld.

AGAMEMNON   Son of Atreus, grandson of Pelops; joint ruler with Menelaos of Argos.

AIGEIAN SEA   Named after Aigeus, this sea divides mainland Greece from Asia Minor.

AIGEUS   An early king of Athens; father of Theseus.

AIGISTHOS   Thirteenth child of Thyestes; the only survivor of Atreus' massacre of Thyestes' children.

ALEXANDER   See PARIS.

ALTHAIA   Wife of Oineus and mother of Meleager. When Meleager was born, the Moirai prophesied that he would live no longer than a brand then burning on the fire; she snatched it from the flames and kept it. The adult Meleager quarrelled with Althaia's brothers, and killed them. In revenge she deliberately burnt the brand, and so killed her son.

AMAZONS   Warrior women from the Black Sea coast. They attacked Athens during the reign of Theseus, camped on the hill subsequently called the Areopagos, and sacrificed there to their patron god Ares. Theseus subsequently defeated them and married their queen.

APOLLO   Son of Zeus and Leto, and brother of Artemis; a major Greek god, worshipped especially at Delos and Delphi. God of archery (and so particularly able to protect his friends and send sudden death on his enemies); music and painting; purification from *miasma*; healing from disease; and prophecy.

ARACHNEION   See BEACONS.

AREOPAGOS   'Place of Ares': seat of Athens' aristocratic and most ancient court.

ARES   The god of war.

ARGOS   A principal city of the Peloponnese, royal residence of the descendants of Atreus and therefore the scene of the action in *Ag* and *LB*. *Eu* refers to the major shift in Athenian foreign policy in 462/1, when the Athenians broke with oligarchic Sparta and concluded a treaty with democratic Argos.

ARTEMIS   Sister of Apollo; a virgin goddess, imaged as a huntress, who protects wild creatures, especially young ones.

ASOPOS   See BEACONS.

ATHENA   Virgin goddess of wisdom, sprung fully armed from the head of her father Zeus. Patron goddess of Athens, and a major supporter of the Greeks in the Trojan War (cf. *Eu* 397f.).

ATHOS   See BEACONS.

ATREIDAI   The sons of Atreus, i.e., Agamemnon and Menelaos.

ATREUS   Father of Agamemnon and Menelaos. He avenged himself on Thyestes, who had seduced his wife and fraudulently claimed the kingship, by murdering Thyestes' children and serving their flesh and vitals to him at a banquet.

AULIS   A port on the coast of Boiotia, from which the Greeks sailed to Troy.

BAKCHANTES   See DIONYSOS.

BEACONS   Klytaimestra's relays started at Mt Ida near Troy and went (1) to the rock of Hermes, on Lemnos; (2) to Mt Athos, the easternmost promontory of Chalkidike; (3) to Mt Makistos on the island of Euboia; (4) to Mt Messapion, on the coast of Boiotia; (5) across the Asopos valley to Mt Kithairon; (6) to 'the mountain of the roving goats', probably on the island of Aigina; (7) across the Gulf of Saron, which separates Aigina from the Peloponnese, to Mt Arachneion between Epidauros and Argos.

CHALKIS   A town on the south-west coast of Euboia.

DAULIS   A small town in Phokis.

DELOS   An island in the Aigeian Sea; birthplace of Apollo.

DELPHI   A town in Phokis, on the slopes of Mt Parnassos, site of Apollo's principal oracle.

DELPHOS   Legendary eponymous king of Delphi.

DIONYSOS   Son of Zeus and Semele; god of ecstatic possession, fertility, and the life-force, both creative and destructive – especially as manifested through liquids, the sap of young trees, the blood of young animals and humans, and wine. His followers are called Bakchantes, after his cult-title Bakchos.

ELEKTRA   Second daughter of Agamemnon and Klytaimestra, sister of Iphigeneia and Orestes.

ERECTHEUS   One of the earliest kings of Athens.

EUMENIDES   'The Kindly Ones', a euphemistic name for the Furies.

EURIPOS   The strait dividing Euboia from the mainland.

FATES   See *moira*/Moirai.

FURIES   Female *daimones* of the underworld (Gk 'Erinyes'), who spring from the spilt blood of murder victims and pursue vengeance – normally working through natural forces (e.g. inflicting madness or disease), or spurring on the conscience of the nearest male relative until he acts as an avenger. For obvious reasons, Klytaimestra's Furies cannot do this; they therefore materialize and pursue Orestes themselves.

GERYON   A three-bodied monster killed by Herakles.

GORGONS   Three winged, female monsters with bronze claws, and hissing serpents instead of hair. One of them, Medusa, turned to stone anyone who looked at her.

HADES   Brother of Zeus and Poseidon and husband of Persephone. Zeus' counterpart below the earth, the ruler of the underworld to which human souls pass after death.

HARPIES   Foul winged female creatures, who seized and befouled the food of Phineus, q.v.

HELEN   Daughter of Zeus and Leda; half-sister of Klytaimestra; wife of Menelaos; later mistress of Paris.

HEPHAISTOS   The god of fire.

HERA   Wife of Zeus and goddess of marriage.

HERAKLES   The greatest Greek hero – the only one to receive the same worship as a god after his death – was the son of Zeus by Alkmene. He was once enslaved to Eurystheus, king of Tiryns, and required to perform twelve Labours at his command.

HERMES   Son of Zeus and Maia; herald and messenger of the gods; the god who escorts travellers, and conducts souls between the worlds of the living and the dead; also the guardian of paternal rights, and the god of deception and trickery.

IDA   A mountain near Troy; see BEACONS.

ILION   Troy.

INACHOS   The main river of Argos.

IPHIGENEIA   Eldest daughter of Agamemnon and Klytaimestra, sacrificed at Aulis so the fleet could sail to Troy.

IXION   King of the Lapithai in Thessaly. He killed his father-in-law to avoid paying the bridal gifts he had promised, and became the first suppliant for purification from the *miasma* of homicide. This was granted by Zeus; but Ixion then attempted to seduce Hera, and was punished with eternal torment.

KALCHAS   The seer accompanying the Greek expedition to Troy.

KASSANDRA   A daughter of Priam and Hekabe. She promised her body to Apollo in return for the gift of prophecy, and then broke her word. The god could not take back his gift; he therefore punished her by ensuring that her prophecies would never be believed.

KILISSA   Orestes' old wet-nurse, named after the coastal region of Asia Minor opposite Kypros. Slaves were often named after their place of origin.

KITHAIRON   See BEACONS.

KLYTAIMESTRA   Daughter of Tyndareus and Leda; half-sister of Helen and wife of Agamemnon.

KOKYTOS   A river in the underworld; its name means 'wailing' (lamentation).

KORYKIS   A large cave high on Mt Parnassos above Delphi; sacred to the local nymphs.

KRANAOS   An early, almost unknown ancestor of the Athenians.

KRONOS   A Titan, son and (by force) heir of the first supreme god, Ouranos; father of Zeus, who in turn overthrew him in the battle of gods and giants on the plain of Phlegra.

KUPRIS   Aphrodite, goddess of love; she was born from the foam of waves on the coast of Kypros.

LEDA   Wife of Tyndareus, mother of Klytaimestra and (with Zeus as the father) of Helen.

LEMNOS   A large island in the Aigeian Sea. The Argonauts found it inhabited only by women; they had killed all the men in revenge (except that Hypsipyle saved her own father) when they imported concubines from Asia Minor.

LIBYA   Traditional birthplace of Athena. In 458 the Athenians were providing military assistance to the Libyan warlord in his attempted revolt against Persian hegemony.

LOXIAS   Probably 'the crooked one'; a cult title of Apollo, referring to the obscurity of many of his oracles.

MAKISTOS   See BEACONS.

MENELAOS   Son of Atreus, husband of Helen; joint leader of the expedition to Troy with his brother Agamemnon.

MESSAPION   See BEACONS.

MINOS   See SKYLLA.

NIGHTINGALE   Prokne killed her son Itys to take revenge on her husband Tereus for raping her sister Philomela. Prokne became a nightingale when she prayed to be changed into a bird to escape from Tereus' pursuit; the sad song of the nightingale is her lament for Itys' death.

NISOS   King of Megara, father of Skylla, q.v.

ODYSSEUS   Son of Laertes, husband of Penelopeia and father of

Telemachos; king of Ithaka. The cleverest hero to go to Troy, he went unwillingly (feigning madness in an attempt to avoid enlistment), and reached his homeland after the sack of Troy only after ten years of further wanderings. His homecoming is the theme of Homer's *Odyssey*.

ORESTES   Only son of Agamemnon and Klytaimestra.

ORPHEUS   A musician from Thrakia, whose songs were so sweet that trees and wild animals followed him.

PALLAS   A cult-title of Athena, of unknown origin and meaning.

PAN   A god of nature, fertility, and animals and birds.

PARIS   A son of Priam and Hekabe, often called Alexander. His abduction of Helen caused the Trojan War.

PARNASSOS   The mountain in Phokis which towers over the town and oracle at Delphi.

PELOPS   Founding father of the royal house of Argos; father of Atreus and grandfather of Agamemnon and Menelaos.

PENTHEUS   King of Thebes, son of Echion and grandson of Kadmos; he denied that Dionysos is a god, and was torn apart by maddened Bakchantes, including his own mother Agauë.

PERSEUS   The hero, son of Zeus by Danaë, who killed Medusa, looking at her image in a mirror given him by Athena.

PHERES   Father of Admetos. Apollo made the Moirai drunk, and persuaded them to let Admetos live beyond his *moira*, if he found someone else prepared to die in his place. Admetos' wife Alkestis offered herself, but was then rescued from Death by Herakles.

PHINEUS   King of Salmydessos, who blinded his sons after a false accusation by their stepmother; the gods punished him by sending the Harpies.

PHLEGRA   The plain, probably on the promontory of Pallene in the north Aigeian, where Athena once took a prominent part in the battle of the gods and giants.

PHOIBE   A Titan, mother of Leto and grandmother of Apollo and Artemis.

PHOIBOS   Cult title of Apollo, meaning 'bright'.

PHOKIS   The region of central Greece surrounding Mt Parnassos.

PLEIADES   The 'doves', a constellation visible in Greece from May to November. The moment at which the constellation sets could be used to indicate a particular time of night.

PLEISTHENIDAI   The house of Atreus (from Pleisthenes, a relative of Atreus whose place in the family tree is uncertain in other sources, and not specified in the *Oresteia*).

PLEISTOS   The river which runs through the deep gorge below Delphi.

PLUTO   The god of the underworld; giver of wealth, since crops and minerals come from the earth.

POSEIDON   Brother of Zeus, god of the sea.

PRIAM   King of Troy.

PROTEUS   A sea-god, living on the island of Pharos off the coast of Egypt, whom Menelaos encountered and had to outwit on his way home from Troy (Homer *Odyssey*, 4.351f.). This incident is the subject of the lost satyr-drama which concluded the *Oresteia* tetralogy.

PYLADES   Son of Strophios; companion of Orestes since childhood.

SARONIC GULF   See BEACONS.

SIMOIS   A river of the Trojan Plain.

SKAMANDER   The main river of the Trojan Plain.

SKYLLA   (1) The dangerous female monster which preyed on ships opposite the whirlpool Charybdis, in the straits of Messina between Sicily and the Italian mainland. (2) The daughter of Nisos; when Minos of Knossos was beseiging Megara, she accepted his bribe to cut off the purple (or golden) hair which grew on top of Nisos' head and gave him life; the Kretans were then able to capture the city.

STROPHIOS   King of Phokis; Orestes grew up in his home.

STRYMON   The large river, flowing into the north Aigeian, which formed the boundary between Makedonia and Thrakia.

TANTALOS   Son of Zeus, father of Pelops, founder of the house of Atreus.

TARTAROS   A place of punishment in the underworld.

THEMIS   Right, the titan daughter of Earth whose main role is to see that crime is punished; first giver of oracles at Delphi.

THESEUS   A great king of Athens in early times.

THYESTES   Son of Pelops, brother of Atreus. His seduction of Atreus' wife Airope is the 'first-beginning crime' (*Ag* 1192) in the house of Atreus.

TRITON   A river in Libya (q.v.); traditional birthplace of Athena.

TROY   A city in Phrygia in modern Turkey; sacked after a ten-year seige by the Greek expedition commanded by Agamemnon and Menelaos.

TYNDAREUS   King of Sparta, father of Klytaimestra.

ZEUS   The most powerful god; son of Kronos and Rhea. Originally a sky and weather god, his weapon is the thunderbolt. He punished several kinds of wrongdoing, including oath-breaking; in particular, the table of hospitality was sacred to him as the protector of the rights of guests – strangers, beggars and suppliants – and hosts. However, Zeus did not make the world, and he was not omnipotent or omniscient. Despite his great and wide-ranging powers, both other gods and human beings could defy him (at their own risk).

GREEK WORDS

agathos   A good or noble man; head of an *oikos* by virtue of a combination of birth, wealth and military ability.

agôn   Contest.

agora   The market-place or city square; the centre of political, legal and social life in the city-states of ancient Greece.

aigis   Literally, 'goat-skin'; a miraculous cloak worn by Athena.

amoibaion   An exchange between solo actor and *choros*, in which one or both sing.

amphisbaina   A mythical snake with a head at each end.

anapaests   The metre of the chanted sections of a Greek tragedy, midway in intensity between speech and lyric song. Often used, as in *Ag*, as accompaniment for the entrance-march of the *choros*.

antistrophe   See *strophe*.

choros   Lit. song (and dance); denotes either the group of twelve choros members or the odes (songs) that they perform.

daimôn   A god or godlike power; *daimônes* are often what we, like later Greeks, would call personifications of abstract forces, e.g. Madness, Fear, Persuasion.

drama   Lit. 'thing done/enacted'; the normal term in Athens for the combination of speech and song, movement and dance which comprises a tragedy or comedy.

ekkuklêma   The rolling-out machine, used in tragedy when the pressure of events inside the building represented by the *skene* has such implications for the public forum outside that they must be seen (as they could not if simply displayed in the entrance, because of shadows).

ephymnion   A lyric refrain added between the responding *strophic* stanzas of a *choros*.

epode   A non-strophic stanza used sometimes to conclude a sequence of three stanzas after the alternation of strophe and antistrophe.

kommos   A lyric lamentation sung by the choros and one or more solo actors.

mainads   Followers of the god Dionysos, possessed by the bakchic frenzy – a trance-like state in which superhuman feats of strength are possible.

mesode   A non-responding lyric stanza inserted between a metrically responding *strophe* and *antistrophe*.

miasma   Pollution; the word embraces both literal dirt and what we

would call psychic pollution automatically incurred by breaches of
taboo.

moira   A person's share or lot in life; the 'destiny' which is not a
predetermined fate, but gradually takes shape as a human life unfolds,
under the guidance of three ancient goddesses, the Moirai.

oikos   The great household, consisting of an *agathos'* family and the
dependants who work for him, which was the basic unit of Greek society.

omphalos   Lit. 'navel'; the sacred stone, in Apollo's temple at Delphi,
believed to mark the centre of the earth.

orchêstra   The dance-floor, almost certainly circular, on which
tragedies were performed.

parodos   One of the two entrance ways on each side of the *orchêstra*. By
a convention reflecting the reality of the theatre's location, the *skene* left
parodos was imagined as leading 'downtown' from the place where the
action was set; the *skene* right *parodos* to the countryside and to other
poleis.

philos   Friend and ally, bound by loyalty or blood-relationship; especi-
ally relatives and other members of one's own household.

poiêtes   Lit. 'maker', 'creator'; the man who was writer, composer,
choreographer and director of a *drama* (also, until Sophokles, the leading
actor).

polis   A city which, with its surrounding territory, was also an
independent state; the largest social unit in ancient Greece.

prosôpon   Lit. 'face'; the Greek term for the larger-than-life (but
realistic) masks which ensured that the age, gender and status of
characters was visible even to distant members of the audience.

skene   Lit. and orig. a tent in which the actors changed masks and
costumes. By the time of the *Oresteia* it was a wooden building behind the
orchêstra, with a pair of double doors and a practicable roof; it could be
used to represent for example a palace, house, temple or tent. Decorating
its front to indicate details of a specific location, as in modern 'scene-
painting', was not introduced until much later in the fifth century.

stele   Tall, thin stone column, usually erected to mark the grave of the
dead *agathos*.

stichomythia   Lit. 'step-speech'; a dialogue sequence of rapid cut and
thrust, in which the speaker changes with every line spoken.

strophe, antistrophe   Lit. 'turn' and 'counter-turn'; corresponding
stanzas in solo and choral lyrics, with different textual content but
written in identical 'responding' verse metre and danced to matching
choreography.

theatron   The 'seeing-place'; the part of the theatre in which the
audience sat.

theios   Divine; marvellous.

timê   Honour or status; always in terms of concrete possessions and/or privileges.

tragoidia   Literally 'song for a goat'; the Greek term for the genre; of wider application than modern 'tragedy' since it includes dramas (e.g. *Eumenides* and Sophokles' *Oidipous at Kolonos*) in which catastrophe is avoided or survived, and dramas which modern critics would regard as nearer to melodrama (e.g., Euripides' *Orestes* and *Helen*).

xenia   Abstract noun denoting the act of hospitality and exchange of gifts and/or the consequent *xenos* relationship between members of two households.

xenos   A person who has contracted or inherited a relationship with the head of an *oikos*, or has arrived and is about to contract a relationship by exchange of gifts, which binds them and their descendants whenever they visit each other's territory. The relationship is reciprocal, regardless of who is acting as 'guest' or as 'host' at any one time, and it transcends any regional grievances or enmities.

SUGGESTIONS FOR FURTHER READING

Arnott, P. (1989) *Public and Performance in the Greek Theatre*, London. The best recent book on the subject, covering a wide range of features of Greek theatre.

Easterling, P. (1973) 'Presentation of Character in Aeschylus', *Greece and Rome*, 20, 3–19. A balanced contribution to an important subject; includes a fine discussion of the tapestry scene.

Ewans, M. (1982a) 'The Dramatic Structure of *Agamemnon*', *Ramus* 11:1, 1–15. Argues that Agamemnon's homecoming provides the structural basis of the plot.

Ewans, M. (1989) 'Aischylos: for Actors, in the Round', in Rosanna Warren (ed.), *The Art of Translation: Voices from the Field*, Boston, 120–42. A detailed discussion of the principles behind this translation.

Ewans, M. (ed.) (1996) *Aeschylus, Suppliants and Other Dramas*, London. The companion volume to this text, including the other surviving dramas and the major fragments.

Goldhill, S. (1986) *Reading Greek Tragedy*, Cambridge. A good, modern study for university students.

Goldhill, S. (1992) *Aeschylus: The Oresteia*, Cambridge. An up-to-date introduction, designed for the general reader.

Gould, J. (1985) 'Tragedy in Performance', in P. Easterling and B. Knox (eds), *The Cambridge History of Classical Literature*, Vol. 1, 263–80, Cambridge. The best short survey of the evidence.

Herington, J. (1986) *Aeschylus*, New Haven. A rhetorical book, excellent in its insistence on the animate nature of Aischylos' universe; flawed by the conviction that *Prometheus Bound* is authentic.

Jones, J. (1962) *On Aristotle and Greek Tragedy*, London and New York. Despite an opaque prose style, and a tendency to overstress those aspects of Greek drama which are remote from us, this presents one of the best approaches to the trilogy.

Kitto, H. D. F. (1956) *Form and Meaning in Drama*, London. Apart from a reading of the action as taking place on two separate levels (which does little justice to the interpenetration between human and divine in Aischylos' universe) this study presents an interpretation, and a comparative reading of *Hamlet*, which are still worth considering today.

Lattimore, R. (1964) *Story-Patterns in Greek Tragedy*, Ann Arbor,

Michigan. An underestimated monograph on the influence of certain basic patterns on the playwrights' shaping of their plots.

Neuburg, M. (1981) *An Aeschylean Universe*, Ann Arbor, Michigan. A densely argued Ph.D. thesis, which offers the only full, credible and coherent account of the ethical world in which the characters of the trilogy move.

Rehm, R. (1992) *The Greek Tragic Theatre*, London. The most recent introduction to the nature and context of Greek tragic performance; it includes an analysis of the *Oresteia*.

Taplin, O. (1977a) *The Stagecraft of Aeschylus*, Oxford. Primarily concerned with establishing the exact moments at which the named characters enter and exit, this large book also provides insights on many other staging matters. It blends lucid, sometimes excellent discussion of important issues with pedantic scholarly disputation. A knowledge of Greek is required for full understanding.

Taplin, O. (1978) *Greek Tragedy in Action*, London. Though its layout is irritating, this book, which is accessible to the non-Greek reader, provides good discussion of gestures, props, tableaux and other important aspects of the subject.

Vickers, B. (1973) *Towards Greek Tragedy*, London. This highly stimulating, often controversial book still offers one of the best interpretations of the *Oresteia*.

Walcot, P. (1976) *Greek Drama in its Theatrical and Social Context*, Cardiff. A short and excellent study.

Walton, J. Michael (1980) *Greek Theatre Practice*, Westport, Connecticut. An important contribution to the study of stagecraft.

Winnington-Ingram, R. P. (1983) *Studies in Aeschylus*, Cambridge. Essays on various topics, offering excellent literary interpretations of the dramas.

Other References Cited in the Introduction and Notes

Adkins, A. W. H. (1960) *Merit and Responsibility: a Study in Greek Values*, Oxford.

Adkins, A. W. H. (1970) *From the Many to the One*, Ithaca, NY.

Anti, C. (1947) *Teatri Greci Arcaici da Minosse a Pericle*, Padova.

Arnott, P. (1962) *Greek Scenic Conventions in the Fifth Century* BC, Oxford.

Ashby, C. (1987) 'The Case for the Rectangular/Trapezoidal Orchestra', *Theatre Research International*, 13, 1–20.

Aylen, L. (1985) *The Greek Theater*, Cranby, NJ.

Bain, D. (1981) *Masters, Servants and Orders in Greek Tragedy*, Manchester.

Baldry, H. C. (1971) *The Greek Tragic Theatre*, London.

Bowen, A. (ed.) (1986). Aeschylus, *Choephoroi*, Bristol.

Brown, A. (1982) 'Some Problems in the *Eumenides* of Aeschylus', *Journal of Hellenic Studies*, 102, 26–32.

Bryant-Bertail, S. (1994) 'Gender, Empire and Body Politic as *Mise en Scène*: Mnouchkine's *Les Atrides*', *Theatre Journal*, 46:1, 1–30.

Buxton, R. G. (1982) *Persuasion in Greek Tragedy*, Cambridge.

Conacher, D. J. (1987) *Aeschylus' Oresteia: A Literary Commentary*, Toronto.

Conington, J. (ed.) (1857) Aeschylus, *Choephoroi*, London.

Connor, W. R. (1989) 'City Dionysia and Athenian Democracy', *Classica et Mediaevalia* 40, 7–32.

Dale, A. (1969) *Collected Papers of A. M. Dale* (ed. Turner and Webster), Cambridge.

Denniston-Page (1957) See Page, D. (1957).

Ewans, M. (1971) *Aeschylean Inevitability: a Study of the* Oresteia, Ann Arbor, Michigan.

Ewans, M. (1975) 'Agamemnon at Aulis: a Study in the *Oresteia*', *Ramus* 4:1, 17–32.

Ewans, M. (1982b) *Wagner and Aeschylus: the* Ring *and the* Oresteia, London.

Ewans, M. (1993) 'Racine's *Phèdre* and Greek Tragedy', *Prudentia*, suppl. vol. 1993, 89–102.

Ewans, M. (1995) 'Patterns of Tragedy in Sophokles and Shakespeare', in M. Silk (ed.) *Tragedy and the Tragic*, Oxford.

Fagles, R. (trans.) (1977) *Aeschylus: The Oresteia*, Harmondsworth.

Forrest, G. (1966) *The Emergence of Greek Democracy*, London.

Fraenkel E. (ed.) (1950) *Aeschylus: Agamemnon*, Oxford.

Garvie, A. F. (ed.) (1986) *Aeschylus: Choephoroi*, Oxford.

Gebhard, E. (1972) 'The Form of the Orchestra in the Early Greek Theatre', *Hesperia*, 41, 428–40.

Goheen, R. (1955) 'Aspects of Dramatic Symbolism in *Agamemnon*', *American Journal of Philology*, 76, 113–37.

Goldhill, S. (1984) *Language, Sexuality, Narrative: the Oresteia*, Cambridge.

Gould, J. (1989) 'Law, Custom and Myth: Aspects of the Social Position of Women in Classical Athens', *Journal of Hellenic Studies*, 109, 38–59.

Hammond, N. G. L. (1972) 'The Conditions of Dramatic Production to the Death of Aeschylus' *Greek, Roman and Byzantine Studies*, 13, 387–450.

Headlam, W. (1906) 'The Last Scene of the *Eumenides*', *Journal of Hellenic Studies*, 26, 268–77.

Henderson, J. (1991) 'Women and the Athenian Dramatic Festivals', *Transactions of the American Philological Association*, 121, 133–47.

Hester, D. (1981) 'The Casting Vote', *American Journal of Philology*, 102, 265–74.

Hormouziades, N. (1965) *Production and Imagination in Euripides*, Athens.

Hornby, R. (1977) *Script into Performance*, Austin, Texas.

Houseman, A. E. (1989) *Collected Poems and Selected Prose*, Harmondsworth.

Hunningher, B. (1956) 'Acoustics and Acting in the Theatre of Dionysus Eleuthereus' *Mededelingen der Kon. Nederl. Akad. van Wetenschappen, Afd. Letterkunde* 198, pp. 303–38.

Kells, J. (ed.) (1973) *Sophocles: Electra*, Cambridge.

Kranz, W. (1933) *Stasimon*, Berlin.

Lebeck, A. (1971) *The Oresteia: a Study in Language and Structure*, Washington.

Ley, G. and Ewans, M. (1985) 'The *Orchestra* as Acting Area in Greek Tragedy', *Ramus*, 14:2, 75–84.

Lloyd-Jones, H. (1961) 'Interpolations in *Choephoroi* and *Electra*' *Classical Quarterly*, 11, 171–84.

Lloyd-Jones, H. (1971) *The Justice of Zeus*, Berkeley.

Lloyd-Jones, H. (trans.) (1979) *Aeschylus: Eumenides*, 2nd edn, London.

Macleod, C. (1982) 'Morals and Politics in the *Oresteia*', *Journal of Hellenic Studies*, 102, 124–44; or *Collected Papers* (Oxford, 1983), 20–40.

Mastronarde, D. (1979) *Contact and Disunity: Some Conventions of Speech and Action on the Greek Tragic Stage*, Berkeley.

Melchinger, S. (1974) *Das Theater der Tragödie*, Munich.

Melchinger, S. (1979) *Die Welt als Tragödie*, vol. 1, Munich.

Page, D. (ed.) (1957) *Aeschylus: Agamemnon* (with J. D. Denniston), Oxford.

Peradotto, J. (1964) 'Some Patterns of Nature Imagery in the *Oresteia*', *American Journal of Philology*, 85, 378–83.

Pickard, J. (1893) 'The Relative Positions of Actors and Chorus in the Greek Theatre of the Fifth Century BC', *American Journal of Philology*, 14, 68–89, 199–215 and 273–304.

Pickard-Cambridge, A. W. (1968) *The Dramatic Festivals of Athens*, 2nd edn, Oxford.

Podlecki, A. (1966) *The Political Background of Aeschylean Tragedy*, Michigan.

Podlecki, A. (ed.) (1989) *Aeschylus: Eumenides*, Warminster.

Pöhlmann, E. (1981) 'Die Proedrie des Dionsostheaters im 5 Jahrhundert und das Bühnenspiel der Klassik', *Museum Helveticum*, 38, 129–46.

Pool, E. H. (1983). 'Clytemnestra's First Entrance in Aeschylus' *Agamemnon*', *Mnemonsyne*, 36, 71–116.

Postgate, R. (ed.) (1969) *The Agamemnon of Aeschylus*, Cambridge.

Rehm, R. (1985) 'Aeschylus and Performance: a Review of the National Theatre's *Oresteia*', *Themes in Drama*, 7.

Rehm, R. (1988) 'The Staging of Suppliant Plays', *Greek, Roman and Byzantine Studies*, 29, 263–307.

Reinhardt, K. (1949) *Aischylos als Regisseur und Theologe*, Bern.

Rosenmeyer, T. G. (1982) *The Art of Aeschylus*, Berkeley.

Scott, W. C. (1984) *Musical Design in Aeschylean Theater*, Hanover.

Seaford, R. (1989) 'The Attribution of Aeschylus *Choephoroi* 691–9', *Classical Quarterly*, 39, 302–6.

Seale, D. (1982) *Vision and Stagecraft in Sophocles*, London.

Segal, C. P. (1981) *Tragedy and Civilisation*, Cambridge Massachusetts.

Sommerstein, A. (ed.) (1989) *Aeschylus: Eumenides*, Cambridge.

Stanford, W. B. (1983) *Greek Tragedy and the Emotions*, London.

Steiner, G. (1975) *After Babel*, Oxford.

Taplin, O. (1972) 'Aeschylean Silences and Silences in Aeschylus', *Harvard Studies in Classical Philology*, 76, 57–98.

Taplin, O. (1977b) 'Did Greek Dramatists Write Stage Instructions?', *Proceedings of the Cambridge Philological Society*, 203, 121–33.

Thomson, G. (ed.) (1966) *The Oresteia of Aeschylus*, 2nd edition, Amsterdam and Prague.

Vernant, J. P. (1981) *Tragedy and Myth in Ancient Greece*, (with P. Vidal-Naquet), Brighton.

Walton, J. Michael (1984) *The Greek Sense of Theatre*, London.

Winnington-Ingram, R. P. (1980) *Sophocles; an Interpretation*, Cambridge.

Zeitlin, F. (1965) 'The Motif of the Corrupted Sacrifice in Aeschylus' *Oresteia*', *Transactions of the American Philological Association*, 96, 463–508.

TEXT SUMMARY

The dramas are set in early Greece *c.* 1100 BC. The action spans twelve to fifteen years in the fortunes of the royal house of Argos, beginning immediately after the end of the Trojan War.

Agamemnon

The action dramatizes the return home of Agamemnon from the Greek expedition against Troy. Aischylos shows the perversion of the rituals of homecoming by his wife Klytaimestra, leading to her murder of Agamemnon and Kassandra, and the increasing disillusion of the Elders of Argos who attempt, with diminishing success, to portray the sack of Troy as an act of divine justice deserving nothing but acclaim. The drama ends when the immediate consequences of this murder have been explored.

In the first half Klytaimestra establishes her dominance over the Elders of Argos and Agamemnon's advance Herald. At the midpoint, Agamemnon returns; Klytaimestra converts his victorious arrival into a dangerous situation by persuading Agamemnon to incur the jealousy of the gods by walking into his house over fine crimson tapestries. However, she cannot persuade Agamemnon's new mistress, the Trojan prophetess Kassandra, to go inside. Kassandra only enters the house after prophesying her own and Agamemnon's death.

At the climax, Klytaimestra appears over the bodies of Agamemnon and Kassandra, and defies the Elders. In the last two scenes first she, and then her lover Aigisthos, attempt to justify the murders; but the drama ends in an unresolved conflict with the Elders, as Aigisthos and Klytaimestra impose a tyranny on the city.

Libation Bearers

The first half of the drama is set around Agamemnon's grave. Agamemnon's son Orestes returns from exile, accompanied by Pylades, to avenge his father's death on the morning after Klytaimestra has been terrified by an ominous dream. Afraid to go herself, she sends her daughter Elektra and some foreign slave women, the Libation Bearers, with offerings to propitiate Agamemnon's spirit. The Libation Bearers easily persuade Elektra to change the purpose of the offerings, and pray instead for vengeance on Agamemnon's murderers.

Her prayers are answered, and after their reunion Orestes, Elektra and the Libation Bearers join in an intense scene of lamentation and invocation around the grave, to gain the support of Agamemnon's spirit for their attempt to overturn the usurping régime of Klytaimestra and Aigisthos.

The second half of the drama is set in front of the house of Atreus. Orestes is at first refused admission to the house by a Servant, but is welcomed in by Klytaimestra when he claims to bring news of Orestes' death. She sends a message to Aigisthos, who is not at home, to come back with bodyguards and question the strangers; but her messenger is Orestes' old Nurse, who is upset by the news of 'Orestes' death', bears no love for the usurpers, and is easily persuaded by the Libation Bearers to change the message. Accordingly Aigisthos arrives alone, and the Libation Bearers lure him into the house.

His death-cry is heard; the Servant runs in calling for Klytaimestra, who attempts a counter-attack; but she is too late. She is confronted by Orestes who – after a moment of hesitation, in which he is given confidence by Pylades – implacably rebuts all her pleas to be spared, even when she threatens him with pursuit by a mother's Furies. He escorts her inside the house to die.

The Libation Bearers sing a choros of rejoicing; but this mood is destroyed by the sight of Orestes standing – as did his mother at the climax of the previous drama – over the bodies of two victims, one of each sex. While he attempts to justify his deed, madness begins to set in. Orestes is pursued from the *orchêstra* by Klytaimestra's Furies, as yet visible only to him.

Eumenides

The opening location is in front of the temple of Apollo at Delphi. Klytaimestra's Furies have now materialized to pursue Orestes, since no living avenger will take revenge on her behalf. Apollo overcomes them by trickery, and allows Orestes to escape, promising him release from his sufferings if he can get to Athens. A dream-image of Klytaimestra stirs them up to resume the pursuit.

Orestes successfully reaches Athens ahead of the Furies, and clasps the image of Athena, imploring her to come and give him sanctuary. The Furies soon arrive and surround him.

Athena arrives in answer to Orestes' prayer, and asks both sides about their dispute. She realizes that the consequences for Athens are serious whether she gives Orestes sanctuary or hands him over to the Furies. Accordingly she resolves to found a court, in which she and some of the wisest of her citizens may judge between them.

She returns shortly with eleven Citizens of Athens, with whom she joins to try Orestes, in the first trial before the Areopagos (in real life, Athens' oldest and most aristocratic court). Apollo appears, defends Orestes, and is shrewdly cross-examined by the Furies.

In the outcome the jurors' votes are exactly tied; Athena, following what became the normal procedure of Greek courts, gives Orestes the benefit of the deadlock. Apollo disappears, and Orestes, after making a speech of thanks, sets out on his way back to Argos.

Athena and the jurors are left to face the anger of Klytaimestra's Furies. She manages to persuade them that they were not really beaten, and the verdict did them no injustice. In return for the slight they feel, she offers them an honoured place in Athens: they will live in the city, and in return for offerings will provide many blessings to Athens. The trilogy ends as Athena and the jurors are joined by Women and Girls of Athens. They clothe the Solemn Goddesses (as these Furies are now to be called) in ceremonial robes and escort them to their new home below the earth.

ACKNOWLEDGEMENTS

This book would not exist without the devoted collaboration of the students and colleagues at the University of Newcastle, NSW, who worked with me on the 1983, 1985 and 1986 productions, and I would like to thank them all. Though it is invidious to single out individuals from three large casts and production and recording crews, I especially wish to name my colleague Barry O'Connor (Agamemnon and Apollo); Vanessa Turton and Jan Hunt (Klytaimestra, Kassandra); Justin Collins and Dimity Raftos (Orestes, Elektra); Katherine Westbury (Athena), and Bruce Copping (Aigisthos); choreographer Ellen Caryanides; and above all the individual members of the three choroses. The productions were funded by the Drama Department and the Senate Research Committee of the University of Newcastle, NSW.

I was subsequently greatly aided by my appointment as a Visiting University Professor at Boston University in 1986–7, where I was able to develop a first, rough version of the commentary and submit it to critical scrutiny. Professor Pat Easterling sent helpful comments on the first full draft; and the criticism and encouragement given by Graham Ley and Dr Greg McCart have been of the greatest value. Special thanks should also go to Dr Richard Seaford, who drew this translation to the attention of Everyman Classics.

ANCIENT CLASSICS
IN EVERYMAN

A SELECTION

The Republic
PLATO
The most important and enduring of
Plato's works **£5.99**

The Education of Cyrus
XENOPHON
A fascinating insight into the culture
and politics of ancient Greece **£6.99**

Juvenal's Satires with the
Satires of Persius
JUVENAL AND PERSIUS
Unique and acute observations of
contemporary Roman society **£5.99**

The Odyssey
HOMER
A classic translation of one of the
greatest adventures ever told **£5.99**

History of the
Peloponnesian War
THUCYDIDES
The war that brought to an end a
golden age of democracy **£5.99**

The Histories
HERODOTUS
The earliest surviving work of
Greek prose literature **£7.99**

£5.99

AVAILABILITY
All books are available from your local bookshop or direct from
**Littlehampton Book Services Cash Sales, 14 Eldon Way, Lineside Estate,
Littlehampton, West Sussex BN17 7HE.** PRICES ARE SUBJECT TO CHANGE.

To order any of the books, please enclose a cheque (in £ sterling) made payable to
Littlehampton Book Services, or phone your order through with credit card details (Access,
Visa or Mastercard) on 0903 721596 (24 hour answering service) stating card number and
expiry date. Please add £1.25 for package and postage to the total value of your order.

In the USA, for further information and a complete catalogue call 1-800-526-2778.

DRAMA
IN EVERYMAN

A SELECTION

Everyman and Medieval Miracle Plays

EDITED BY A. C. CAWLEY
A selection of the most popular medieval plays **£3.99**

Complete Plays and Poems

CHRISTOPHER MARLOWE
The complete works of this fascinating Elizabethan in one volume **£5.99**

Complete Poems and Plays

ROCHESTER
The most sexually explicit – and strikingly modern – writing of the seventeenth century **£6.99**

Restoration Plays

Five comedies and two tragedies representing the best of the Restoration stage **£7.99**

Female Playwrights of the Restoration: Five Comedies

Rediscovered literary treasures in a unique selection **£5.99**

Poems and Plays

OLIVER GOLDSMITH
The most complete edition of Goldsmith available **£4.99**

Plays, Poems and Prose

J. M. SYNGE
The most complete edition of Synge available **£6.99**

Plays, Prose Writings and Poems

OSCAR WILDE
The full force of Wilde's wit in one volume **£4.99**

A Doll's House/The Lady from the Sea/The Wild Duck

HENRIK IBSEN
A popular selection of Ibsen's major plays **£4.99**

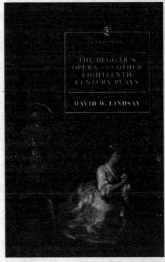

£6.99

AVAILABILITY

All books are available from your local bookshop or direct from
Littlehampton Book Services Cash Sales, 14 Eldon Way, Lineside Estate, Littlehampton, West Sussex BN17 7HE. PRICES ARE SUBJECT TO CHANGE.

To order any of the books, please enclose a cheque (in £ sterling) made payable to Littlehampton Book Services, or phone your order through with credit card details (Access, Visa or Mastercard) on 0903 721596 (24 hour answering service) stating card number and expiry date. Please add £1.25 for package and postage to the total value of your order.

In the USA, for further information and a complete catalogue call 1-800-526-2778.

SAGAS AND OLD ENGLISH LITERATURE IN EVERYMAN

A SELECTION

Egils saga
TRANSLATED BY
CHRISTINE FELL
A gripping story of Viking exploits in Iceland, Norway and Britain **£4.99**

Edda
SNORRI STURLUSON
TRANSLATED BY
ANTHONY FAULKES
The first complete English translation **£5.99**

The Fljotsdale Saga and The Droplaugarsons
TRANSLATED BY
ELEANOR HAWORTH
AND JEAN YOUNG
A brilliant portrayal of life and times in medieval Iceland **£3.99**

The Anglo-Saxon Chronicle
TRANSLATED BY
G. N. GARMONSWAY
A fascinating record of events in ancient Britain **£4.99**

Anglo-Saxon Poetry
TRANSLATED BY
S. A. J. BRADLEY
A widely acclaimed collection **£6.99**

Fergus of Galloway: Knight of King Arthur
GUILLAUME LE CLERC
TRANSLATED BY
D. D. R. OWEN
Essential reading for students of Arthurian romance **£3.99**

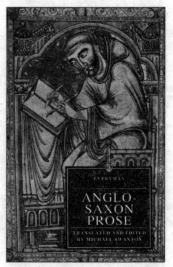

£4.99

AVAILABILITY

All books are available from your local bookshop or direct from
Littlehampton Book Services Cash Sales, 14 Eldon Way, Lineside Estate, Littlehampton, West Sussex BN17 7HE. PRICES ARE SUBJECT TO CHANGE.

To order any of the books, please enclose a cheque (in £ sterling) made payable to Littlehampton Book Services, or phone your order through with credit card details (Access, Visa or Mastercard) on 0903 721596 (24 hour answering service) stating card number and expiry date. Please add £1.25 for package and postage to the total value of your order.

In the USA, for further information and a complete catalogue call 1-800-526-2778.

MEDIEVAL LITERATURE IN EVERYMAN

A SELECTION

Canterbury Tales
GEOFFREY CHAUCER
EDITED BY A. C. CAWLEY
The complete medieval text with
translations £3.99

Arthurian Romances
CHRÉTIEN DE TROYES
TRANSLATED BY D. D. R. OWEN
Classic tales from the father of
Arthurian romance £5.99

Everyman and Medieval Miracle Plays
EDITED BY A. C. CAWLEY
A fully representative selection
from the major play cycles £3.99

The Vision of Piers Plowman
WILLIAM LANGLAND
EDITED BY A. V. C. SCHMIDT
The only complete edition of the
B-version available £4.99

Sir Gawain and the Green Knight, Pearl, Cleanness, Patience
EDITED BY A. C. CAWLEY
AND J. J. ANDERSON
Four major English medieval poems
in one volume £3.99

The Piers Plowman Tradition
EDITED BY HELEN BARR
Four medieval poems of political
and religious dissent – widely avail-
able for the first time £5.99

The Birth of Romance: An Anthology
TRANSLATED BY JUDITH WEISS
The first-ever English translation of
these fascinating Anglo-Norman
romances £4.99

Of Love and Chivalry: An Anthology of Middle English Romance
EDITED BY JENNIFER FELLOWS
A unique collection of tales of
courtly love and heroic deeds £5.99

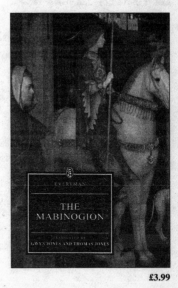

£3.99

AVAILABILITY

All books are available from your local bookshop or direct from
**Littlehampton Book Services Cash Sales, 14 Eldon Way, Lineside Estate,
Littlehampton, West Sussex BN17 7HE.** PRICES ARE SUBJECT TO CHANGE.

To order any of the books, please enclose a cheque (in £ sterling) made payable to
Littlehampton Book Services, or phone your order through with credit card details (Access,
Visa or Mastercard) on 0903 721596 (24 hour answering service) stating card number and
expiry date. Please add £1.25 for package and postage to the total value of your order.

In the USA, for further information and a complete catalogue call 1-800-526-2778.

PHILOSOPHY AND RELIGIOUS WRITING IN EVERYMAN

A SELECTION

Ethics
SPINOZA
Spinoza's famous discourse on the power of understanding **£4.99**

Critique of Pure Reason
IMMANUEL KANT
The capacity of the human intellect examined **£6.99**

A Discourse on Method, Meditations, and Principles
RENÉ DESCARTES
Takes the theory of mind over matter into a new dimension **£4.99**

Philosophical Works including the Works on Vision
GEORGE BERKELEY
An eloquent defence of the power of the spirit in the physical world **£4.99**

Utilitarianism, On Liberty, Considerations on Representative Government
J. S. MILL
Three radical works which transformed political science **£5.99**

Utopia
THOMAS MORE
A critique of contemporary ills allied with a visionary ideal for society **£3.99**

An Essay Concerning Human Understanding
JOHN LOCKE
A central work in the development of modern philosophy **£5.99**

Hindu Scriptures
The most important ancient Hindu writings in one volume **£6.99**

Apologia Pro Vita Sua
JOHN HENRY NEWMAN
A moving and inspiring account of a Christian's spiritual journey **£5.99**

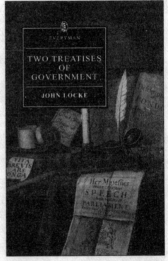

£3.99

AVAILABILITY

All books are available from your local bookshop or direct from
Littlehampton Book Services Cash Sales, 14 Eldon Way, Lineside Estate, Littlehampton, West Sussex BN17 7HE. PRICES ARE SUBJECT TO CHANGE.

To order any of the books, please enclose a cheque (in £ sterling) made payable to Littlehampton Book Services, or phone your order through with credit card details (Access, Visa or Mastercard) on 0903 721596 (24 hour answering service) stating card number and expiry date. Please add £1.25 for package and postage to the total value of your order.

In the USA, for further information and a complete catalogue call 1-800-526-2778.

clarity and power, in the B stanzas; each dance here opens with an image of gentleness and subtlety, and ends in the desolation of personal loss.

Stanzas C1 and C2 call for choreography of even greater intensity and gravity, leading to an extremely ominous conclusion, as the Elders' celebration finally reaches its denouement in apprehension. It is effective for this choreographic sequence, as it ends for the second time, to echo the end of the prelude for a moment in a tableau – before suddenly dissolving, in the epilogue 475f., into dislocated, sudden individual movements.[26]

Scene 3

Following normal practice, Agamemnon has sent a Herald ahead to the city on his landfall, while he sacrifices to the gods of his homeland. The Herald's arrival instantly punctures the fantasy with which the Elders tried to escape in 475f. from the burden of their reflections. Klytaimestra was right, and all they can do is hope that the more ominous implications of the sack of Troy will not be fulfilled. (They will be; cf. 527–8.)

The build-up to the Herald's entry is of unusual length, and it gives the opportunity for the Elders to break up, individually and slowly, from the defiantly bold positions which they have taken up in the closing epilogue of Choros 2. They now cluster hopefully around and behind the one of their number who has crossed to EBR to tell them about the Herald's imminent arrival.[27] But a pattern for the scene is set at once, by the way in which even this functional speech has a dying fall built into it. The speaker shies away in 499f. from the fear of disaster, and this must be brought out in the movement. He should turn away from the R *parodos*, and carry his meditation into the rear centre of the *orchêstra*. This establishes a mood-pattern which will then be developed, when the blocking later reflects the ways in which the Herald also tries desperately to hold on to his unwarranted optimism – and loses it.

[26] These should prefigure, on a smaller scale, the much greater chaos into which the Elders will be plunged by the death-cry of Agamemnon at the start of Scene 7.

[27] This sequence works so well in the theatre that there is no need to bring Klytaimestra back on – spoiling the effect of her entry at 587, see below – and assign the speech to her simply because there is no 'parallel' (in the minute number of surviving Athenian tragedies) for such a long speech by a choros member (*pace* Dale 1969, 215).

her commanding position to seek the Elders' involvement, coming forward towards them in gestures of appeal as she explores emotionally the fate of the victims – and also prefigures the dangers that await the conquerors (341f.)

She will also leave BC, of course, for the last three lines, but this time ironically, as she prepares to part by deprecating herself as (merely!) female and echoing the motif 'yet may the good prevail'. She should then exit at once, not waiting for a reply,[25] and so undermine by her contempt both the Elder's grudging concession of victory and his attempt at sarcasm in 352.

Choros 2

The Elders embark on their official celebration of the sack of Troy, in fulfilment of the duty which they have twice promised to Klytaimestra; but the rejoicing quickly turns sour. This ode presents one of the most striking demonstrations of the drama's underlying pattern: expectation met by fulfilment, and then followed by apprehension. The Elders brood on what Klytaimestra has told them, trying to focus their feelings on an analysis of the ways in which the capture of Troy has fulfilled the traditional belief that Zeus himself protects the rights of guests and hosts. They prove this to their satisfaction; but their thoughts lead them on to a very different perspective, in which the conquerors of Troy are almost as overshadowed by the potential consequences as the defeated Trojans themselves.

In the choreography, the prelude and epilogue have to be marked off clearly from the three strophic pairs, in which there must be a continuous pattern of movement to match the seamless development in the Elders' thoughts. Severe, abrupt images of power are appropriate in the prelude, as the Elders invoke Zeus while taking up their positions for the dance proper. Then the A stanzas invite a highly complex and subtle response from the choreographer, who must match both the remarkable sequence of the imagery and the ways in which the tentative initial picture in each stanza gradually develops towards a terrible certainty in the last four lines. This mood must be continued, with gathering

[25] Taplin (1977a, 290). He is of course also right (ibid.) to take Klytaimestra off at the end of this scene; his arguments are not damaged by Mastronarde (1979, 21).